THEATRE OF CATASTROPHE

THEATRE OF CATASTROPHE

New Essays on Howard Barker

EDITED BY
KAROLINE GRITZNER AND **DAVID IAN RABEY**

OBERON BOOKS
LONDON

First published in 2006 by Oberon Books Ltd., 521 Caledonian Road, London N7 9RH

Tel: 020 7607 3637 / Fax: 020 7607 3629 / info@oberonbooks.com / www.*bloomsbury*.com

A catalogue record for this book is available from the British Library.

ISBN: 1 84002 672 3

Cover photography & design: Dan Steward

To HB

Our Honorary Professor

penblwydd hapus

CONTENTS

NOTES ON CONTRIBUTORS

ELISABETH ANGEL-PEREZ is Professor of English Literature at the University of Paris-Sorbonne (Paris IV). She is a specialist in contemporary English theatre and drama. Her most recent publications include a book on post-traumatic theatre (*Voyages au bout du possible: les théâtres du traumatisme de Samuel Beckett à Sarah Kane*, Klincksieck, 2006) and a collective opus about Howard Barker's theatre (*Howard Barker et le Théâtre de la Catastrophe*, Éditions Théâtrales, 2006). She has also collaborated and coordinated the translation of *Arguments for a Theatre* (*Arguments pour le théâtre*, Les Solitaires Intempestifs, 2006) and translated several plays by Howard Barker, Martin Crimp and Caryl Churchill.

MARY KAREN DAHL is a Professor of Theatre at Florida State University. She has a longstanding interest in the relationship between performance and politics. Her book *Political Violence in Drama: Classical Models, Contemporary Variations* was selected a Choice Outstanding Academic Book. Related essays include 'Postcolonial British Theatre: Black Voices at the Center' in *Imperialism and Drama* for Routledge; 'Stage Violence as Thaumaturgic Technique' in *Violence in Drama* for Cambridge University Press; and 'State Terror and Dramatic Countermeasures' in *Politics and Terror in Modern Drama* for Edinburgh University Press. Her current work poses questions about political theory and citizenship and includes essays on media and theatrical treatments of contemporary events such as the case of Stephen Lawrence and the *Behzti* affair.

KAROLINE GRITZNER is a Lecturer in Drama in the Department of Theatre, Film and Television Studies at the University of Wales, Aberystwyth. Her research interests include contemporary British and Irish theatre; modern European drama; theatre, gender and critical theory; and the philosophy and aesthetic theory of Theodor W Adorno in relation to theatre and the arts. She is currently working on a monograph on contemporary British Theatre in the context of Adorno's aesthetic theory (for Edward Mellen Press).

HELEN IBALL is a Lecturer in Drama at the University of Hull. Her interests in contemporary theatre and live art, identity politics, and performance aesthetics, are reflected in her contribution to *Casting Gender: Women and Performance in Intercultural Contexts* (Peter Lang, 2005). Her essays have appeared in the journal *Performance Research* in special editions 'on food' and 'on archiving'. Helen has published on the work of Sarah Kane in *Contemporary Theatre Review*, and is completing a monograph on Kane's play *Blasted* (Continuum, 2007). She is currently engaged in research for a study of British theatre and theatricality, 1990s – present.

CHRISTINE KIEHL teaches English Literature and Drama at the University of Lyon 2. She has assisted various drama productions for Lyon-based companies. She writes articles on contemporary English drama and more exclusively on Howard Barker's Theatre of Catastrophe. She participated in the Wrestling with Barker Summer School (July 2003) and in the international colloquium on Howard Barker held in Paris-Nanterre (January 2004). Her PhD thesis (December 2005) is entitled 'Le Corps dans le théâtre de la catastrophe de Howard Barker'.

CHARLES LAMB is Head of Performing Arts at Bournemouth and Poole College. Born in 1947, he studied literature and drama at the Universities of Aberdeen, Essex and Warwick. His career has been mainly as a teacher of drama in schools and colleges. Of the fifty or so productions he has directed, many have been by contemporary writers. His association with Howard Barker, extends back over twenty years to his production of *Fair Slaughter* at the Quay Theatre in Suffolk. He subsequently directed the premiere production of *Crimes in Hot Countries* and has also staged *The Possibilities* and *Wounds to the Face* by the same author. He has written a number of articles on contemporary theatre including 'A Conversation' with Howard Barker in his *Arguments for a Theatre* (Manchester University Press, 1993, 1997). He is the author of *Howard Barker's Theatre of Seduction* (Harwood Academic, 1997) and *The Theatre of Howard Barker* (Routledge, 2005). Charles Lamb is an Associate of The Wrestling School.

CHRIS MEGSON is Lecturer in Drama and Theatre at Royal Holloway College, University of London. He has previously worked as an actor and political researcher. His recent publications include essays on Howard Barker (Blackwell), David Hare (Oxford University Press), British theatre during the Cold War (Routledge) and the impact of 1968 on British playwriting (*Contemporary Theatre Review*). He is currently researching contemporary approaches to documentary and 'verbatim' theatre.

ROGER OWEN is a Lecturer in Theatre and Performance Studies at the Department of Theatre, Film and Television Studies, University of Wales, Aberystwyth. He has published in English and Welsh on theatre in Wales, and has also worked as a performer with Brith Gof and Eddie Ladd. He is a nucleus member of the Lurking Truth Theatre Company / Cwmni'r Gwir sy'n Llechu and has collaborated over a number of years with David Ian Rabey on such productions as *Victory: Choices in Reaction*, *The Castle* and *The Early Hours of a Reviled Man* by Barker, *The Sons of Light* by David Rudkin, and *The Back of Beyond* and *The Hanging Judge* by Rabey.

DAVID IAN RABEY is Professor of Drama and Theatre Studies at the University of Wales, Aberystwyth. His publications include the first book-length study of Barker's work, *Howard Barker: Politics and Desire* (Macmillan, 1989), *David Rudkin: Sacred Disobedience* (Harwood/Routledge, 1997) and *English Drama Since 1940* (Longman's Literature in English series, 2003). He is an Associate of The Wrestling School theatre company, and Artistic Director of Lurking Truth / Gwir sy'n Llechu theatre company, for whom he has written the plays *The Back of Beyond* and *The Battle of the Crows* (published together as *The Wye Plays*), *Bite or Suck* and *Lovefuries*. He has directed and/or acted in ten Barker productions to date, directing or co-directing *Pity in History*, *Victory*, *The Castle*, *The Europeans*, *(Uncle) Vanya* and *Ursula*, and performing as Scrope/Undy (in *Victory*), The Exaggerater in *Don't Exaggerate*, Sleen in *The Early Hours of a Reviled Man*, Vanya in *(Uncle) Vanya* and Isonzo in Barker's own production of *The Twelfth Battle of Isonzo*. He is currently under contract to Palgrave Press to write his second critical study of Barker's work, *Howard Barker: Ecstasy and Death*, covering the period 1988–2007, and is scheduled to direct a production of *Gertrude – The Cry* for 2007.

JAMES REYNOLDS graduated from Rose Bruford College with an MA in Theatre and Performance Studies, with Distinction. His dissertation thesis explored Howard Barker's performance practice with The Wrestling School. James is currently undertaking PhD research into the theatre practices of Robert Lepage and Ex Machina at Queen Mary, University of London.

ELIZABETH SAKELLARIDOU is Professor of Drama and Theatre Studies in the School of English at Aristotle University of Thessaloniki. She has published extensively on contemporary British theatre. Her latest book is *Women's Theatre and the Brechtian Tradition* (Athens, 2006, forthcoming). Her current research focuses on the performativity of pain and melancholia in tragedy.

ANDY W SMITH is Senior Lecturer and Subject Leader in Performing Arts in the International Film School Wales, University of Wales, Newport. His teaching and research interests include: site-specific theatre and video installation; post-war British and American theatre; American television and cinema; screen acting and media performance. Andy has written journal articles on cult television, and for the *Dictionary of Literary Biography* (Thomson-Gale) has published on Welsh dramatists Ian Rowlands and Ed Thomas. Andy has forthcoming publications on postmodern teen horror in contemporary American cinema (Manchester University Press) and the relationship of graphic novels to Gothic literature and film (Routledge).

LIZ TOMLIN is Research Fellow in Performing Arts at Manchester Metropolitan University, and Playwright and co-Artistic Director of Point Blank theatre, who have produced her plays *Dead Causes* (2000), *Nothing to Declare* (2002/3), *Operation Wonderland* (2004), *Roses & Morphine* (2005),

Last Orders (2006). Her critical writing includes 'English Theatre in the 1990s and Beyond' in *The Cambridge History of British Theatre vol 3* edited by Baz Kershaw (Cambridge University Press, 2004), 'Innocent Tourists? Neo-Colonialist Narratives in Contemporary Performance' in *Contemporary Theatre Review*, 16, 1 (Routledge, 2006) and 'Transgressing Boundaries: Postmodern Performance and the Tourist Trap' in *TDR* 162 (1999).

HEINER ZIMMERMANN taught Drama and Theory at the Department of English at Heidelberg University. He has published a monograph on Shakespeare and over forty articles on Shakespeare, Fielding, Yeats, Pinter, Stoppard, Wesker, Crimp and Barker in books and periodicals.

RAISING HELL

An Introduction to Howard Barker's Theatre of Catastrophe

DAVID IAN RABEY

1. BARKER: AN ODYSSEY OF RESTLESSNESS

The English dramatist-director Howard Barker (b. 1946) has, through a unique combination of style, content, theoretical argument and *mise-en-scène*, persistently countered conventional presumptions and propositions of the supposedly 'natural' or 'inevitable' restrictions of how one might think, feel, speak, act, love and exist. His plays and productions refuse to offer an immediately, readily or completely recognisable world. They offer something more profoundly alluring and haunting: the resonant collisions, surprising embraces and mesmeric duels of characters who advertise their theatricality and stake everything on their own powers and politics of performance. His work offers a purposefully anti-naturalistic expansion of vocabulary: of language, terms of experience, scenic and physical expression, and being.

Barker aims to create an authentically theatrical art, different in style and objectives from film and television; he sees no point in the theatre trying to compete with these other media, or seek a reflected glamour by what must inevitably remain a second-hand association with their style and effects. He aims to move theatre onto a different ground. He repudiates both entertainment and pedagogic enlightenment (which both offer to answer all questions and resolve all contradictions) as ultimate objectives of the theatrical experience. Rather, he creates a theatre which offers a deeper imaginative opposition to society through speculations involving a questioning relief from prevalent social ideals. This theatre becomes a space which is resistant to social pressures and necessities; and the suspension of these forces and promises entails anxiety, rather than more conventional forms of pleasure. Here the actor, through her/his diction, rhythm and movement, has to mesmerise and fascinate the audience to continue and extend their considerations of possibilities. It may be that the audience for this theatre does not yet go to the theatre. But

it might, if it encountered a theatre (as Barker calls it, an Art of Theatre) which offered
something more than what is currently conventionally associated with 'theatre'. This is a
theatre that proposes that nothing is impossible.

Barker's stage plays first appeared in British theatres in the early 1970s, at the Royal
Court's Theatre Upstairs and the Open Space, at which time his first radio plays were also
broadcast by the BBC. In 1975, *Claw* premiered at the Open Space, and *Stripwell* opened
on the Royal Court main stage, as did *Fair Slaughter* in 1977. Always prolific, Barker was
active with and produced by the Royal Shakespeare Company at the Warehouse Theatre
(*That Good Between Us*, 1977; *The Hang of the Gaol*, 1978; *The Loud Boy's Life*, 1980),
Oxford Playhouse and Sheffield Crucible (*The Love of a Good Man*, 1978/9; *No End of
Blame*, 1981; *A Passion in Six Days*, 1983). At this stage, Barker's plays were muscular,
savagely comic attacks on the promises of social authority; an authority which achieves
its ends through various forms of confidence trickery. Those in power establish rules and
principles (based on justice, law, democracy) by which they themselves are unconstrained.
They provide distractions, incentives and promises of security to prevent their subjects
from recognising and emulating their deceit. Moreover, Barker's plays depict political
power shaped and complicated by the urgings of sexual passion, sometimes unlived but
always eruptive. This passion may not always be a force of disclosure; sometimes personal
pathology informs and shapes social repression. Barker's imaginative compulsion to push
beyond surfaces and current reflexes was exemplified by the way that whilst, like some of
his contemporaries, he analyzed the rhetoric and historical mission of the British political
Right (in *Loud Boy* and *Birth on a Hard Shoulder*, 1980), he presented in *That Good* a
dystopian view of an imagined future Labour government. Barker's drama was also keenly
and unusually aware of counterpoints between the English present and the European past,
especially in *Fair Slaughter*, *The Love of a Good Man* and *The Power of the Dog* (1984), and
his finest achievement of this period and style is his first major consideration of power and
the artist, *No End of Blame*.

However, Barker's imaginative restlessness and stylistic self-development drove
him to new forms, plays of contradiction rather than of analytic thesis. These plays often
excavated a startlingly re-visioned history which challenged conventional obedience to the
moralities of documentary and theatrical realism; they discarded satire of the contemporary
in order to glimpse what Barker termed 'anti-history': an unofficial (indeed, anti-official)
account of formative and recurrent historical events, in the tragic odysseys of marginalised
and obscured figures, who demonstrate the promptings of passion (the pain of wanting),
melancholy (the sensed inevitability of irrevocable loss) and the illogical persistence of the

human spirit. This period begins with the abrasive, fractured landscape of *Victory* (1983), the sexual yearning and enquiry into national promise in *Crimes in Hot Countries* (1983) and leads to Barker's first major tragedy *The Castle* (1985), a densely brooding and deeply resonant excoriation of the psychic entanglements of gender, sexuality, war and power. *The Castle* was premiered by the Royal Shakespeare Company at the Barbican Pit, as the centrepiece of an unfortunately brief retrospective season ('Barker at the Pit'), which also included the professional premiere of *Crimes in Hot Countries* and the hitherto unperformed *Downchild* (written 1977), a fine example of Barker's earlier style which subverted the form of the comedy thriller to condemn the imaginative failures, betrayals and constrictions of the Harold Wilson era which, in the words of that play's protagonist, 'made stupor rhyme with socialism'. Also in 1985, the BBC production of Barker's radio play *Scenes from an Execution* won the Prix Italia; this dramatisation of artistic impulse, political assimilation and state ownership became recognized as a classic of the radio drama form, and also had an extended life as a frequently and internationally revived stage play.

Women *Beware Women* (1986) and *The Bite of the Night* (1988) were the final two flowerings of Barker's associations with the Royal Court and the RSC, respectively. *Women Beware Women* was the first major example of Barker's so-called 'conversations with dead authors', his reanimations of classic texts to pursue new enquiries from the springboard of familiar theatrical and cultural conclusions: here he hi-jacked the form and characters of Thomas Middleton's Jacobean tragedy to present a more disruptive speculation on sexual transformation and its threat to civic discipline. Rejected by the Royal Court (as the RSC would in turn reject *The Europeans*), *The Bite of the Night* was his most ambitious play to date, an innovative four-and-a-half-hour investigation of the mythic imagination of successive societies, and the prescriptive gesture politics of various representatives of different sexual conditionings, delineated in terms and images which were both visceral and increasingly poetic. Indeed, *Bite* represents a full breakthrough into Barker's unique form of poetic theatre, a politically resonant form of expressionism he termed Theatre of Catastrophe, which was developed by *The Europeans* (written 1987) and *Rome* (written 1989, published 1993, and still awaiting a full professional production). *The Europeans* (staged at the University of Aberystwyth in 1991 and by The Wrestling School in 1993) is one of Barker's most masterful and continuingly resonant works, a harrowing love story set in the aftermath of Islamic-Christian cultural war, and dramatising the power of the individual to re-perform and subvert the political mayhem which political systems impose on people.

1988 saw the formation of The Wrestling School, a theatre company founded by the actor-director Kenny Ireland with the main objective of premiering and reassessing Barker's plays in production. Ireland directed *The Last Supper* (1988), *Seven Lears* (1989), a revival of *Victory* (1991) and *The Europeans* (1993), but his humanist directorial instincts were increasingly at odds with Barker's ever more searching and uncompromising texts. Barker directed his own work with *Ego in Arcadia* (Italy, 1992) and *Hated Nightfall* for The Wrestling School in 1994. Indeed, from then on, Barker became the principal director of his own theatre company, The Wrestling School, and expanded his verbal and dramatic ambition and experimentation into a unique theatrical style involving a distinctive boldness in movement and scenographic effects. Barker has developed a sense of pictorial stage composition, informed by his work as a painter, in which movement acquired a near-balletic choreographic precision and the soundscape became an additional 'sonic character' alongside scrupulously delivered language of operatic reach and scale. His theatre is uniquely distinguished by its classical discipline, visual imagery, and moral ruthlessness. His combination of text with precisely orchestrated *mise-en-scène* makes him a British composer of theatre comparable to Robert Wilson, and the publication of the theoretical essays which underpin his practical experimentations (in the volumes *Arguments for a Theatre* and *Death, The One and the Art of Theatre*) emphasise the ways that his forms of artistic enquiry involve challenges to social objectives: here, the aesthetic (and the poetic) is political.

2. THE FORTIFIED CASTLE AND THE FLAYED SKIN

Barker's work exemplifies and demonstrates the power and principles of seduction as characterised by the French philosopher Jean Baudrillard. I here wish to acknowledge, in appreciation, the writing of Charles Lamb (latterly in *The Theatre of Howard Barker*, Routledge, 2005), which first makes the link between Baudrillard and Barker, with specific references to their theories of performance, and self-performance; but I would like to develop the range of associations which one can project (in the geometric sense) from this link. This initiative might appropriately begin with a consideration of what I would suggest to be Barker's principal artistic project: the reassessment of all values, by a formal estrangement of what might conventionally be recognisable or familiar. His repudiation and defiance of the familiar and recognisable terms of so-called 'real life', and of conventional theatrical naturalism, finds argumentative support in Baudrillard's rhetorical assertion:

The real, moreover, has never interested anyone. It is a place of disenchantment, a simulacrum of accumulation against death. And there is nothing more tiresome. What sometimes renders the real fascinating – and the truth as well – is the imaginary catastrophe which lies behind it.[1]

This links with Barker's assertion, 'Only catastrophe can keep us clean', and his refinement of the terms of his form of tragedy, Theatre of Catastrophe. In words from his 1986 revisioning of Thomas Middleton's *Women Beware Women*:

> Catastrophe is also birth. Out the ruins crawls the bloody thing,
> unrecognizable in the ripped rags of former life. Ghastly breaths of
> unfamiliar air! Like the infant, expelled from the silent womb, screams red its
> horror, then tastes oxygen. I have to find my life![2]

Compare Baudrillard's valorisation of the catastrophe which lurks behind the accepted terms of 'real life', where 'real life' is something hitherto accepted and apparently inclusive, now perforated and undermined by the principles of seduction and reversibility:

> Suddenly this seizure rebounds on the so-called 'real' world, to reveal that this 'reality' is
> naught but a staged world, objectified in accord with the rules of perspective... A hole in
> reality, an ironic transfiguration, an exact simulacrum hidden at the heart of reality, and on
> which the latter depends for its functioning. This is the secret of appearances.[3]

And, indeed, Baudrillard's account of the process and dynamics of seduction might also serve as a description of the duels at the centre of Barker's dramas, their struggles for the terms of power and sexuality (which are usually shown to be linked):

> Seduction always seeks to overturn and exorcize a power. If seduction is artificial, it is also
> sacrificial. One is playing with death, it always being a matter of capturing or immolating
> the desire of the other [...] The seductress [...] survives because outside psychology,
> meaning or desire [...]
>   There is something impersonal in every process of seduction, as in every crime,
> something ritualistic [...] Dramaturgy without a subject. The ritual execution of a form
> which consumes its subjects. This is why the piece takes on both the aesthetic form of a
> work of art and the ritual form of a crime.[4]

Barker's drama proposes, in the words of his play *Golgo*, that 'There are those recorded, and those who fail to be recorded, obviously there is OTHER TESTAMENT!... ALWAYS OTHER TESTAMENT!'. Thus Barker opposes History – the imposition of ideological and moral narrative form – with Anti-History – the disruptive fragmentation of this form by the testimony and performance of individual pain, a pain articulated by characters who are socially marginalized but capable of displacing the labellers and 'Historical Authorities' from centre stage; thereby these characters demonstrate the insecurity of all promised reconciliation and the instability of all order. The very spatial dynamic of plays such as *Hated Nightfall*, *(Uncle) Vanya*, *The Early Hours of a Reviled Man*, *Golgo* and *The Fence* are strong examples of a literally 'hell-raising' Barkerian trope, in that some personified force conventionally repressed or marginalised as 'abject' erupts into the centre of the stage action to claim dramatic primacy and wreak havoc (Dancer in *Hated Nightfall*: 'The world abhors me. It writhes to know I walk upon its surfaces... I JUMP ON IT'; 'Chaos. How it suits me. It's my medium'). Such transgressive protagonists are sometimes in turn catechised by choric figures, resembling the classical Eumenides or furies, except that this outraged chorus represents a moral-historical order, which would reclaim and/ or prosecute the transgressor(s). However, the fundamentally conventional terms of this chorus are eluded, questioned and/or reversed by the protagonists' sense of what Stephen Greenblatt – of whom more later – would call 'absolute play' (Dancer: 'What you describe as a rebuke to me, is no more or less than my desire').

   In their provocation and examination of the catastrophic collapse of conventional values, Barker's plays necessarily interrogate myths of political totality, and generate imaginative seismic reverberations into various areas of global political tensions. Either metaphorically or literally, these tensions are centred upon what the French philosopher Julia Kristeva calls 'that fragile spot of our subjectivity', a vulnerable part of the self 'where our collapsed defenses reveal, beneath the appearances of a fortified castle, a flayed skin'.[5] Indeed, Barker's plays *The Castle* (1985), *The Europeans* (1987) and *A Hard Heart* (1992) take as their central images fortification and sieges. They demonstrate an incessant drive for one-upmanship, escalating terms, outbidding, ostentatious performance and concessionary sacrifice – crucially, of other people – in the interests of a supposed larger game-plan. This drive is often associated with the sexual reflexes of an individual psyche, projecting itself onto others, because insecure and therefore paranoically desperate to establish a control, or monopoly, of definition – which inevitably turns out to be doomed and flawed. The architect of The Castle, in the play of that title, creates an edifice which will re-present and amplify the sexual conditioning of his captor and ruler; the architect knows that The

Castle 'will create enemies where there are none', and the more insistently it escalates, the more devastating are the repercussions when its inevitable Achilles heel is discovered, and its weight of invested definition is turned against itself in collapse.[6] I hope, from even this brief account, you will glean a sense of how these plays predict aspects of post-9/11 global politics and the paradoxical reflexes of the so-called 'war on terror'.

3. SHATTERED MIRRORS AND ABSOLUTE PLAY

But I would also argue that Barker's drama offers further insights, in terms which other theories might help us to appreciate fully. Stephen Greenblatt's theories of Self-Fashioning start from the argument that 'in sixteenth-century England there were both selves and a sense that they could be fashioned', where 'the power to impose a shape upon oneself is an aspect of the more general power to control identity – that of others at least as often as one's own'.[7] Perhaps one might identify an affinity of impulse and cultural climate between 'sixteenth-century England' and late twentieth and early twenty-first century Britain (both Thatcherite and Blairite), highlighted by Greenblatt's terms:

> If we say there is a new stress on the executive power of the will, we must say that there is the most sustained and relentless assault upon the will; if we say that there is a new social mobility, we must say that there is a new assertion of power by both family and state to determine all movement within the society; if we say that there is a heightened awareness of the existence of alternative models of social, theological, and psychological organization, we must say that there is a new dedication to the imposition of control upon those modes and ultimately to the destruction of alternatives.[8]

Put simply, Greenblatt suggests that the Renaissance saw 'an increased self-consciousness about the fashioning of human identity as a manipulable, artful process'.[9] He argues that the Renaissance was a time of unprecedented negotiation between, on the one hand, the experience of being moulded by political, social and cultural forces outside one's control, forces which were apparently benign and neo-liberal but ultimately totalitarian; and, on the other hand, the imaginative effort to shape one's own identity. Of course, human nature cannot exist independent of culture and its control mechanisms (plans, rules and instructions) for the governing of behaviour: this is a system of meanings, Greenblatt claims,

…that creates specific individuals by governing the passage from abstract potential to concrete historical embodiment. Literature functions within this system in three interlocking ways: as a manifestation of the concrete behaviour of its particular author, as itself the expression of the codes by which behaviour is shaped, and as a reflection on these codes.[10]

Barker's imagining, and increasing control of the theatrical production, of his dramatic works is consciously and purposefully performed in these philosophical and practical terms. His Shakespearean re-evaluations and reanimations of historical figures, literary characters and existing dramatic texts are a conscious address to the poetics of an English (-speaking / -reading) culture, frequently and startlingly (re)located in a European context. In such instances, existing texts and characters are viewed 'as the focal point for converging lines of force'[11] in culture, sites of interplay between structures and interpretations which inform the constructions of identity. Greenblatt notes how: 'We respond to a quality, even a willed or partially willed quality, in the figures…who are, we assume by analogy to ourselves, engaged in their own acts of selection and shaping and who seem to drive themselves towards the most sensitive regions of their culture, to express and even, by design, to embody its dominant satisfactions and anxieties'.[12] This is, if anything, more consistently true of Barker's characters than even Shakespeare's or Marlowe's; Barker's characters are frequently, if not always willingly or enviably, propelled into particularly stark forms of 'cultural embodiment'. They are, in current performance terms, 'explicit body performers', *dramatically fictional* but at least to some degree authentically *theatrically manifested* by the courage of the performer, as in efforts of will involving speech, action and physical disclosure (such as nakedness) which throw notions and criteria of 'authenticity' into play.

Moreover I would propose that both Barker's drama and his theatrical productions exemplify and explore what Julia Kristeva identifies as the effect of abjection: the imperfect process whereby the symbolism of a dominant social system tries to exclude some embarrassing thing or body which calls its boundaries into question, but finds it cannot part with, or separate from, it completely; the creature who represents embarrassing possibility comes back, even more compulsively, to call the prevailing notion of (im)possibility into question. The social and theatrical space that surrounds the Barker protagonist is, as in Kristeva's terms, 'essentially divisible, foldable and catastrophic'. This unforgivable protagonist constantly (re)describes her/his self in her/his social surroundings, whose 'fluid confines…constantly question his solidity and impel him to start afresh'.[13] Violent and painful passions generate tensions which erupt and burst, as the protagonist decides to shatter the mirrors of conventional reflection which surround them.

A striking example of these effects occurs in Barker's play *The Early Hours of a Reviled Man* (broadcast by BBC Radio 1988; directed for the stage by Roger Owen, Aberystwyth Theatr y Castell 1990), in which Sleen, a doctor and eminent novelist of reactionary views, takes his regular perambulation through the streets where he has loved, triumphed and suffered. He is accosted by old friends and new enemies, all invoking a sense of justice he is determined never to satisfy. The play's inspiration is the historical figure of the French novelist Louis-Ferdinand Céline, whose writing depicted life fatalistically as a series of catastrophes, in which only death and the process of dying have dominion, and only the energy of hatred promises relief from feelings of personal emptiness and persecution.[14] Barker's Sleen is a masterful dramatisation of the compulsive drive and stealthy ability to defy all forms of moral superiority; Sleen defines himself through doing the 'Unfashionable / And / Untolerated / Thing',[15] and, like other charismatic Barker protagonists, his potency resides in his command of imaginative (self-) invention. These characters achieve what Greenblatt identifies as the quintessential sign of power, 'the ability to impose one's own fictions on the world'.[16] The persistence of Céline/Sleen's offensiveness, and the resentment which his paradoxical qualities inspire, makes him an appropriate figure for Barker's exploration: he is self-armoured in pessimistic fatalism which does not inhibit his wilful refusal to submit or be 'smothered' by conventional ideals of happiness, rationality, longevity or utilitarianism. Sleen exposes the insecurity underlying his enemies' insistence on separating themselves from him: 'I deserve everything I get, but so do you'. Indeed, their moral outrage is revealed as a hysterical compulsion to distinguish or redeem themselves by asserting their own superiority over him, a reflex of abjection which nevertheless gives Sleen an irrational power, to dissolve their limits of identity.

Kristeva, in her book of theoretical poetics *Powers of Horror*, identifies the Abject as

> something rejected from which one does not part... What does not respect borders, positions, rules. The in-between, the ambiguous, the composite. The traitor, the liar, the criminal with a good conscience, the shameless rapist, the killer who claims he is a saviour [17]

The figure of Sleen, a brilliant novelist and doctor to the poor who is also anti-semitic, and his progress through the city exemplify and dramatise the very effects of which Kristeva writes; appropriately, since her study is partly concerned to identify the dynamics of mutual degradation in the writings of Céline, his assault on the dichotomy of the sacred and the profane. She notes how such a figure calls all borders into question, because abjection 'is above all ambiguity. Because, while releasing a hold, it does not radically cut off the subject from what threatens it – on the contrary, abjection acknowledges it to be in perpetual danger'.[18] In this sense, *The Early Hours* is a jet-black comedy of abjection and contamination, in which Sleen's pursuers represent the subjects who wish to separate themselves from his unforgivably questioning presence, but who find their boundaries continually problematized or dissolved by his sheer persistence in existence, and their inability to murder him. His very presence conducts the others through a series of revelatory scenes which demonstrate to them how their dependency on postures of correctness and self-identifications with moral superiority *debar* them from his unshakeable purchase on the imagination – even on theirs. *The Early Hours* is one of Barker's most profoundly comic disruptions of the terms of moral identity, and examples of what Greenblatt calls 'absolute play', the pursuit of the unforgivable through shameless performance which disrupts the containments of conventional morality:

> The will to play flaunts society's cherished orthodoxies, embraces what the culture finds loathsome or frightening, transforms the serious into the joke and unsettles the category of the joke by taking it seriously, courts self-destruction in the interest of anarchic discharge of its energy. This is play on the brink of an abyss, *absolute* play.[19]

4. THE CULTURAL NEGOTIATIONS OF A SHAKESPEAREAN DRAMATIST

The interrogation of received cultural forms and associated moral wisdoms is an important, and often particularly subversive, strategy available to all artists, beyond the potentially sterile literary fashion for (identifying) intertextuality. Jeanette Winterson, for example, argues how, in her chosen realm of fiction, texts are 'always in dialogue' with other texts in a process which is importantly dynamic, rather than static for both reader and writer; her own process of making what she terms 'cover versions of stories that we know very well' is a way of finding new angles and possibilities with which to inject 'fresh material into what already exists, so the story changes' and is 'kept alive by the retelling, by the changing… I think of it not as a literary game, nor as an exercise, but as a necessary nourishment from one text to another'.[20] I have noted elsewhere, not only how the work of Shakespeare provides richly fertile ground for such re-evaluative imaginings, but how his work is itself the most vibrant classical exemplification of this very strategy, and how we might speak with proper accuracy and seriousness of someone 'Being a Shakespearean Dramatist':

> The genius of Shakespeare's drama might aptly be said to reside in the *incompleteness* of its *prescriptions*: hence its challenging power and its infinitely renewing fascination. I would also add that the 'necessary choice' of the dramatist, like that of the performer, also excludes, but simultaneously illuminates, others... It is worth reminding ourselves in this context that this is how Shakespeare himself usually worked. With the exceptions of the three apparently 'sourceless' plays (*Love's Labour's Lost*, *A Midsummer Night's Dream* and *The Tempest*), every Shakespeare play is a consciously surprising re-emphasizing re-animation of some pre-existing story or play, and the explosive power of *King Lear* is amplified by its startling final departure from the happy ending of its chrysalis play, *King Leir*.[21]

Barker was significantly nominated by the late Sarah Kane as 'the Shakespeare of our age'.[22] However, Barker's own model of practice might be at least as much influenced by classical traditions of painting, wherein numerous artists present their distinctive and distinguishing compositions of and perspectives on subjects, such as the Crucifixion, narratives from the Apochrypha and images from classical epics and myths, as part of a continuum of both *hommage* and making new argument from old matter. A fine example is provided by Barker's *(Uncle) Vanya* (produced at the University of Aberystwyth in 1995 and by The Wrestling School in 1996). As Barker observed in 1994 about his imaginative reconsiderations of 'voids and absences':

> Sometimes these resonant spaces, when investigated, have led me to an interrogation of the function of the text – and the cultural status of the author – in contemporary society, an elision which is perhaps inevitable in confronting authors who are now much more significant than the sum total of their works. I am here thinking not so much of Shakespeare, now a negligible influence on the tone of contemporary writing in Britain – itself a tragedy for the theatre of our time – as Chekhov, whose uncontested authority in British theatrical and cultural circles has made of him a more luminous icon in this part of Europe even than in his country of origin.[23]

Barker's *(Uncle) Vanya* begins with a savagely comic condensation of Chekhov's world, in which the characters perform extreme versions of their monotonous self-preoccupation. Only Vanya has the painful emotional and imaginative mobility to step outside the frame of the action, to express with extravagant ruthlessness his (conventionally subtextual) agonized passions to the audience; but, even though he can pause and comment on the action of the play, he seems powerless to alter its course. In his articulate despair, Vanya invites audience judgement on other characters and his own motives whilst artfully challenging their terms of definition and reaches of imagination: 'Do you agree the professor is vile or do I slander him am I correct or extreme HE GOES TO BED WITH SUCH A YOUNG WOMAN am I poisoned by sexual jealousy or HE PUTS HIS FLESH INSIDE HER BODY or or or'.[24] Even the object of his adoration Helena tells (taunts?) him, 'You should stop grumbling and reconcile people to one another' (p 302) and his beloved niece Sonya drones the mantras of conventional futile hope: 'Uncle Vanya will be happy one day, won't you Uncle, happy one day?' (p 303). However, Barker's Vanya successfully shoots Serebryakov (whereas Chekhov's Vanya repeatedly misses), and is thereby committed to a life outside conventional morality. Even Helena expects him to turn himself in to the police. However, Vanya is defiantly, exhilaratingly unrepentant, even when her husband reappears as a ghost and tries to make Vanya stop his rebellion. Barker's Vanya seems prepared to break from the melancholy of Chekhov's world, crucially and defiantly preferring to accept consequences:

SEREBRYAKOV: The problem with an action Chekhov says is that it leads to consequences

VANYA: I do not wish to know what he says

SEREBRYAKOV: Each action more ridiculous than the last

VANYA: So be it

SEREBRYAKOV: Ramifications of such outlandish character the perpetrator forfeits every sympathy

VANYA: I DON'T REQUIRE SYMPATHY TELL HIM. It is possible I am not human. I was comic and now I am inhuman. The comic, the pathetic, the impotence, made me lovable, but underneath I was not human. And nor is anyone. Underneath, Human. TELL CHEKHOV! (p 309)

As I have commented elsewhere, 'Barker's Vanya reveals that Chekhov's play is only nominally play: it is more accurately an essay in…limitation…Vanya bursts the walls of Chekhov's play by pursuing the unforgivable'.[25] However, Chekhov enters the play as a character and force seeking to reassert control, maintaining that the characters' attempted revolution was only an adolescent rebellion, 'A mutiny is merely the affirmation of things after all' (p 329). Indeed, when Chekhov himself dies, the other characters apart from Vanya seem to find it necessary to reinvent and incorporate him in their habitual reflexes and fears of freedom. Finally even Vanya seems ready to accept the judgement and death sentence issued by the chorus of remaining characters, now a mixture of dead and living ghosts, but at the fateful moment he chooses not to yield, not even to his grief at the suicide of Helena. He chooses to live further in instinctive imaginative defiance of the limitations which all the other characters have enviously sought to place upon him. Struggling with shock and grief, he nevertheless identifies a responsibility towards his own potential and discovers the '*effort of will*' which takes him out of the room.

Barker's play *(Uncle) Vanya* offers the audience an experience in which the theatrical conventions of Chekhovian naturalism are exposed and vividly dramatised as forms which permit and reflect an imaginative self-limitation, even the dignifying of depression, in distinctively English rather than Russian terms of systematic self-abnegation and limitation. *(Uncle) Vanya* dramatises and demonstrates the possibility of broaching the definitions inherent in Chekhovian form and, analogously, its attendant enshrinement of social and personal determinism in the theatres of both national culture and personal consciousness. The effects of delimitation in this play importantly extend to the space and setting, the plasticity of which reflects the human upheaval, for example in the fragmentation of the house and the incursion of the sea, whilst replacing the stage conventions of theatrical naturalism and realism (which are explicitly identified with conformity in objectified imaginative defeat) with unpredictable effects of rupture and transformation.

5. A LAW UNTO HIMSELF

Hated Nightfall (1994) offers in many ways a classical example of Barker's work: a figure usually excluded from or submerged by history – the tutor of the Romanoff children, Dancer – pursues his own claim to significance, an apotheosis of absolute play, murderous abandon and vengeful erotic dedication, with wry but lethal disregard for the agents of historical order and official ideologies who attempt to interrupt him. In a speculation about the last hours of the Russian Imperial family in 1918, the play imagines the brief incandescence of Dancer, whose sexual fixation on his mistress is permitted tortured expression amidst the social reversals; he offers himself as a self-consuming harbinger of death. As Barker observes in the programme essay for the 1994 Wrestling School production of the play, entitled 'Saintliness, Death and the Perfect Family':

> Catastrophe is also opportunity, and Revolution's seductive fallacy has always been the promise of absolute licence…in the exhilaration of the vortex the ordered life dissolves and what beckons through chaos is PERMISSION. Here, one who aspires to sainthood might rinse his personality in the foaming hydrants of a collapsed authority, wring himself

out in a new shape and discover performances of self which, however insubstantial their foundations, are incandescent with INVENTION...[26]

Dancer seizes the opportunity for an orchestrated expression of his own precisely excessive eroticism to take centre stage. Johan Engels's set for the Wrestling School production of *Hated Nightfall* featured plastic walls, apparently firm boundaries which could suddenly deliriously warp, as the obscured faces of the Chorus pressed their clamouring features through the fabric to pronounce on the central action before vanishing or being banished again by Dancer, who, like Sleen, defies the ostentatious moral incomprehension and terms of permission of his adversaries. When a Romanoff daughter suggests 'you are not really bad, citizen', he insists 'I am / I am that bad (*Pause.*) / Believe me. / You merely cannot bear to contemplate it'.[27] When Dancer kills a bureaucratic representative of the new historical order, the Chorus protest, 'We can forgive the revolutionary death but this' (p 7) and denounce Dancer as 'INSANE', he contemptuously replies, 'You would say that! How Necessary you should think I am insane! Think so if it relieves you!' (p 8). He refuses terms of legitimacy: 'I do not call myself History. The Agent of Destiny. Justice. The People's Will. I don't drape myself'; 'This is not History. This is the opposite of History' (p 33). Master of a crucially limited time and space, Dancer is determined to be 'a law unto myself' (p 9) (a principle of the Barker aesthetic), a master of anti-official ceremonies. However, '*The spell is broken*' (p 42) when Romanoff re-establishes the hierarchy of his family relationships and forges a brief alliance with the revolutionaries to deny Dancer his apotheosis; this resurgence of moral consensus brings down Dancer, literally and physically, for his crimes of 'ARROGANT / AND / PETULANT / DISHARMONY' (p 46); but most injuriously, it threatens a death which Dancer fears will be 'poorer than my imagination predicted' (p 47).

In some respects, Barker's theatre reaches into effects associated with what Hans-Thies Lehmann has termed 'postdramatic theatre', in which the spectators 'are no longer just filling in the predictable gaps in a dramatic narrative but are asked to become active witnesses who reflect on their own meaning-making':[28]

> Here everything depends on not understanding immediately. Rather one's perception
> has to remain open for connections, correspondences and clues at completely unexpected
> moments, perhaps casting what was said earlier in a completely new light.[29]

Barker's own productions have certainly pushed his plays further into scenically dynamic formations, what Lehmann calls a 'disposition of spaces of meaning and sound-spaces';[30]

and Barker's play *Found in the Ground* (published 2001, as yet unproduced) represents his most ambitious landscape play, a scenic poem set in a continuous present which nevertheless creates 'new accents in subtle variations and loops'.[31] On the other hand, Barker is the modernist theatre *auteur par excellence*, insisting on constructing in its wholeness 'an aesthetic theatre composition of words, meanings, sounds, gesture', rather than demonstrating the 'fragmentary and partial character' which characterises much contemporary performance.[32] Barker's degrees of non-/accordance with Lehmann's terms of postdramatic theatre might be usefully identified in full elsewhere. If one accepts Barker's distinction between the conventions of 'the theatre' and the objectives of his 'Art of the Theatre',[33] one might even argue that Barker is developing a post-theatrical drama, which reaches imaginatively beyond received and current notions of stageability and fashion.

Consider Patrick McCarthy's observations on Céline:

His life was dedicated to probing the pain that men feel at their contact with the world. Each person knows, as he goes about his daily round, that one part of him does not join in. It remains outside, permanent and untouched... It was Céline's destiny to face this 'otherness': to look hard at it and liberate it... It explains why reading Céline is such a shattering experience. It is not that fate dominates or that death lies in wait. It is that at every moment the 'otherness' is rampant. It runs around screaming that the nightmare is real and the waking hours only a dream. It imposes on the reader a very special kind of pain – reminiscent perhaps of Shakespeare's wildest moments in *King Lear*.[34]

McCarthy's terms are also relevant to Barker, except that Barker avoids what McCarthy identifies as Céline's fundamental 'sense of fear of man abandoned to himself',[35] through his exploration of the theatrical medium. However, in Barker's hands, the theatrical medium and event avoids and deconstructs the conventional clichés of collective event and experience, whilst nevertheless demanding that the audience engage with the work in an imaginatively creative way, by confronting and engaging with the dissolution of the conventional definitions upon which recognisable 'reality' depends. Rather, Barker's theatre shows, through its demonstrative entwinements of individual solitudes, how the theatricality and performance of political obsessions inform our most intimate personal configurations; but his theatre also insists that private and secret feelings may have public consequences, as the fences which constitute our separateness and selves may invite, compulsively, the broaching of their own limitations and the redefinition of identity. His work stands at, and extends, the boundaries of what is possible in theatre.

NOTES

1. J Baudrillard, *Seduction*, tr. Brian Singer (Basingstoke, Macmillan, 1990), p 46

2. H Barker, *Women Beware Women* in *Collected Plays vol 3* (London, Calder, 1996), p 180

3. Baudrillard, *Seduction*, pp 63, 65–6

4. *Ibid.*, pp 87, 100

5. J Kristeva, *Powers of Horror*, tr. L S Roudiez (New York, Columbia University Press, 1982), p 135

6. The ruler, Stucley, exemplifies and embodies Kristeva's description of 'an ego, wounded to the point of annulment, barricaded and untouchable', alternately cowering and fantasising hostile phantoms with a fearsome eloquence which nevertheless only permits and creates antagonistic relationships with others. The central process of *The Castle* is strikingly, if unintentionally, summarised by Kristeva's writing: 'Separation exists, and so does language, even brilliantly at times, with apparently remarkable intellectual realizations. But no current flows – it is a pure and simple splitting, an abyss without any possible means of conveyance between its two edges. No subject, no object; petrification on one side, falsehood on another'; Kristeva, *Powers of Horror*, p 47

7. S Greenblatt, *Renaissance Self-Fashioning from More to Shakespeare* (Chicago, Chicago University Press, 1980), p 1

8. *Ibid.*, pp 1–2

9. *Ibid.*, p 2

10. *Ibid.*, pp 3–4

11. *Ibid.*, p 5

12. *Ibid.*, pp 6–7

13. Kristeva, *Powers of Horror*, p 8

14. See P McCarthy, *Céline* (London, Allen Lane, 1975) for a good introductory critical biography of this writer.

15. H Barker, *A Hard Heart* and *The Early Hours of a Reviled Man* (London, Calder, 1992), p 51

16. Greenblatt, *Renaissance Self-Fashioning*, p 13

17. Kristeva, *Powers of Horror*, p 5

18. *Ibid.*, p 9

19. Greenblatt, *Renaissance Self-Fashioning*, p 220. See also Barker's *Downchild*, and the protagonist's climactic literal 'play on the brink of an abyss'.

20. J Winterson, *Lighthousekeeping* (London, Harper Perennial, 2005), 'PS' section, pp 2–3

21. D I Rabey, 'On Being a Shakespearian Dramatist' in *The Wye Plays* (Bristol, Intellect, 2004), p 4

22. Quoted in D Rebellato, 'Sarah Kane: An Appreciation', in *New Theatre Quarterly* (August 1999), 280–1, p 280. In this Rebellato also recalls Kane's passionate performance as Bradshaw in a production of Barker's *Victory* at Bristol University, and her enthusiasm at the thought of playing Skinner in Barker's *The Castle* (Kane: 'the part I was born to play').

23. H Barker, *Arguments for a Theatre* 3rd edn (Manchester: Manchester University Press, 1997), p 153

24. H Barker, *(Uncle) Vanya* in *Collected Plays vol 2* (London, Calder, 1993), p 299. Subsequent quotations from this play will be indicated by page numbers for this edition until otherwise indicated.

25. D I Rabey, 'For the Absent Truth Erect: Impotence and Potency in Howard Barker's Recent Drama', *Essays in Theatre/Études Théâtrales* 10, 1 (November 1991), 31–7, p 35

26. H Barker, programme essay, *Hated Nightfall* (The Wrestling School production) 1994

27. H Barker, *Hated Nightfall* in *Hated Nightfall* and *Wounds to the Face* (London, Calder, 1994), p 6. Subsequent quotations from this play will be indicated by page numbers for this edition until otherwise indicated.

28. K Jürs-Munby, 'Introduction' to H-T Lehmann, *Postdramatic Theatre* (London, Routledge, 2006), p 6

29. Lehmann, *Postdramatic Theatre.*, p 87

30. *Ibid.*, p 32

31. *Ibid.*, p 63. Lehmann's account of the landscape play is based on Gertrude Stein's work.

32. *Ibid.*, pp 56–7

33. See H Barker, *Death, The One and the Art of Theatre* (London, Routledge, 2005)

34. McCarthy, *Céline*, pp 316–7

35. *Ibid.*, p 316

HOWARD BARKER IN CONVERSATION

WITH **DAVID IAN RABEY** AND **KAROLINE GRITZNER**

RABEY The exordium has become an increasingly important ingredient in your
direction: sometimes specified in the text, sometimes not, and sometimes developed
differently in rehearsal to the scripted abstract (as for your own production of *He
Stumbled*). The exordium is a sequence and proposition combining recorded sound
with strong visual images and rhythmic movement, presenting the audience with
striking imagery as soon as they enter the space; so that the audience enter the
space on the performers' terms, rather than on those of their own daily routines and
discourses of 'sense'. These images then resolve into a narrative when the performers
are released into language. *Found in the Ground* begins with a scripted exordium, but
in this play more than any other of yours to date, the aesthetic drive and rhythm of
the exordium seems extended into the scenographic propositions and drive of the
entire play, and we lose any Interlude (such as we formerly encountered in *The Bite
of the Night*, *Rome*, or *The Last Supper*). In *Found in the Ground* you seem to invoke
and orchestrate an opera for a moving landscape, in a way which is perhaps only
comparable to Robert Wilson's scenographic direction.

BARKER The exordium is my substitute for properly possessing the performance
space. I have often said that the foyer is an obstacle to a spiritual experience, an area of
trivia littered with the distractive detritus of entertainment. I cannot own a theatre, so
I am compelled to create the conditions for my work in that critical time-lapse between
the auditorium doors being opened and the beginning of the performance. Naturally
the audience are not expecting this environment as they take their seats – they may
even resent it – but it is a necessary break with the normal continuum of street-foyer-
performance-street, an admonition that they will not be seeing or hearing according to
the conventional rules of social-realist theatre, comedy or what is routinely on offer.

   The routine of the exordium has to be repetitive, however complex it can sometimes
appear, partly for practical reasons, such as its late arrival in the rehearsal, when the
actors are already fully occupied with the technical, so it cannot be too demanding of
their time and resources…an example might be provided by the Wedding Machine in

my 2003 production for the Wrestling School of *13 Objects*: as a simple fulcrum rises and falls, lifted on a pulley by a seated, visible actor, one end plunging a collection of objects – lilies, a clock, a trowel – into a tank of fluid, and the other simultaneously lifts a framed wedding photograph high, away from a half-naked bride who is contemplating it…she rises to follow it and turns to accuse another seated bride…as her gesture is completed a shriek comes from the sound system (pre-recorded of course) …it's a simple rhythm…but I have to say actors lack physical training and often cannot do it…Victoria Wicks is exemplary but she has a dancer's rhythms…in *A House of Correction* an actress doing a similar series of movements never got over an innate feeling that it was 'silly', and one failed element sinks the whole thing…again and again you are brought back to the value of the ensemble…you have to recruit people who want your sort of aesthetic and believe in it.

You are right to observe that in *Found in the Ground* some of the choreographic features of my exordia remain…the choruses of nurses with trays…the march of the headless victims…the racing approach of the dogs. Perhaps I was thinking here of sustaining the musical nature of the exordium…so that the play is like a string quartet by Bartók…the themes keep returning always developed and furthered, the torsion increased…

RABEY   You often use sound as an invasive force and factor, in your exordia and subsequently.

BARKER   I have nearly eliminated music from my theatre but instead use drones or reassembled cuts from a small number of modern composers, or recorded cries and breaths. I use the cries to punctuate the image.

RABEY   Your use of costume has become increasingly distinctive and important, through realisations of the designs of Billie Kaiser. They are often simple, blending the modern with the classical or 1940s/50s, monochrome features combining with set and lighting in a highly painterly stage image.

BARKER   The Barker/Kaiser designs are part of an overall vision of the stage, part of the de-naturalising imagery. For one thing, they tend to be monochromatic, as the sets do, creating a flat plane for voice to dominate…the costumes are beautiful and as you have observed owe a great deal to classic *haute couture* of the 1930s, 40s and 50s, not least in their hats. They are intended to raise the status of the female characters both socially and sexually, hence the common use of the half-veil and high heels. They have a profound relationship with the naked body because in some sense they almost command their own desecration, the unveiling of the female characters. Of course here again the designs make demands on the actors, you have to know how to walk in these costumes. Wicks, Jessop, Bertish know how to walk and the sound of the heel on the floor is critical. The use of the narrow range of shades in the clothing of the performers asserts the non-naturalism of the production, and obviously the eruption of one colour becomes powerfully suggestive: I'm thinking of Gertrude's sudden appearance in yellow in *Gertrude – The Cry*. Inversely, the collapse of a character's moral status might show itself in the poverty of a garment, as at Doorway's dying speech in *The Fence*.

RABEY In *The Fence*, Photo is blind, as are his father and sister, a recurrent motif in your work to suggest a particularly thin-skinned character (such as Isonzo in *The Twelfth Battle*, Smith in *Rome*…); paradoxically, you create increasingly visual landscapes in production, through which these blind characters must move…

BARKER Blindness in my plays has something intensely and fundamentally *of theatre* about it…it has an irresistible moral value, which is nothing to do with pitying blind people, I mean a moral aesthetic. It has its supreme moments in *Isonzo* and *The Fence* in a similar context, when a loved woman is exposed in her nakedness to eyes that cannot see. It is densely metaphorical in *The Fence* when Istoria goes to her friend and undresses her for the sightless eyes of Photo, a gesture of sexual possession, and of course the triangularity between what the audience *can* see and what the character *cannot* is full of exquisite contradictions. In *Isonzo*, the old man's entire store of sexuality is invested in sound or in his imagined ability to hear what the sighted cannot…the *interior* of his loved one…blindness is licence to penetrate more deeply than the sighted might require.

RABEY You have spoken of your aesthetic objective being anxiety, rather than more conventional theatrical forms of pleasure. The audience encounter a spare, often monochromatic, energetically costumed production, with excessive language at the core of the event, and focus shifted onto the actor's body as an instrument of speech and movement; with sound (rather than music) cues adding a further processed, spatial quality to create a soundscape to stress the audience, rather than comfort them or create an emotional climate within which to engage sympathetically. As Chris Corner has observed, this is an aesthetic density, rather than an opulence or richness of detail, a richness which does not overwhelm the actors. As you have said, this is work which offers an obligation rather than a conventionally recognisable pleasure, presenting extreme situations which can answer a boredom with the status quo and recognise a hunger to search.

BARKER   Beauty and anxiety are not strangers to one another, and because beauty is something of a privilege, it is privileged in my *mise-en-scène* also, where the effects are most carefully prepared, and – might I say – the result of a single vision and not a compromise of competing imaginations however 'collaborative' they might seem to be. I am attempting two things simultaneously: to draw the audience into a relationship with the stage which eradicates sympathy at the outset as a prime condition and replaces it with an obsessive gaze and its audial equivalent, both overwhelming and both a plethora. If the exordium announces new terms of seeing and hearing, the play confirms it and, for those who are willing, frees them of the common expectations of 'understanding' and replaces it with a hypnotic regard. The anxiety comes from what's said and what's done, because they are profoundly resistant to conventional morality, obviously. This moral refusal has produced a wall of resistance to my work in the critical and theatre worlds, revealing in itself of the collusive nature of these bodies, but also making it painfully (once) and luxuriously (now) clear that 'I do not know the theatre and the theatre does not know me'.

RABEY   However, it also strikes me that the invocations and manipulations of anxiety are very much the currency of recent reactionary politics associated with the so-called 'War on Terror', in which political leaders of various ideologies seek to 'bind' their subjects 'with fear', to recall a resonant phrase from your 1980 play *The Loud Boy's Life*. This political climate, with its ideal of an impossible 'security', makes it particularly difficult to advance the offer and characterisation of anxiety as exhilarating – difficult, but perhaps particularly necessary, to unlock prevalent associations. How would you distinguish your ideal form (and sensation) of anxiety from indiscriminate fearfulness and contraction?

BARKER   Let us not confuse fear with anxiety. Fear exists between men in all social situations, and politics sometimes manipulates it. Social democracies like ours create fear whilst attempting to ameliorate pain, a dazzling contradiction. Fear of sickness and death is obsessive here, and the state in its medicalisation of all human experience makes itself a body-snatching agency in the process. Organ removal, an extreme form

of the impertinence of the *demos* and the eradication of the private, is justified only by
dread of death. But I think of anxiety in my theatre as a state quite different to fear…
rather it is a troubling of the fixed strata of moral conventions…a sort of low quaking
that threatens the foundations of the stable personality…the public doesn't quite
know where to place its feet, there is an insecurity, but one which is simultaneously
exhilarating – surely the best example is the shock and freedom lent to Katrin by the
fall of the social system in *The Europeans*. I think of these plays as types of prayer, they
demand something of a world which won't give it, but one does not cease praying…
Isn't one anxious when one prays? Tragedy originates from these same sources.

RABEY   As Brendan Kennelly puts it in his version of *Medea*, 'Prayer…is anger at what
is, and a longing for what should be'…?

BARKER   No, I think that would be to reduce prayer to a practical statement of aims
and desires. It is without anger, it is uttered without hope, to a wall of silence…the
cosmological oblivion to which it is addressed does not, however, detract from its
passionate need, its value as *expression*… I tried to introduce this in *Two Skulls* [Danish
radio, 2002].

RABEY   Nakedness is another recurrent motif in your plays and productions, but you
characteristically combine elements of erotic allure with associations and experiences
of fear, a horror which may potentially be common to characters, actors and audiences.
This is a further feature of your landscape of anxiety, in which (self-) exposure is
simultaneously fixing and unsettling.

BARKER   As Gay says in wonder at the state of nakedness in *The Bite of the Night*, to be
naked is to be weak in some ways, but potentially powerful in others. For example, the
authority of the final naked moment in *The Fence* isn't simply erotic. In that final image,
Algeria's nakedness is a supreme rebuke to the forces that overthrew her regime, it is
a triumphant reversal of the sordid nakedness of the dead dictator, as when Mussolini
and his mistress were suspended upside down and humiliated in 1944. It is such
a mobile surface of concepts, the unclothed body, a surface which, no matter how
overwritten, still has the power to be discovered *differently*…it mocks pornography,
which plays with the secret, by being authentically secret.

RABEY   However, there is a powerful element of eroticism in the mesmerism of your
plays in performance: though this eroticism may be more to do with the sense of

anticipation, which can prolong excitement or 'stretch pleasures...to their breaking point' (to use a phrase from *Isonzo*). Perhaps there is here an unconventional acknowledgement of the *instability* of eroticism: a staged awareness of how easily it can turn into, and back from, its opposite.

BARKER I should not want to suggest that I don't employ the erotic in the naked. Obviously in *Gertrude – The Cry* the triangular agony of the opening scene is deeply erotic: two lovers kill for passion and find deeper desire through their own cruelty, and a victim must watch the taking of his own sexual property by another (and I say 'property' here deliberately...the queen is the property of the king, primarily for procreating the line of dynasty; see *The Gaoler's Ache*) ...hence the three cries, each one musically distinct for the emotion it contains. Nakedness was critical in this scene, and when I saw the play in Vienna, in a good production, much was forfeited because the actress declined to be naked but wore underwear to protect her modesty, and I don't criticise, the stage is terribly revealing, but I must also praise Victoria Wicks in the Wrestling School premiere production, for her phenomenal bravery in her playing of the sexual moment and its complete success. And yes, she wore high heels throughout, I was constructing a sexual moment of intensity which necessarily employed the erotic conventions of its day. What I did not want to do was to imitate a sexual act naturalistically...it was an exquisite metaphor made vivid by the language spoken. You are right to suggest that such scenes always risk bathos...it is in the actor's power, if she trusts the director's concepts, to keep that at bay.

RABEY In the context of eroticism, I am also interested in allusions you have made to sex as a potential basis for religion, or neo-religious beliefs; and also in your developing sense of 'the religious' in your work, which seems neither institutional nor conventional, but a passionate rejection of conventional worldliness.

BARKER Why do I sometimes speak of the religious aspect of sexuality? I think because religion shares its ecstatic potential, but more, because religion is the study of secrets, and the secret retreats always before knowledge and takes up residence somewhere else...so does sexuality, it is self-inventing, it has its great books, its great testaments, perhaps I have written one or two myself, and it is also irreducible to anything else...look how pitiful the sex manual is...the scientific is abolished here...and it entails the prayer...what lover has not looked on the nakedness of his/her desired one without uttering a prayer of devotion? What is the demand in that prayer? The hope that this is the doorway to some other truth…

GRITZNER   The catastrophes of the twentieth century feature strongly in your work. Many of your protagonists devise precarious ways of stepping out of their historical moments. Social context does not seem to restrict the possibilities of their actions.

BARKER   Yes, the world wars are in *The Love of a Good Man* and *The Power of the Dog*. In the latter the two egoists, the beautiful fashion model and the dreamy philosopher, try to escape the elimination of the individual by faceless bureaucrats and policemen in Stalin's Europe. The protagonists are discriminating in their unconscious. Suicide is a way of avoiding the historical moment: you might say most of my protagonists are suicides, even if they don't perform it. Their absolute solitude is probably a form of suicide also. I write plays in which the social context is diminished but not overcome – hence the absence of authentic victims from my work. The social context might be oppressive or catastrophic, but few of the protagonists allow that to extirpate their spiritual or erotic ambition. It is this resistance to the moral and political climate that might be said to constitute the milieu of the action, and whilst I deny the value of terms like optimism or pessimism with regard to tragedy, this self-assertion is clearly a moral confidence and not a nihilism.

GRITZNER   Would you agree that there is an underlying tension or contradiction between intellectual argument and emotional response in much of your work?

BARKER   I don't think ideas are the material of my plays or poems, though characters ponder their circumstances at length, they are meditative even in surroundings that abhor meditation. But this exercise, startling though it is in some instances, only thinly disguises the crucial operation of instinct, the all-powerful coercion of desire. The twin poles of my 'realism' are coercion and decay. Between these absolutes, men and women struggle to find love and meaning.

GRITZNER   Many of your characters are involved in complex processes of self-exploration and self-definition which, in a cultural context of post-modernity, could almost appear anachronistic.

BARKER   The self is a vital component of culture, and to talk of dissolving the self is to usher in a terrible nihilism masquerading as popular democracy. Perhaps the dubious aspect of the self is the idea of the 'authentic' self – rather we can evolve and invent ourselves from a disparate store of private sources, which to me are sacred. Everything tends to violate these, now more than ever.

GRITZNER   Do you perceive a crisis of theatre in the current political and cultural climate?

BARKER   Yes, but crisis is the essential condition for art forms, without crisis they are unlikely to reinvent themselves spontaneously, that much goes without saying. But this particular crisis? It's a transitional moment, because there is a dominant theatre ideology which is decayed. This is social realism, with all its political ambitions, its projects of enlightenment (i.e. social control) and so on. It's very close to the functioning of *socialist* realism in the Stalin era and has the same kind of critical police working it up all the time. The 'crisis' in this is manifold, but perhaps the worst aspect is that the decline of a theatre language and form has done deep damage to acting training, so skills in voice and body, on which it is necessary to build the new forms, are being lost. We know how voice and its trained modulations are now persecuted as 'elitist'. This is sham democracy, with Robespierrist rhetorics, but no one much notices it. One has to note also that the function of the writer in all this continues to decay… what he had, which is imagination, is the very thing *the theatre* most likes to stamp on, after all, imagination is never *relevant*, and relevance is the slogan of a people's society…ask any dramaturg…it's his favourite word…and meaningless.

GRITZNER   What does it mean to be 'European'?

BARKER   To be European is to hold to opposites and live, if not rejoice, in the contradictions. Read Céline, and read Thomas Mann. Look at Bosch, and look at Rembrandt. Read Voltaire and de Maistre, or place Camus beside Cioran. What is more, migrate from one to the other, for it's impossible to extend one's treasured *tolerance* to all of these. The individual and the collective are never more embattled than they are here, and reconciliation is impossible given the now ancestral nature of the conflict. It is perpetual oscillation, and all talk of harmony is false, a self-deception. Further, whether or not Europeans invented beauty, they have argued beauty to an extreme, it dominates every street in an old city, and we sense the agony of these streets, that also is our way…if you cannot relate pain to beauty, I think you are not a European in your soul.

'I AM NOT WHAT I WAS'

Adaptation and Transformation in the Theatre of
Howard Barker and The Wrestling School

ANDY W SMITH

In 1988 Kenny Ireland and Hugh Fraser formed a theatre company that was to have an unusual and specific remit: to bring together a group of like-minded actors, designers and musicians who would concentrate all their creative energies on staging the plays of Howard Barker, whose work at that time was in danger of being neglected by the major commissioning centres of British theatre.[1] The company was to be called 'The Wrestling School' as a reference towards the intellectual and practical 'wrestling' with the problems posed by Barker's plays. With the support of Howard Barker, Ireland and Fraser cast actors for the first proposed Wrestling School production *The Last Supper* (1989). In his essay 'Towards a theory of production', Barker outlines the practical and artistic necessity for The Wrestling School:

> Its starting principles related to the complexity of its chosen texts, the explosion of which dictated the manner of production and its values. These texts were texts of ideas perhaps, but, more crucially, texts of emotions... Speech therefore, the mastery of rhythm, the passionate plasticity of language was its first requirement in the actor.[2]

Taking the primacy of the actor as its first principle, The Wrestling School sought to express a vision of the 'possible' through the demands of its 'chosen texts'. Barker's 'poetic text' is brought into existence in performance by a number of factors that are distinctive to the company's rationale: an emphasis on the actor's voice concordant with the *body-in-extremis*, opening up unstable worlds that are governed not by causality but by irrational actions and scenarios that force the actor *and* the watching spectator into the most extreme emotional states. Barker writes that:

Only a pitch of emotional complexity could overwhelm the resistance of an audience educated in the disciplines of meaning and the habits of entertainment. The culture is not neutral, but flogs its publics into obeisance to governing modes, political, aesthetic systems of seeing, hearing, demanding.[3]

With hindsight, Barker's short essay can be seen as a manifesto for creating a live performance context that is (almost) unique in contemporary British theatre: an Arts Council funded company dedicated to performing the work of one writer.[4] As such, The Wrestling School can be viewed as an anomaly in contemporary performance practice, created specifically for a neglected writer. The organic development of the company since 1989 has involved utilising the skills of different actors, designers and musicians who have each contributed to the specific performance style of the company's productions.

Barker *is* the authorial voice of the company, but the movement towards a performance context is necessarily collaborative; the contributions made by the set designer Tomas Leipzig and the costume designer Billie Kaiser are as crucial to The Wrestling School experience as other related elements. In particular, the development of The Wrestling School as a production company opens up new areas of discussion in relation to Barker and contemporary British theatre. First, the adoption of specific performance practices and aesthetic forms has created a signature 'style' for the company. Second, this signature 'style' is integral towards the development of Barker's drama as 'poetry of transgression', primarily through his adaptation and transformation of dramatic icons in his plays *(Uncle) Vanya* (1996) and *Gertrude – The Cry* (2002). This debate is not conditioned solely by an analysis of dramatic text; an interrogation into the performance style of The Wrestling School is inextricable from the exploration of adaptation in Barker's work from 1994 onwards.

CONTRADICTION EXEMPLIFIED AS GRACE

One of the consequences of The Wrestling School's formation is its impact upon the staging of Barker's work, particularly the development of a specific performance choreography that is commensurate with the poetic features of the text. This choreography became more defined as Barker himself took on responsibility for the artistic direction of The Wrestling School following the departure of Kenny Ireland in 1993. As Barker's essay 'Towards a theory of production' states:

[…] the creation of visual metaphors whose melancholy lay essentially in a decay, and the aggregration of a musical score whose ambition gradually rose to equal the ambition of the text itself, gave The Wrestling School a context of such sympathy that the violently disordered, broken narratives of the production are unified; contradiction exemplified as grace, and the whole experience immunized against the cramping verdicts of a utilitarian critical ideology.[5]

Having spent the best part of ten years constructing a series of polemic arguments for a Theatre of Catastrophe, Barker was now in the position of being able to marry his theoretical propositions with intensive practice. Always a prolific writer, Barker's output since the formation of The Wrestling School seemed to be even more productive than before. Between 1988 and up until June 2005 The Wrestling School has produced 24 plays written by Barker. Most of these productions have been 'new' texts, with the exception of three revivals from the 1980s: *Victory* (1991), *The Castle* (1995) and *Scenes from an Execution* (1999). Of these 24 plays Barker has himself directed 16 productions. Of these 24 productions, three have seen Barker entering the territory of appropriating classic texts: Shakespeare's *Hamlet* (1604) and *King Lear* (1606) and Chekhov's *Uncle Vanya* (1899).[6]

THE WRESTLING SCHOOL: TOWARDS A NEW AESTHETIC

In *Seven Lears* (1989) Barker constructs a prequel to *King Lear*, starting from the observation that the maternal figure is entirely absent from Shakespeare's play. *Seven Lears* marks an important moment in Barker's development with The Wrestling School; straddling the recognisable traits of previous Barker texts (the episodic structure, the evasions and elisions of language, the occasional flashes of satire) and the attempt to open up the drama into new territory (the development of the choric interjections, the suggestion of a more formal physical choreography conditioned by the text). In performance (Leicester Haymarket, November 1989) *Seven Lears* came across as an exercise in intellectual conjecture, the conceit of the play (the re-imagining of a classic tragic text) driving forward the episodic narrative, creating a strange disjunction between the directing and the writing. Despite being an entirely unredeemable character, Nicholas le Prevost's sensitive portrayal of Lear *was* sympathetic, suggesting that the text and Kenny Ireland's direction of the production were at odds with one another, a conflict brought into sharp relief by the consequent disagreement between Barker and Ireland over the interpretation of his texts. Barker explains why he took over the directing of Wrestling School productions:

It was important for me to take on the direction of The W/S because traditional methods
as employed by our original artistic director Kenny Ireland had increasingly frustrated me
and seemed in contravention of certain aesthetic principles I had evinced in the Theatre of
Catastrophe. This wasn't specific to him – nearly all text theatre has the same career.[7]

The consistent rupturing of humanist platitudes (meaning / purpose / value) in Barker's
work become even more pronounced as he moved towards incorporating a vision of
catastrophic tragedy, using the means of The Wrestling School to deliver the experiential
act for the spectator. Most importantly, for Barker's directorial practice the catastrophic
theatrical experience cannot be facilitated through the use of multimedia techniques that
locates a tension between the live body and its mediation through a plethora of recorded
visual forms[8] but by the 'creation of stage discourses which are wholly incapable of
annexation by film'.[9]

Instead, Barker's development as a theatre director is conditioned by what he views
as 'the reoccupation of abandoned aesthetic territory' and the rejection of the 'instinct to
entertain and educate the audience'.[10] As Barker notes, 'My own development as a director
has taken me further and further away from this [Ireland's methods], but at the same
time, I write more and more in a way which renders such kinds of direction impossible.'[11]
It is the *writing* of this new work that dictates the staging choices, as Barker explains: 'The
rhythmic nature of the modern texts, even their poetry, the stress on imagery and extreme
articulation, abolish the usual style-language of naturalism, which just about does for a
play like *Victory*.'[12] This emphasis on the 'rhythmic nature' of speech and movement is an
obvious de-naturalising strategy, as Barker notes:

> [...] I have to achieve a company that has the spiritual/physical articulation, and a taste for
> significant gesture, that accommodates the text. The text has a music that compels these
> moves in those predisposed to respond to it...[13]

Barker's emphasis on the actor's physical response to poetic language creates what he
describes as 'theatre-speech'.[14] Allied to this is the specific construction of the *mise-en-
scène* of a Wrestling School production, formulated and refined across several different
productions over a period of time. As the artistic director, Barker was able to put into
place the conditions that created the type of production values now associated with The
Wrestling School: 'monochrome, high-style in costume, austerity but severe beauty in sets,
and a chiaroscuro lighting manner, as well as the now well-known Exordium, an opening
mystification of sound and action'.[15]

This combination of visual and auditory stimuli is designed to intensify the audience's emotional response to the theatrical experience. David Ian Rabey has argued that Barker's work as a director 'reflects the precision and boldness of his other work as a visual artist, and combines this with a compositional emphasis on surprising physical movement and imagery and disturbingly unforeseeable sound'.[16] The combination of the balletic actor, coupled with the musicality of the text, creates a dramatic form that is relentless in its verbal intensity and physical action. This performance register is even more pronounced in the plays that follow *Seven Lears*, and coincides with Barker's development as a director of his own plays for The Wrestling School.

Barker's artistic direction of The Wrestling School has resulted in a unifying of his role as writer and director: 'I don't know the writer/director relation any more. They are thoroughly merged.' [17] In order to critique fully Barker's adaptations of *Uncle Vanya* and *Hamlet* it is also necessary to analyse their production contexts. Instead of viewing Barker solely as a dramatist, it may be more useful to view his merging of the director/writing role from the perspective of practice.

ENTERING THE CHEKHOVIAN MADHOUSE

Barker's careful insistence that the poetic text remains at the centre of his work is best demonstrated by the series of plays that follow on from *Seven Lears*. Between 1993 and 2004, fourteen of Barker's plays have received productions from The Wrestling School, all but one being directed by Barker. The first three productions that Barker directed for The Wrestling School were *Hated Nightfall* (1994), *Judith* (1995) and *(Uncle) Vanya* (1996). *Hated Nightfall*, which ran from April to May 1994 at the Royal Court theatre, is a play that interrogates spiritual revolution and its aftermath, taking as its starting point the execution of the Russian royal family by the Bolsheviks at Ekaterinburg in July 1918. *Hated Nightfall* stands as an important moment in the development of The Wrestling School, the first play that Barker could direct according to the aesthetic principles laid down in *Arguments for a Theatre*. Its influence can be seen in the Barker directed productions that followed it: *Judith* and *(Uncle) Vanya*. *Judith* is a short, one-act play that dramatises the story of Judith and Holofernes from the Apocrypha, a subject Barker had already explored in *The Possibilities* (1988), a series of short scenes linked by ethical dilemmas. The erotic symbiosis between love and death is explored through Judith's assassination of Holofernes, a moment where the subject's body becomes immersed within the wider body politic of the state. The relationship of moral and ethical transgression encased within the seductive act is a recurrent tension in Barker's drama. The Barker directed plays of The Wrestling School intensify this correlation further, particularly *(Uncle) Vanya*, *Ursula* (1998), *He Stumbled* (2000), *Gertrude – The Cry* and *Dead Hands* (2004).

(Uncle) Vanya sees Barker rejecting the Chekhovian urge for nostalgic introspection that results only in stasis. In choosing Chekhov as his object of revision Barker is moving his dramatic trajectory towards a direct confrontation with the naturalist orthodoxy in English drama, engaging with a dramatist who is arguably the most revered writer in the theatre canon after Shakespeare. Barker's *(Uncle) Vanya* changes the relationship dynamic between the characters by doing something Chekhov rejected – he allows Vanya the chance to act on his urges by shooting at *and* killing Serebryakov, thus fulfilling the will to live that Chekhov's characters are constantly deferring:

> *A shot. They are silent. Suddenly SONYA gets to her feet.*
> SONYA: Our paralysis is nothing more than the reflection of our economic crisis the
> decline of rents and the aggressive style of capitalism in a backward economy we –
> *Another shot. Pause.*
> The rise of the proletariat and the exploitation of rural labour by –
> *And another.*
> Interest rates which –
> *And another.*
> STOP! STOP!
> *Pause. At last VANYA enters, with the gun.*
> MARYIA: Who gave you that gun…?
> VANYA: Chekhov. Chekhov did.
> *They stare at him.*
> SONYA: Uncle Vanya, what have you –
> VANYA: (*Quietly.*) Ivan.
> SONYA: Have you hurt anyone, have you –
> VANYA: Ivan. (*Pause.*)
> Hatred.
> Hatred.
> How perfectly it guided me.
> *Pause. ASTROV goes to move.*
> ASTROV: Oh, God, he's –
> VANYA: (*Levelling the gun at ASTROV.*) Don't go.

He stops.

SONYA: Uncle, have you –

VANYA: Ivan. (*Pause.*) The word uncle castrated me. I forbid the word.

SONYA: (*Defiantly.*) You are my uncle and I'll –

VANYA slaps SONYA's face. She reels.

MARYIA: Jean!

VANYA: No, that's French. And Vanya is diminutive.

No more diminutives, or endearments, abbreviations or

THINGS TO HANG YOURSELF ON

IVAN IS THE NAME.[18]

This climactic moment in the first act contains a number of important moments for breaking the connection to Chekhov's *Uncle Vanya*. The shooting of Serebryakov is obviously the most catastrophic, followed by Vanya's violent rejection of his 'diminutive' and 'familial' name. Barker attempts to resuscitate Vanya from what he describes as the 'cult of futility and impotence' [19] by giving him the will to carry through the murder of the old professor, a tyrannical force in Chekhov's play whose marriage to Helena is a constant source of frustrated desire for Vanya. In The Wrestling School programme notes for *(Uncle) Vanya*, Jonathan Dollimore writes of Vanya quitting 'the Chekhovian madhouse':

> Barker works from within as well as against an aesthetic tradition so powerful it cannot be blamed entirely on the critical establishment (though there is such an establishment, and it does police art, the more effectively for believing in itself). No, this is a tradition that has been internalised by art itself. The most effective way of undermining this tradition is not to repudiate it – the total gesture of rejection which simply leaves everything in place, unchanged – but to turn it yet further against itself. Chekhov dramatised the deadlock of false society as a deadlock within the self (Raymond Williams). By turning the play against itself, Barker releases the energy deadlocked in both society and the self. [20]

Barker achieves this 'release of energy' not only through the disruption of the original narrative but by the dismantling of the dramatic conventions that govern the Chekhovian text. Thus the play begins with the indolent strumming of a guitar, so prevalent in Chekhov's plays, followed by Vanya's violent disavowal of that trope: 'STOP STRUMMING STOP THAT IDLE FUTILE STRUMMING YOU STOP IT. (*It ceases, then continues.*) I'LL KILL YOU I'LL' (p 295). Barker transforms Chekhov's monologues into a series of précised solipsisms. Astrov's speeches about deforestation become paragraphs unbroken by punctuation:

ASTROV: Man is endowed with reason and creative power so that he can enhance what
    he has been endowed with but up till now he has been destroying not creating there
    are fewer and fewer forests the rivers are drying up the wild creatures are almost
    exterminated the climate is being ruined the land is becoming poorer and more
    hideous every day when I hear the rustling of the young saplings I (*Pause.*) (p 295)

Barker's revision of *Uncle Vanya* is an attempt to return the iconic text to the moment
where death and desire are not held in temporary stasis but become the very drive of the
play. *Uncle Vanya* was the first major Chekhov play in which a character does not die,
and the restoration of melodrama by Barker denies the 'misery of the Chekhovian world,
where love falters in self-loathing and desire is petulance'.[21] The actor Michael Pennington
writes of *Uncle Vanya* that, 'Chekhov has achieved a true tragedy in which nobody dies – in
which indeed the idea of sudden death becomes ridiculous'.[22] In bringing sudden death
back into the play Barker creates a dramatic world that ruptures the comforting nostalgia
of Chekhovian naturalism, a world where the sea crashes into a room thousands of miles
from the coast, bringing with it a shipwrecked man who is Chekhov himself, heading for
a confrontation with his own characters.

    Ultimately, it is the character of Helena, the repository of desire, who unmakes herself
in defiance of Chekhov's admonishments in the face of his character's mutiny:

HELENA: I want to say
    Without temper
    If possible without the least sense of the heroic
    Without even the measured ambition to speak the truth
    which is only another vulgarity
    To say
    I am not what I was
    Indeed
    I was nothing and now I am at least the possibility of
    something
    And this
    I will defend (p 329)

Helena's speech can be read as a palimpsest for the Barkerian urge for reinvention,
an attempt to restore the self-fashioning malcontent as the prime violator of an ethical
consensus. Helena's 'I was nothing and now I am at least the possibility of something'

is an echoing refrain in Barker's plays, reminiscent of his rationale for The Wrestling School:

> The play of The Wrestling School requires nothing of the impossible, but insists on the far reach of the possible, its speculations far outstripping tolerance, its imagination too unstable for enlightenment. It proclaims the world unstable, but in the apertures of pain, discovers beauty.[23]

The Wrestling School production team creates this instability through a combination of unsettling theatrical *mise-en-scène* and the placement of characters within those dramatic worlds that are systematically taken to the limits of their emotional, physical and moral capabilities. Thus in *(Uncle) Vanya* the familial set up is undermined and destroyed through the active transgressions of Vanya and Helena (murder and desire), each finding an action or expression through which to invalidate the nausea of their Chekhovian worlds. Dollimore writes of Barker's *(Uncle) Vanya* that

> [...] the truly sacrilegious know more about the sacred than those who believe that they have moved into some (postmodern) space beyond the sacred; the sacrilegious know the great paradox of transgression, namely that it occurs in a state of loving vengeful intimacy with that which it violates.[24]

It is in this violation of the sacred (text) that Barker merges his double role as director and writer, where the *performance* of bodily transgression becomes the radical moment in a culture that seeks to sublimate liminality, extricating order from the limits of ethical values. Barker confronts modernity with what is essentially unrepresentable, albeit in a form that primarily uses language to (literally) strip away the eroticised subject, as Helena testifies to:

> HELENA: This thinness of mine. I am a rack of bones from which swords might be
> made. Did you know the body was a resource for instruments, the ribs for needles,
> and the shoulder blades, what are they for, axes probably I AM A LETHAL OBJECT
> careful you might cut your fingers and bleed from a caress. (p 337)

(Uncle) Vanya is arguably the play that consolidated The Wrestling School design style which can be seen in many of the subsequent productions. The set for *(Uncle) Vanya* was a metallic box, a trap for the characters through which the remarkable motif of the sea

flooding the stage occurred. The designer Tomas Leipzig has subsequently returned to the design of the metallic scenic space, notably in *He Stumbled*, a set made out of steel shutters that opened up apertures to reveal headless naked torsos. Both Leipzig and the costume designer Billie Kaiser have worked extensively in opera and film, and their focus on the relationship of texture, sound and colour in their designs has an operatic feel to it; what could be described as a baroque formalism which complements the emphasis on expressive movement and language in Barker's writing.

Barker's imagined worlds are often defined in Wrestling School productions by the disjunction between what is *seen* and what is *heard*: the dropping of paper leaflets in front of fans to simulate the effect of aeroplanes dropping propaganda in *A House of Correction* (2001), or aural environments created in the opening exordiums. Barker describes these environments as 'imagined spaces…where people with not very complicated intentions encounter others with very complicated intentions', and he is adamant that they are 'hardly expressionistic, I would say, they must be experienced as actual'.[25] *Gertrude – The Cry* stands as a recent example of a Wrestling School production where all elements coalesced to create a performance that was the very embodiment of Barker's work as a dramatist *and* practitioner.

THE AMATORY FLASH

The eroticised subject and its annihilation by the *logos* have remained at the margins of acceptable literature, though their power to fascinate is apparent in writings by the Marquis de Sade in the eighteenth century, through to those of surrealist Georges Bataille. This power is the subject of what Susan Sontag has described in her 1967 essay as 'The Pornographic Imagination'.[26] In this essay Sontag outlines the tradition of erotic writing as literature, arguing for an understanding of pornography as art, where 'pornography is one of the branches of literature – science fiction is another – aiming at disorientation, at psychic dislocation'.[27]

Using the examples of De Sade and Bataille (among others), Sontag writes that 'the "obscene" is a convention, the fiction imposed upon nature by a society convinced there is something vile about the sexual functions, and, by extension, about sexual pleasure'.[28] For Sontag, the repression of sexuality by Western Christianity results in extremities of action and desires, 'pushing us at intervals close to taboo and dangerous desires, which range from the impulse to commit sudden arbitrary violence upon another person to the voluptuous yearning for the extinction of one's consciousness, for death itself'.[29]

The writing of such desires, a documentation of the obscene, the unacknowledged, the taboo, is often configured as perversion because it overtakes and destabilises humanist values that view sexuality as a positive rather than a degrading force. It is in the voyeuristic exposure to transgressive sexual energies that results in a contamination of ethical postures, and the reason why sin, repression and confession are so intimately related in the 'pornographic imagination', reflected in the chorus taunting the Empress in Barker's *Hated Nightfall*: 'SHE FUCKED WITH PRIESTS'.[30]

Barker's play *Gertrude – The Cry* has at its core a similar obsession with sexual abjection and its rejection by Judaeo-Christianity as obscene and forbidden. The character of Gertrude is a force so potent in Barker's reinvention that her erotic existence becomes the very cause of extinction in the play. Gertrude is a character so fraught with transgression that her every action becomes the progenitor of agony. Barker's resuscitation of Gertrude, like that of his Vanya, is based on the stripping of her guilt and giving her a sense of autonomy that she lacks in Shakespeare's play. The conflict between Gertrude and Hamlet in Shakespeare's play forms the basis of T S Eliot's 1922 essay 'Hamlet and his problems':

> Hamlet is up against the difficulty that his disgust is occasioned by his mother, but that his mother is not an adequate equivalent for it; his disgust envelops and exceeds her. It is thus a feeling which he cannot understand; he cannot objectify it, and it therefore remains to poison life and obstruct action. None of the possible actions can satisfy it; and nothing that Shakespeare can do with the plot can express Hamlet for him. And it must be noticed that the very nature of the *données* of the problem precludes objective equivalence. To have heightened the criminality of Gertrude would have been to provide the formula for a totally different emotion in Hamlet; it is just *because* her character is so negative and insignificant that she arouses in Hamlet the feeling which she is incapable of representing.[31]

Barker, in criminalising Gertrude, creates a Hamlet whose anger at his mother is clearly justified. As Barker writes in the programme notes to The Wrestling School production of *Gertrude – The Cry*:

> [...] Gertrude's sketchily described character is soddened with shame and regret. The unevenness of her portrayal, which T S Eliot famously drew attention, compelled me, a tragic writer not burdened with Shakespeare's religious sentiments, to attempt a new Gertrude. This one was to be passionate, defiant and more authentically tragic than the

adolescent prince himself. Gertrude is bound to Claudius by an exquisite crime or the play hardly hangs together.[32]

The key to the play lies in what Barker describes as the sexual complicity between Gertrude and Claudius in plotting the death of old Hamlet, 'a three way moment of ecstasy, intercourse and murder' that results in an 'orgasm of tremendous proportions'.[33] This is 'The Cry', Gertrude's moment of 'erotic exclamation' over the prostate body of her husband as her lover pours poison into the ear. Gertrude implores Claudius to kill her husband, whilst he demands that she strips naked for the act of murder:

GERTRUDE: Do it now

CLAUDIUS: If anyone's a dog

GERTRUDE: DO IT NOW

CLAUDIUS: It's me

   GERTRUDE positions herself above the head of the sleeping man, tilted, provocative.

GERTRUDE: Poison him

   CLAUDIUS goes to kiss GERTRUDE. She shuts her eyes, averts her face.

Poison him

   CLAUDIUS takes the phial from his clothing. He kneels by the sleeping man. He pours the fluid into the man's ear. GERTRUDE seems to vomit in her ecstasy. Her cry mingles with the cry of the sleeping man who shudders.

Fuck me

Oh fuck me

   CLAUDIUS and GERTRUDE couple above the dying man. All three utter, a music of extremes. A servant enters holding a garment, and attends.[34]

This 'cry' becomes the transcendental moment that claims Gertrude as the object of this particular tragedy, leaving her son Hamlet as the subject of ridicule, his infantile response over his father's body undermining any romantic expectations of the 'sweet prince':

HAMLET: I expected to be more moved than this

   Pause.

Cascades

Storms of

Torrents of emotion

Never mind these things will come later when I least expect them in bed with a bitch
or on a horse eyes full of tears you're crying she will say you're crying the horse will
neigh yes horse yes bitch I am and I don't know why I'm blind I'm choking silly ha ha
forgive me ha I'll get off the bitch off the horse have you a handkerchief
He laughs briefly.
Horses don't have handkerchiefs but bitches might to wipe their crevices that stinks
I'll say that stinks of filthy copulations am I to wipe my eyes with that yes wipe away
and fuck your finicky fastidious and
He laughs, shuddering.
WOMEN ARE SO COARSE (p 13)

Barker transforms Hamlet's misogyny into the very *raison d'être* of the character.
Hamlet's lack of distinction between a horse and a 'bitch' (both 'things' to ride) in the
first paragraph is tempered by their sexualised difference in the second paragraph, the
imagined handkerchief used to wipe away his grief-stained tears is the same handkerchief
that wipes 'crevices…that stink[]' of filthy copulations'. The bodily excretions so important
as metonyms to 'the pornographic imagination' are realised by a series of powerful images
and phrases: Gertrude appears to 'vomit in her ecstasy' as Claudius pours the fatal 'fluid'
into the ear; the 'Cry' itself is followed by the extraordinary copulation of Claudius and
Gertrude over the shuddering body of a dying man.

In the 2001 Wrestling School production of *Gertrude – The Cry*, Hamlet was dressed
as an English public schoolboy in blazer, shorts, long socks and trainers adding to the
impression of a petulant adolescent, supplemented by the actor Tom Burke using a high
pitched voice for the character. Gertrude's elegant, singular sexuality, performed by
Victoria Wicks, was referenced visually through a selection of high style costumes, vibrant
pastel colours that contrasted with the other female characters' dark browns and blacks,
who were covered up from neck to toe in a metonymic suppression of their sexuality. The
design of the show complemented the intensity of the performances, creating the requisite
atmosphere of anxiety for the audience. Claudius, transfixed by Gertrude's cry, seeks out
the source but is fooled by the moment: it is not him that is the cause of the Cry but the
betrayal of Old Hamlet:

CLAUDIUS: I must have it
The cry Gertrude

I must drag that cry from you again if it weighs fifty bells or one thousand carcasses I
must

IT KILLS GOD (p 22)

This cry that 'kills God' happens twice more in the play – at the death of Hamlet and the
death of Claudius. This philosophical abstraction is at the very centre of the 'pornographic
imagination'; the killing of God is the replacement of the *logos*, or belief in a totality of
being, by the profanity of excess – the individual reduced to a series of 'erotic exchanges',
to paraphrase Sontag.[35] Julia Kristeva has written of Bataille's fiction that:

> The contemporary amatory narrative thus tries to convey at the same time the idealization
> and the state of shock germane to amatory feeling: the sublime is this neither-subject-
> nor-object entity that I have called 'abjection'. Erotic fantasy merges with philosophical
> meditation in order to reach the focus where the sublime and the abject, making up the
> pedestal of love, come together in the 'flash'.[36]

Kristeva's 'amatory flash' reveals a merging of 'erotic fantasy' with 'philosophical
meditation', the melding of the sublime and the abject that results in Gertrude's 'Cry'. The
obscenity of the action lies in its visual representation of the 'flash': the on-stage murders
of old Hamlet, Hamlet and Claudius are all prefaced by Gertrude's 'Cry', each moment a
signature of erotic frenzy, as Gertrude responds to Claudius poisoning Hamlet:

GERTRUDE: My belly
  My womb
  The rivers
  Boiling through
  Latin names now
  Urethra
  Vulva
  Mammary
  Surging as the blood goes flooding more blood
  Than any body can contain
  The brain however
  THE AGONY OF THE BRAIN (p 79)

Gertrude's interior body is here configured as 'flow', blood, urine and faeces responding to the primal psychic dislocation of witnessing her child's death. The intellect ('Latin names now') fights against this flow as she recognises that the surging of blood through her veins is miniscule compared to the 'agony of the brain', her physical pain matched with her mental anguish concomitant with childbirth. The rupturing of moral and social taboos in the play (the 'fucking' over the body of a dying man, the sex act performed in the graveyard, the infanticide of the baby) is a consequence of Gertrude's amatory flash and has wider connotations regarding the type of theatre on display. Kristeva writes that, 'The contemporary narrative (from Joyce to Bataille) has a post-theological aim: to communicate the amorous flash.' [37] Kristeva further notes that the concentration of the abject and the sublime opens up the representation of the invisible, of what was previously unrepresentable, whereby 'written eroticism is a function of verbal tension, an "in-between-the-signs".' [38] Barker's *Gertrude – The Cry* operates in much the same way as Bataille's writings, as Sontag notes: 'What Bataille exposes in extreme erotic experience is its subterranean connection with death'.[39]

In *Gertrude – The Cry* Barker creates an 'erotic, meditative narrative – an amorous one', as Gertrude becomes the 'death-mother',[40] poised between *Eros* and *Thanatos*, 'a (preoedipal) mother who knows no taboo'.[41] Her final action is to cradle Claudius's dead body as her 'great cry comes, not from herself, but from the land'. (p 92) As her putative husband Albert enters, she is left with a 'ruined face', a mask of complicity in the deaths of all who desire the Cry: Hamlet, Cascan and Claudius. It is at this point that the sublimation of eroticism encases the whole scenic space, as Claudius guesses before his death:

> Always I thought the cry was in you
> But it's not
> It's outside (p 87)

By this point the very world of the play becomes the 'Cry': it obliterates all meaning and becomes its own referent, a world of grey death covered with the ashes of the murdered. Gertrude taunts the dying Claudius:

> The making of a garden grey this garden everything I plant grey we are northern are
> we not great is the grey stone and the moss grey grey waves and me grey naked I'll
> stoop even in frost boots on my feet grey socks
> *She seems to laugh.*
> And he shaving in a so-high window will glance from the mirror to my arse

> Grey garden
> Grey garden
> Ashes scattered on it
> Scattered ashes of burned men
> HE'LL RUSH TO FUCK
> HE'LL RUSH TO FUCK
> AND OUR SLIDING HEELS WILL TREAD YOU IN (p 92)

The last words of the play belong to the new king Albert, untouched by Gertrude's death drive, who orders the destruction of the bodies that litter the ground: Claudius, his mother Isola, and the baby daughter: 'BURN THESE BURN AND SCATTER THESE' (p 93).

The smell of burnt flesh is the final metonymic act of the play, a consumption of the body consumed by a cry of apocalyptic proportions. Howard Barker has written: 'I regard *He Stumbled* and *Gertrude* as major works, and in this climate, revolutionary works.' [42] *Gertrude – The Cry* stands as one of the most important Wrestling School productions, for in its adaptation of a canonical text and transformation of a neglected character it exposes an audience to the most extreme limits of the 'pornographic imagination'. As Susan Sontag writes:

> That discourse one might call the poetry of transgression is also knowledge. He who transgresses not only breaks a rule. He goes somewhere that the others are not: and he knows something the others don't know. [43]

Barker's directorial work with The Wrestling School has transformed his drama from speculative satire to poetry of transgression, taking us somewhere that very few contemporary British dramatists and practitioners dare to go.

NOTES

1. The key defining point in the formation of The Wrestling School appears to be the rejection of Barker's commissioned play *The Europeans* by the RSC in 1987. In several essays and articles since, Barker returns to this moment as an example of how his dramatic vision was (and is) desperately at odds with the ruling theatrical orthodoxy.

2. H Barker, 'Towards a theory of production' in *Arguments for a Theatre* 3rd edn (Manchester, Manchester University Press, 1997), p 134

3. *Ibid.*, p 134

4. The Welsh dramatist Ed Thomas has also been in the rare position of having a theatre company created solely to perform his work: Y Cwmni / Fiction Factory has been performing his plays since 1988.

5. Barker, 'Towards a theory of production', *Arguments for a Theatre*, p 134

6. Barker has used the technique of adapting classical drama before, notably with Middleton's *Women Beware Women* (1986) and Lessing's *Minna* (1994).

7. H Barker, letter, 7 April 2003

8. Multimedia techniques that are usually associated with post-modern performance companies like Complicite or the Wooster Group.

9. H Barker, 'The Ethics of Relevance and the Triumph of the Literal' in M Rubik & E Mettinger-Schartmann (eds) *(Dis)Continuities – Trends and Traditions in Contemporary Theatre and Drama in English vol IX* (Trier, Wissenschaftlicher Verlag Trier, 2002), p 90

10. H Barker, 'A bargain with impossibility: the theatre of moral speculation in an age of accord' in *Arguments for a Theatre*, p 96

11. Barker, letter, 7 April 2003

12. *Ibid.*

13. *Ibid.*

14. *Ibid.*

15. *Ibid.*

16. D I Rabey, 'Barker: Appalling Enhancements' in *English Drama Since 1940* (London, Pearson Education, 2003), 182–90, pp 182–3

17. Barker, letter, 7 April 2003

18. H Barker, *(Uncle) Vanya* in *Collected Plays vol 2* (London, Calder, 1993) p 305. Subsequent page numbers indicate quotations from this edition until otherwise indicated.

19. H Barker, programme notes, *(Uncle) Vanya*, The Wrestling School, 1996

20. J Dollimore, programme notes, *(Uncle) Vanya*, The Wrestling School, 1996

21. Barker, programme notes, *(Uncle) Vanya*, 1996

22. M Pennington, *Are You There Crocodile? Inventing Anton Chekhov* (London, Oberon, 2003), p 79

23. Barker, 'Towards a theory of production', *Arguments for a Theatre*, p 134

24. Dollimore, programme notes, *(Uncle) Vanya*, 1996

25. Barker, letter, 7 April 2003

26. S Sontag (1967) 'The Pornographic Imagination', quoted in G Bataille, *Story of the Eye* (London, Penguin, 1982), pp 83–118

27. *Ibid.*, p 94

28. *Ibid.*, p 103

29. *Ibid.*, p 103

30. H Barker, *Hated Nightfall* in *Hated Nightfall / Wounds to the Face* (London, Calder, 1994), p 43

31. T S Eliot (1922) 'Hamlet and his problems' in *The Sacred Wood: Essays on Poetry and Criticism* (London, Faber and Faber, 1997), p 86

32. H Barker, programme notes, *Gertrude – The Cry*, The Wrestling School, 2002

33. H Barker, 'Death, the One and the Art of Theatre', unpublished paper, One-Day Symposium: *Theatrical Aesthetics of Eroticism and Death*, University of Wales, Aberystwyth, 1 May 2004

34. H Barker, *Gertrude – The Cry / Knowledge and a Girl* (London, Calder, 2002), p 10. Subsequent page numbers indicate quotations from this edition until otherwise indicated.

35. S Sontag: 'All action is conceived as a set of sexual exchanges'; 'The Pornographic Imagination' in Bataille, *Story of the Eye*, p 112

36. J Kristeva, 'Bataille and the sun, or the guilty text' in *Tales of Love* (New York, Columbia University Press, 1987), p 368

37. *Ibid.*, p 368

38. *Ibid.*, p 369

39. S Sontag, 'The Pornographic Imagination' in Bataille, *Story of the Eye*, p 107

40. J Kristeva, 'Bataille and the sun, or the guilty text' in *Tales of Love*, p 371

41. *Ibid.*, p 371

42. H Barker, letter, 7 April 2003

43. S Sontag, 'The Pornographic Imagination' in Bataille, *Story of the Eye*, p 116

BARKER DIRECTING BARKER

JAMES REYNOLDS

An analysis of Howard Barker's direction of his own work for The Wrestling School is needed in order to characterise and assess the directorial practices and dramaturgical framework through which he translates his texts and aesthetics into a cohesive style of performance. Such an account may develop understanding of Barker's evolution as a director as well as elucidate his relationship to modernist practitioners such as Samuel Beckett and Antonin Artaud. This analysis draws on rehearsal observation, workshops and correspondence with Barker, as well as interviews with Wrestling School actors who have worked with him since the role of company director passed from co-founder Kenny Ireland to Barker in the mid-1990s.

IN BARKER'S HANDS

What immediately stands out about Barker's directing is his deliberate foregrounding of the irrational in the transgressive acts which are at the core of his writing for the theatre. Barker the writer creates characters who transgress but the preparatory work of Barker the director is not aimed at the creation of a 'comfort zone' between actor and audience. Rehearsal does not function as a framework for the investigation of a subtext which rationalises transgression. Barker explains the significance of this approach:

> The actual practice is in the direction in the end, what *happens* to the text in my hands as opposed to someone else's, and this is much to do with the abolition of the humanist stereotype…in Ireland's *Weltanschauung* the bad act was always dimly lit by the will to goodness…we need 'to understand how he/she got like that…' But the excavation of desire and will in my work doesn't require that protection.[1]

For Barker, taking on the direction of his own work meant realising the style and effect in performance he envisioned. When the 'humanist stereotype' is presented as a model for characterisation the element of the irrational in transgression is explained away. Barker's direction, however, seeks to atomise the entity of the audience by confronting the individual spectator with the anxiety of the irrational in the transgressive fact. Something else happens to the text in Barker's hands because his view of how the human is to be presented is different from Kenny Ireland's, although the same may also be said of Barker in relation to directors who staged his work for the RSC. Barker's characters don't need a reason to cross the line; they cross it because they want to or because they will it.

Ursula (1998) is noteworthy for Barker as it was 'a key moment in the history of the W/S... It was in this particular piece that the acting strength of the company revealed itself, as well as my own way with the work.' [2] *Ursula* was the first play that Barker cast. He chose actors who could move away from humanist notions of character and produce the style of acting relying on the excavation of desire and will which he had envisaged:

[In *Ursula*] All the casting was my own, they were Barker actors as opposed to Ireland actors... If you think of the actresses employed by Ireland...they are altogether more naturalistic and do not have a particular body/voice cohabitation...in brief I was able to assert my own values. [3]

Barker articulates these values in a description of his casting processes:

In auditioning I am primarily interested in voice, technique, the desire in the performer to speak the speech, his avoidance of trivial detail, his ability to move, to have physical confidence, and to reveal whether or not the voice can initiate the move. I do not expect intellectual sophistication, theoretical knowledge or philosophical tendencies in an actor, but I insist they understand the director directs. [4]

It is worth repeating that Barker does not require the actor to match the sophistication of his own ideas and arguments but looks for technical ability, will, speech as a motive force for action, and the capacity to take direction. He begins and continues the process on active terms without referring actors to his theories, indicating that his vision is realised by directorial practices which are appropriate to that vision, but which do not require it to be referenced in order to be realised. Of equal significance is Barker's ability to use the greater control of the directorial role to realise the aesthetics of catastrophic theatre through a holistic methodology in which all elements of form are aligned:

[With] *Ursula* the acting style I encouraged was only possible because of my decisions on set design. Set design is not a separate issue from acting...music, design, costume and so on. All must come from a single source. The set imposes disciplines on actors...we are talking of constraints, not meaningless freedoms. [5]

This is significant as it indicates that even this early in his directing career, Barker was already committed to the dramaturgical framework of the 'total theatre' approach, led by the aesthetic principle that all elements function as a seamless unity in the staging of the text. The crucial contribution of established Wrestling School designers Tomas Leipzig, Billie Kaiser, Helen Morley and Paul Bull should not be ignored [6] but Barker's rehearsal methodology nonetheless remains text-centred.

Claire Price broke a personal tradition to research historical period for her role as Ursula, but at the first rehearsal, 'Howard was totally uninterested in it. For Howard it's a purely imaginative journey. Facts and figures – utterly irrelevant.' [7] Indeed, Barker characterises his approach in early rehearsals thus:

> There is hardly any exploration at all, very little debate about meaning, little time spent round a table. Nothing makes sense until it is stood up, which occurs very swiftly. I rely on the actors' will and ambition and try not to cramp it, but on the other hand, I have very firm ideas and expect them to be fulfilled, even down to detailed moves.[8]

Within the rigid framework provided by the director, the actor is given a wide scope for the excavation of will and desire. Price:

> It [*Ursula*] was the first time as an actor where the quantity of emotion I have to give to a part was welcomed and I was never told to edit. Working with Howard, no extreme is too extreme. Any extreme you've gone to, you can always go further.[9]

A strict directorial framework combined with exploratory freedom for the actor remains at the core of Barker's direction of his own texts. The development of this practice has been described as a process of continual refinement, with director and company continuing to evolve a distinctive style through 'an intensification of the company's style… The company believes ensemble to be the key to style, and style to be produced from a purification of requirements.' [10]

Dead Hands (2004) reflected the refinement of The Wrestling School's distinct style: a razor sharp oneness of actor, text, visual and aural theatre systems, stripped of ornament in its minimalism but with a density of expression borne of the unity forged by Barker's work on the play as its director. Take the final image of the play: Eff's hand was stuck to Sopron's face as he sat, his hand gripped her face with its fingers spread wide as she sank to the floor at the side of his chair in slow-motion, back-lit, her dress mushrooming outwards, the under-frame of the skirt distorting the shape as she sank, a glissando sound effect screeching downward in pitch as Eff pressed her face down and forwards, the light dimming in accompaniment to sound and image.

This carefully layered metaphor of suffocation and entrapment has no stage direction in the published text of *Dead Hands*. In fact, Sopron exits in the published version and the play closes with Eff in solitude. Yet Barker clearly crafted this moment with great exactitude. Such meticulous detailing is a key feature of his directorial practice and is, therefore, an important feature of The Wrestling School's style. Yet the exactness Barker employs as director and the freedom which he offers to the actor would seem to contradict each other.

INVISIBLE FORCES

Nietzsche's description of the self as 'a plurality of energy drives' [11] contextualises Barker's view of character and, by unlocking the potential contradiction in his direction, indicates the key to the liberty of the actor; Nietzsche's argument that 'the subject is not a subject but a creative becoming' [12] underpins the self-creating language of Barker's characters. They remake themselves through speech and they recast their worlds through will. Barker, therefore, directs the actor to abandon the explanation of role, and to commit to its exploration, and in this the actor enjoys artistic freedom. Rehearsal is an excavation of desire and will taking place alongside staging.

In one sense Barker's characters are created only in the moment of performance, requiring the audience to be 'other' in order to attain self-definition, and thereby presence. Subsequently, time exists in the Barker performance as a dimensional aspect of character more than as an aspect of plot. The through-line of action becomes redundant because continuity of character in relation to given circumstances is exploded in catastrophe. Actor and character co-exist in catastrophe through will: the creative struggle of the actor in the present moment becomes a metaphor of the character's struggle for self-definition. The two are connected by the will to speak. The nature of the present in the Barker character's stage reality is thus: saying is being.

Staging desire and will as the sources of behavioural motivation rejects the deterministic and rationalist elements of naturalistic and epic acting. Working outside dominant modes of characterisation is liberating but also challenging for the actor. The practices Barker uses to stage desire and will, therefore, must be a key feature of his work as a director, and even more so bearing in mind his strictly dramaturgical (as opposed to critically discursive) approach to working with the actor. An example in performance:

in *Dead Hands*, Eff's will is constantly threatened with being overwhelmed: he arrives having endured a journey of 'unremitting vileness' [13] and his journey through the play is equally tortured. In the presence of his father's corpse, Eff is confronted repeatedly with his father's naked mistress. Barker augmented Eff's time-dimensionality in performance through sound. Emotion was realistic but accompanied by 'gratingly metallic' [14] sound effects which ensured that style remained firmly non-naturalistic. The aural fracturing elongated the emotional experience, suggesting that for Eff a great deal of time had passed in what was a moment in real time. His attempts to assert his will through speech were renewed after these extended peaks of trauma. In one sense Barker meets the challenge of staging desire and will by relying on the totality of theatre systems: in another sense, he relies on the experience of the pool of actors that makes up The Wrestling School and on the techniques that they have evolved. Desire and will are staged, as in *Dead Hands*, but they are also staging – both performance and process.

Working with Wrestling School associates revealed the core of a performance lexicon of staging desire and will, focused on the self-defining uses of language typical of the Barker character.[15] A common pattern of speech in Barker, which Wrestling School actors know as 'tumult', is characterised by a deliberate excessiveness and rapid changes of focus. The challenge for the actress is neither detachment nor identification: it is the creation of anxiety. In *Gertrude – The Cry* (2002) Isola witnesses Cascan's attempt to strangle Hamlet and provides an exemplar of 'tumult':

> THE KID I SAID
> A miracle
> He never tripped
> These shoes with the steel tips on
> Clatter
> Clatter
> The noise
> A Regiment
> But Hamlet's lost in thought
> He never flinched
> The servant grabs him round the neck
> THE KID I SAID [16]

Furthermore, Isola searches for words through speech in her monologue – again, a linguistic technique common in Barker. Melanie Jessop calls this the 'hunted thought'.

Isola's flow of speech is continuous: the pauses are acted through while she searches with great exactitude for The Word. The self is overcome, its need for deception resisted: only an exact truth can be accepted or spoken. This performance strategy is aimed at the excavation of the character's will. The machinery of the text creates what Wrestling School actors describe as 'pressure' on the will of the Barkerian character, necessary for the creation of a state of anxiety which will resonate in the actor and penetrate the spectator.

These core ideas address the staging of will but also characterise further the nature of Barker's work as a director of his own texts. He directs the ensemble while language functions as a second director for the actor. Barker describes this process in rehearsal:

> The actors play the emotions spontaneously, they are not encouraged to think of a motivation, but to keep all possibilities in play, to seize initiatives where the text permits it (or demands it) but above all to listen to the language. It alone can guide them.[17]

Barker's texts work in the same way a musical score does for conductor and musician. Stage practice is encoded in the use of language, in the use of bold type, syntax, capitals, and limited but specific stage directions. There are other ways in which this 'shadow director' contributes to rehearsals.

Julia Tarnoky writes of Barker's language that 'the shape on the page tells you how it's built'.[18] Melanie Jessop states that through the layout of text 'Howard points…he is describing to you the air around things, silences around them'.[19] These are visual sentences. Jessop performed *Und* (1999) and quotes a section from the play as an example of this, one which demonstrates the shape and building of the text as an encoded stage direction:

> I DO ADMIRE THOSE WHO
>
> MORE THAN TALENT MORE THAN BEAUTY THOSE WHO
>
> Simply
>
> Walk
>
> Walk
>
> Walk
>
> Into
>
> *Pause.*
>
> The terrible [20]

For Jessop, Und's speech reflects through sound and rhythm both the abstract atmosphere, and the concrete rhythm, of the slow walk of the Jews into the gas chambers.[21] Barker writes onomatopoeically: in a way similar to Shakespeare, direction for meaning, movement and delivery is encoded in the sound of the text. Furthermore, Tarnoky writes that 'the journey of each character is word by word. Sounds contain motivation and if you deliver them, they advance the character'.[22] In interview with Jessop, an example of how Barker's onomatopoeia informs staging emerged from her work on *Judith* (1990), one which demonstrates Tarnoky's notion of sound-motivation in action:

> Holofernes is talking about how unhappy he is and he's resisting all of Judith's attempts at seduction. She's really up against it…and as she's listening to him speak this strategy formulates itself: 'I also am unhappy.' There's some big vowel changes in there but not a lot of consonants to hang onto. I remember it being a very difficult line to say and I realised that there's not a single challenging sound in that sentence, it's completely without any spike at all. [23]

The text directs, functioning as a form of shadow direction in the actor's process as well as being the language of the character in performance. The aural sculpture that is Barker's language, and the theatrical presentation of will, combine together with narrative and concept in the delivery of the performer to create anxiety in the audience. These concepts connect the language of the play to the internal dynamics of will, establishing an appropriate source of momentum for the company's style of performance. Barker's directorial practice is twofold, creating a strict expression of will and desire in the staging of this aural sculpture while allowing the actor the freedom to explore the will and desire of the character through the instructional poetry of the text.

THE THEATRE OF ANXIETY

It is important to recognise that the 'mother' principle of Barker's directorial aesthetic is the creation of anxiety in response to the performance, and that this has antecedents. Barker's dramaturgical framework is comparable to Samuel Beckett's in the sense that they both employ a conscious indeterminacy of meaning, avoiding clarity or didacticism in favour of an 'anxious' theatre, in which the creation of anxiety in the spectator is the total of all values. Jonathan Kalb writes of Beckett that

> The action is richly ambiguous [and that] most spectators' entire reaction (to later Beckett) is to 'the overall impact of a single overwhelmingly powerful image'…afterwards they remember bits of the haunting text despite what they think is their lack of understanding, and allow meaning to accrue to the play as its overwhelming effect wears off. [24]

This analysis is applicable to the reception and production of Barker's work. *Gertrude – The Cry* demonstrates these parallels. The image of Gertrude and Claudius performing intercourse over the dying body of old Hamlet dominates its performance. Gertrude's transgression is visual, and as eroticised as it is cruel, yet the image of the sexual murder is followed immediately with Cascan's dislocating speech on the nature of ecstasy:

> All ecstasy makes ecstasy go running to a further
> place that is its penalty we know this how well we
> know this still we would not abolish ecstasy
> would we we would not say this ever-receding
> quality in ecstasy makes it unpalatable on the
> contrary we run behind it limping staggering I
> saw it there I saw it there
> *He laughs.*
> A haunting mirage on the rim of life [25]

Subsequently, young Hamlet's presence repeatedly evokes the image of transgression. Yet, as with Beckett, it is in the afterglow of the performance that the 'attack' of the image begins to melt into different kinds of appreciation. Themes and concepts such as these are expressed in the flow of narrative lyrically, and with overwhelming density. Attempting to capture meaning in the moment of experiencing the performance is futile. It is retroactively, as Kalb suggests of Beckett's drama, that meaning accrues for the individual. As the imagery dissolves into the mind, the interpretive function begins to consider possible meanings. The experience of The Wrestling School performance is anxious and its memory long-lived as, in the same way as Beckett's drama, it cannot be assimilated immediately. In this anxiousness lies its power as a theatre experience.

Appreciation of Barker's praxis is necessary in order to understand how this aesthetic of anxiety is realised in performance. Barker characterises his approach thus:

> I have very firm ideas and I expect them to be fulfilled, even down to detailed moves.
> Nothing is free, open, or democratic in this company, it is wholly visionary in emphasis, a
> working out of the images of the text. [26]

Jane Bertish's description of rehearsals as 'gloriously collaborative' is also, paradoxically, accurate. [27] Having observed Barker directing *Dead Hands* in September 2004, it is clear to me that his directorial practice can be either open or prescriptive according to context, and that he does not play the role of 'writer in rehearsal'. Barker entertains a degree of logical analysis of text but his conclusions are contingent and reveal that the indeterminacy of meaning in his writing is paralleled in his dramaturgy. 'Probably' is a favourite answer – due to an unwillingness to limit possible interpretations. Actors' questions are often answered, 'I don't know,' and left unresolved. While Barker assumes the controlling force of the directing role, he is neither repressive nor unifying despite his presence as 'the writer'. A constant prefix in questions to actors is, 'Do you want to…' and his dialogue with them is characterised by continuous 'optioning'. Barker asks the actors for interpretation of role and dramatic moment rather than prescribing it. Speaking to Justin Avoth in rehearsal for *Dead Hands*, Barker used a series of interrogative, and non-prescriptive, questions to draw him into the text: 'Are you crying?'; 'What's going through his mind?'; 'Why doesn't he particularly want her to do it this time?'; 'Every time she does it you've got to act or not act?' He showed firmer control when necessary, paring down excessively busy characterisation, at other times he relinquished control, saying to Chris Moran, 'Direct it for yourself.' Working with Moran on his 'Barber' monologue generated a plethora of possibilities. Disruption, narrative, symbolism, relationship, personal freedom, rhythm – each providing a focus point for a sequence of attempts at delivery, each layer described by Barker as 'one more thing to add to this construction' – as opposed to one response being the right take.[28]

Similarly, David Ian Rabey, discussing a production rehearsal of *The Twelfth Battle of Isonzo*, describes how Barker 'exploded' his sense of the character by directing him that Isonzo could be sighted but equally he could be blind and pretending sight. Barker's indeterminacy in process emerges as a deliberate strategy in the direction of the actor, 'creating a labyrinth in which to lose oneself', which in turn creates anxiety in performance as the actor keeps contradictory elements in play.[29] Furthermore, the element of the irrational in his writing – Barker states that 'frequently I do not know what I am writing' [30] – provides a source of contradiction for the actor which remains unresolved despite his role as director-dramatist. Claire Price describes encountering such opacity in rehearsal:

> I remember saying, 'What does this mean?' and he said, 'I don't know, you tell me,' and I said, 'Well you wrote it,' and he said, 'Yes, but I may not necessarily know what it means.' It's almost like something comes to him and he's a conduit, and he writes it, and often things will go on the page that he couldn't possibly intellectualise or explain to anybody else.[31]

Barker's unwillingness to provide explanation of character, and desire to leave actors with their questions, characterises the relationship between his directing role and his identity as the writer. It is not a question of having someone there with all the answers: the indeterminacy that causes anxiety in performance is mirrored in directorial practice. In *Dead Hands* for example, Sopron attempts to outmanoeuvre Eff by leaving – a logical move in a realist drama. But her announcement that she has a train to catch is met with Eff's reply that there is no train station, in turn met by her announcement, 'All the same I have a ticket'.[32] In the performance, these exchanges communicated the collapse of logic, adding to the surreal nature of the location both on and offstage: they were not ridiculous and therefore easy to dismiss; they embodied the effect of anxiety in the audience. In rehearsal, it was clear that the illogical nature of the exchange was difficult for the actors. Barker directed by suggesting to the actors that the station and the ticket were both fiction, and that this was a fight for power and a demand for submission over nothing, but to be played as if it were fact.[33] The effectiveness of the actual moment in performance lay in the actors' conviction that this was real – and in the audience's anxiety over whom to believe, an eye-widening suspension of certainty.

Barker indicates what is required to create a 'total' theatre style, combining the discipline of scenographic elements with the freer reign the actor enjoys in creating or expanding anxiety:

> An actor with no sense of musicality can't play me…I am…infinitely tuned to the text for obvious reasons, and orchestrate very carefully. I think of myself as the conductor of an orchestra of voices as well as a ballet master.[34]

The visual and aural disciplines Barker refers to indicate self-awareness of the contribution his direction makes to the performance style. Barker states that 'set design is not a separate issue from acting': this also applies to the orchestration of sound, image and scenography into a unity which I have previously attempted to demonstrate he achieves in his dramaturgy.[35] What requires articulation is the convention of negotiation through which Barker orchestrates the material, so that this can be realised in practice.

In one sense there is nothing exceptional in the process. Barker is privileged in that he is in a position to bond forms prescriptively into a unity of expression, and negotiation between elements of form takes place as it does in all process. Where his practice is of particular interest is in its convention of negotiation between elements of form: namely the 'working out of the images of the text'.[36] The dramatic situation, characters and language are worked up into an aural sculpture by Barker and the actors, and sustaining its anxiety forms the convention through which negotiations in rehearsal are made. In essence this revisits the penetrative power of the single image in Beckett's later works: the contrast is that Beckett's stage directions are exacting and the stage picture is often static; Barker's directions are minimal and the sculptural imagery more fluid.

In rehearsal for *Dead Hands*, Barker worked with the company in a meticulous way on one such moment, the final grieving of Sopron for her dead lover. Her journey across the space to the body was accompanied by a drone sound effect hummed by Barker: her nakedness achieved suddenly as she let her trench-coat fall; her grief expressed in the naked, sobbing embrace of the corpse, accompanied by a note sung by Barker; Eff being drawn across the space to her, raising her up into his arms in a contrasting silence, and crossing the stage to exit. Barker's direction was that this was 'not primarily a sexual thing, it is marked as a ritual by her removing her clothing', and staging it as a ritual was an exacting process, especially given the search for a haunting physical expression which would satisfy another of Barker's directions, 'Let's avoid the normal.' The exactitude given to this short section – possibly thirty seconds in performance – took nearly an hour of the day's rehearsal before Barker was satisfied with its beauty and ritualistic power.[37]

This was not an intellectual process, but a physical one: Justin Avoth describes finding 'the route of the argument physically':[38] the actor's performance deepens alongside physical work on stage imagery and proxemics. Barker directed 'setting the picture up' – a necessity in rehearsal – and talked of 'letting the picture settle' – a necessity in performance.[39] Once the tableau (and accompanying sound effect) has settled, the text overlays the visual/aural impact, which is either sustained through the continuation of the image, through language, or destroyed by a contrast – whatever technique creates further anxiety.

In *Dead Hands* such moments of Artaudian cruelty punctuated the performance. It is important to note that these nodes are a key denominator of The Wrestling School style: stage imagery propelled powerfully enough by sound and emotion to penetrate the spectator, who engages with possible meanings as they emerge over an extended time-frame – not just for the duration of the performance but in the afterglow of the image.

SPECIAL CONDITIONS

The convention of negotiation is witnessed most intensely in Barker's creation of the exordium, which takes place at the opening of each Wrestling School production. Contrasting diegetic and non-diegetic sounds, light, automated scenery, repetitive gestures by characters, erotically charged postures, tableaux, sections of action from the body of the play – such tactics present the audience with abstracted aspects of the performance, creating a surreal pre-performance which sets the tone of anxiety. The exordium foregrounds aspects of the text with a scenographic boldness, announcing an intense focus and disabling realistic registers of interpretation. For the exordium of *(Uncle) Vanya* (1996) characters mounted a raised walkway carrying metal trays and kitchenware, pausing at the top before dropping them to the stage far below. This attacked the nervous system noisily, creating the desired state of anxiety very quickly. The exordium is difficult to characterise completely. There are examples in stage direction which indicate the effect required:

> *The repetitive sound of an industrial process. A naked woman, headless, perambulates in front of three kennels. A pyramid of books smoulders. When the sound ceases, the woman stops.* [40]

Barker describes the purpose of the exordium:

> The first aesthetic is to overwhelm the resistance of the public... Thus the opening of all our work is a surreal action called an exordium – the exordium announces the form. But at once the moral territory starts to break up, and we can only get through the hostility caused by this...by highly finished, stylish performance, costume, set, the whole aesthetic designed to announce the *special conditions* of the play. [41]

The signposting of form through Barker's direction of the exordium is a tactic devised to prepare the audience for the specific theatricality of each Wrestling School performance. The style the exordium announces needs to be distinct and maintained in order to counter-act the audience's loss of moral stability as the play begins and ethical boundaries are transgressed. The distinctive style of performance anchors the audience as the morally speculative content simultaneously destabilises it.

The use of sound in the exordium to establish the convention of its use in performance is one example. In *Dead Hands*, moments of emotional intensity – in particular Sopron's grief – were accompanied by what Barker referred to in rehearsal as a 'Stockhausen ping'. [42] The exordium had already established non-naturalistic uses of sound as a convention. The importance of the aural element as a theatrical 'glue' is such that in rehearsal, and before the completed sound tapes arrived, Barker would hum to indicate the sound effects which would eventually, in the words of Justin Avoth, 'co-act' [43] with the delivery of text. Further evidence of its significance for Barker is his statement that, 'When I see other companies perform my texts, the poverty of the aural ingredient shocks me – Gertrude's cry is a good example. The actress must deliver the cry and not run from it.' [44] That Barker's characters are eloquent is clear, but what is often missed in terms of his aesthetic is that emotional intensity often cannot be conveyed through language: sometimes it causes language to break down. The use of sound, 'co-acting' with the physical portrayal of these moments of extremity, is a key element of the Wrestling School style of performance and recalls Artaud's use of vocal extremities. Significantly, Rabey characterises the effect of Barker's language in performance also as Artaudian:

> Barker's drama fulfils Artaud's personally unrealised call for a theatre rebuilt on a concept of drastic action pushed to the limit... But whereas Artaud urged the pursuit of metaphysical principles...Barker achieves Artaud's less indulgent or mystical desired effects through language.[45]

My suggestion is that Barker's directorial practices achieve an Artaudian cruelty in The Wrestling School's performance work through language, as Rabey suggests, but also through scenographic practices such as the simultaneous employment of theatre systems to overwhelm the audience, the exordium, as well as presentation of voice as instrument, and body as distilled expression. These and other elements connect Barker's Theatre of Catastrophe and Artaud's Theatre of Cruelty through the anxiety they seek to create in the spectator not necessarily in their excess, but certainly in their cruelty. Barker's dramaturgical framework, at least in terms of his directorial practice, shares common ground with Artaud's, whose theories and practices may therefore prove to be an appropriate starting point for further critical appraisal of Barker's plays and theory of theatre.

NOTES

1. H Barker, letter, 11 August 2004
2. H Barker, letter, 22 June 2004
3. Barker, letter, 11 August 2004
4. Barker, letter, 22 June 2004
5. Barker, letter, 11 August 2004
6. And deserves much greater exposition than is possible here.
7. C Price, interview, 1 August 2004
8. Barker, letter, 22 June 2004
9. Price, interview, 1 August 2004
10. H Barker, programme notes, *13 Objects*, 2003
11. S Sheehan, *Anarchism* (London, Reaktion, 2003), p 73
12. *Ibid.*, p 74
13. H Barker, *Dead Hands* (London, Oberon, 2004), p 11

14. S Marlowe, '*Dead Hands*' reviewed in *Theatre Record* (1 October 2004), p 1420

15. 'Wrestling With Barker', a practical workshop held by Wrestling School associates and actors Melanie Jessop, Gerrard MacArthur, Lloyd Trott, Chris Corner and Howard Barker at RADA on 13 November 2004

16. H Barker, *Gertrude – The Cry* (London, Calder, 2002), p 71

17. Barker, letter, 22 June 2004

18. J Tarnoky, letter, 7 July 2004

19. M Jessop, interview, 28 July 2004

20. H Barker, *Und* in *Collected Plays vol 5* (London, Calder, 2001), p 221

21. Jessop, interview, 28 July 2004

22. Tarnoky, letter, 7 July 2004

23. Jessop, interview, 28 July 2004

24. J Kalb, *Beckett in Performance* (Cambridge, Cambridge University Press, 1989), pp 9–10, 22

25. Barker, *Gertrude – The Cry*, p 10

26. Barker, letter, 22 June 2004

27. J Bertish, interview, 26 July 2004

28. Rehearsal observation

29. D I Rabey, 'Two Against Nature: Rehearsing and Performing Howard Barker's Production of his Play *The Twelfth Battle of Isonzo*,' in *Theatre Research International* (UK: International Federation For Theatre Research, 2005) 30, 2, p 177

30. This quotation is drawn from Nick Hobbes's interview with Barker in the production programme for *Scenes from an Execution*, performed at the Dundee Rep, 2004

31. Price, interview, 1 August 2004

32. Barker, *Dead Hands*, p 52

33. Rehearsal observation

34. Barker, letter, 22 June 2004

35. Barker, letter, 11 August 2004

36. Barker, letter, 22 June 2004

37. Rehearsal observation

38. J Avoth, letter, 23 July 2004

39. Rehearsal observation

40. H Barker, *Found in the Ground* in *Collected Plays vol 5* (London, Calder, 2001), p 287

41. Barker, letter, 22 June 2004

42. Rehearsal observation

43. Avoth, letter, 23 July 2004

44. Barker, letter, 22 June 2004

45. D I Rabey, *Howard Barker: Politics and Desire* (London, Macmillan, 1989), p 5

DEAD HANDS AND KILLER HEELS

HELEN IBALL

A man encountering the body of his father for the first time can hardly be expected to bound up the stairs.

Dead Hands [1]

Eff and Sopron are 'united in their grief' (p 8). Howard Barker's *Dead Hands* (2004) literalises and sexualises this platitude, which Eff claims that Sopron addressed to him as they passed on the stairs. Eff has arrived too late to attend the death of his father. He is overcome by his first sight of the dead man's mistress – 'what a look she has […] Cruel is not the word' (p 7). Barker's programme note identifies the force of doubt by which Eff is overtaken: 'if we can bequeath our material property might we not bequeath our emotional property also?' [2] In playing through this doubt, *Dead Hands* performs a particular take on the specific capacities of the theatrical *mise-en-scène*, drawing special attention to aspects of cultural (and, particularly, sexual) iconicity. High heeled shoes have achieved a particular significance in Barker's more recent plays, key to the corporeal and temporal distinctiveness of his style – and, by extension, encapsulating something of the unique capacity of theatre as a space for poetic speculation upon human intimacy. The highly-charged ambiguities of the stiletto-shod female archetype have become an emblem of Barker's aesthetic and of his approach as auteur-couturier.

Barker might be seen to achieve such a totality of expression to an extent that is only possible due to the existence of The Wrestling School as a company dedicated to producing his work and his own role as writer-director in recent years. For example, the exordium to *Dead Hands*, though not referred to in the published text, must be read as integral to Barker's vision. Its effect is to establish Sopron as the sexual keystone in this 'play for three actors and a corpse' [3] and, particularly through repetitive movement, to heighten the style from the outset by focusing attention upon the visual aesthetic. Sopron is seated with her back to the auditorium, her death-bed vigil defined as ritually she drops book by book onto a pile at her side. Her long legs powerfully akimbo, her stiletto-heels and the bentwood chair – all glance at a strong female archetype familiar via the Bob Fosse 'showgirl'. Reference to contemporary (popular) culture – and, particularly, to musical theatre – induces a level of academic anxiety when approaching Barker's determinedly elitist work. It is, however, an axis that relishes a sense of inevitability when addressing the preoccupation with women's footwear and its invocation of sexual archetypes. This trajectory calls up reference to *Gertrude – the Cry* (2002) and to *Knowledge and a Girl* (2002); in which, respectively, Barker revisits Shakespeare's *Hamlet* and 'Snow White' by the Brothers Grimm, to 'redeem' their female antagonists from 'popular contempt'.[4] Thematically, it activates resonances from Barker's recent philosophical framing of his work in *Death, The One and the Art of Theatre* (2005).[5]

TAKING THE TAILOR'S PENCIL

> [O]ne of the characteristics of my tragedy is its way of lifting the life and status of the characters out of the common facts of life, and subsequently, the appearances of common life also. It is a statement of intention about what is being seen but also who is being seen. The haute couture manner – slightly outdated of course – announces a place removed, even individuals *removed* [Barker's emphasis]. That they also carry high status (and the wearers must move in accordance with it) is another aspect of the tragedy – as Nietzsche says, you can't make tragic protagonists out of the chorus.[6]

Within the terms of Barker's reference to haute couture, it is noteworthy that whilst high heels had been around for 300 years it was not until the 1950s that advances in design and technology combined to produce the very thin heel that became known as the stiletto. Furthermore, this style of footwear was developed to complement the Dior New Look which is a predominant silhouette of haute couture. The New Look, with its immaculately fitted bodice, nipped in waist, and the voluminous extravagance of skirts from a post-war moment signalling conspicuous consumption, has clear echoes in the cut of the female protagonists' dress in recent Barker productions. Its visual resonance exudes designer exclusivity through a backward glance, which achieves an immediate heightening of style and deportment. Barker recognises that his project is a tragic theatre demanding a concomitant visual aesthetic which in turn must overcome financial constraints:

> The Wrestling School is a very poor theatre, but you would not guess that from watching the productions, for two reasons: the first is the powerful acting talent we have attracted

(and it is virtually an ensemble) and the second is a strong sense of design throughout, at every level, from costume to sound, all governed by a single imagination.[7]

The *appearance* of Barker's recent female protagonists is compelling – both in the sense of their dress and in terms of their manner of entering the stage space. Indeed, the synthesis of these two aspects is fundamental – these women's clothes, and particularly their stiletto shoes, shift the execution and thus the impact of their entrance. In *Dead Hands*, after Eff's early speculation on Sopron, 'for example (*Pause*.) Marching in here naked but for shoes' (p 8), there is no further talk of shoes, though they remain a persistent visual motif. In the two earlier plays, *Gertrude – The Cry* and *Knowledge and a Girl*, women's footwear is talked about frequently or is directly the subject. It is, in any case, already a central premise of the source text 'Snow White' where the 'Wicked Stepmother' is made to wear red-hot iron shoes. In *Gertrude*, Ragusa is lumbered with a criticism generally levelled at actors, accused of being 'wooden' in the way she inhabits her skirt and shoes,[8] whilst the muscularity of the Queen's gait is described in *Knowledge and a Girl* in terms of her 'taut arse' and 'tense limbs slicing the air in ribbons with each step'.[9] The self-consciously performative aesthetic of high heels bridges both the stylistic and speculative attitude of Barker's theatre, as 'by lifting the hips they propose a sexual act' and, as Barker notes:

> [T]he posture created by them generates a permanent tension which is of course, a factor
> of the body onstage in non-naturalistic theatre such as mine, where the sexual is the lingua
> franca of power and submission.[10]

The designer Tomas Leipzig acknowledged 'all the Barkerian senses of the shoe', placing stiletto heel shoes in small cages for the set of *The Twelfth Battle of Isonzo* in the Lurking Truth / Gwir sy'n Llechu production of 2001/02.[11]

In a play entitled *Dead Hands* the phrase 'on the other hand' (p 9) acknowledges complex and multifaceted response, just as Sopron's own hands function to contradict her general appearance and, in their very contradiction, serve to enhance her beauty. Which is located in the particularising eye of the beholder – Eff is overcome specifically and immediately (not by the legs in the shoes) but by her 'infantile but aged hands' to the extent that 'immediately I knew I'd sleep with her if not today tomorrow' (p 7). This and the other plays under discussion are fascinated by, and redemptive of, female sexuality in middle-age, by 'beauty somehow severed from youth' (p 17). Gertrude is told by her mother-in-law, 'you'll kill men with those legs in those stockings so what if you're 42'.[12]

Her son Hamlet's assertion that 'the world is full of things I do not understand but others understand them evidently' is exemplified by her shoes, which:

> [H]ave heels of such extravagant dimensions how can you move except by dislocating your entire anatomy […] should shoes not enhance the action of our limbs should they not encourage us to act in sympathy with the body's functioning not trick us into grotesque parody.[13]

Reflecting on his work, Barker identifies a similar function and force behind both onstage stilettos and onstage nakedness: that they are staged is the key, a quality which he sets against '*being* naked, or "nude" or simply "unclothed".' He observes this quality as intrinsic to the high heeled shoe which over 300 years has become 'more than a cultural artefact, or even a sexual artefact, it is one of the great tropes of self-consciousness'. Similarly, Barker describes as 'critical, even archetypal' the 'staging of nakedness as self-consciousness, as something profoundly more than itself', contrasting this approach with the circumstantial one common to:

> [A] naturalistic moment of nakedness ('I have come out of the bathroom, and happen to have left my clothes off…perhaps you have noticed…?') where the intention is to seduce […compared with] almost all nakedness in my own work where the gesture of revelation is endowed with performance, above all, challenge to transgress the social/political routine, to subvert the situation and thereby disorientate, to force a collapse on the spectator (by spectator I mean the opposite character in the play…).[14]

This claim prompts investigation of how the strategic use of theatre's multiple modes of signification in *Dead Hands* facilitates a self-conscious shift of perspective, enabling the 'gesture of revelation' Barker describes above to be 'endowed with performance'.

TA(L)KING DOWN THE WALLPAPER

> 'I admit at one stage I had thought of the set having wallpaper'.[15]

Camille Paglia noted in *Sexual Personae* that 'society's repressions increase sexual pleasure'.[16] Earlier in her study, Paglia has observed that eroticism may be perceived as 'our imaginative lives in sexual space, which may overlap social space but is not identical with it'.[17] One way into *Dead Hands* is to recognise the energisation of the erotic as a result of this overlap, causing friction between the social and sexual spaces. Throughout the play, etiquette functions both as a restraint upon impulsive behaviour and as a signalling system in, for example, ritualised seduction. Gestures are archetypal in such scenarios: Barker talks of the retrieval of the dropped handkerchief which is 'to begin. We both know this will perhaps be fatal'.[18] This dynamic is heightened by the setting of the play at a final moment in the lifecycle, (incompletely) cushioned by socialised behaviours, and which in turn exhorts an impulse to 'live while you can'. This offers particular opportunity for Barker's theatrical dissidence in relation to a theatrical space that is more often than not limited by domestic verisimilitude. Thus, the 'promiscuity' [19] ascribed to Barker's theatre can only be defined in relation to an established norm, which Barker himself described in *Arguments for a Theatre* as emerging from the 1980s culture which:

> [P]ermitted philistinism to parade as democratic art. The managers leapt to sham renaissance postures, wanting power, gold and spectacle, while the fringe, which had sheltered even those whose aesthetic was not oppositional, suffered a double relapse, a miniaturist art no longer fitting the ambition of writer or actor and shrivelling again into scenes of domestic life.[20]

Dead Hands is a chamber piece that relies for its concentrated impact upon, among other aspects, the disorientation of social realist domesticity. More than other of his work, due to its themes, single setting, and fundamentally domestic landscape, the play depends upon the invocation of the very mimetic strategies that Barker dismisses out of hand. He is widely known to be driven by the urge to distinguish his work from all other theatre, maintaining a determinedly elitist project, which he has described recently and in detail as 'the art of theatre'. In *Death, the One and the Art of Theatre* the assertion is made repeatedly: 'all I describe is theatre even when theatre is not the subject'. In terms of the art form, however, there is a crucial distinction to be made:

> What distinguishes 'the art of theatre' from 'the theatre' is its insistence on going through the actual, the conventional, the representative, to the speculative, the territory where social hygiene has no application, and the rupture of the social moment of bereavement, to gaze into the abyss behind or under it, is a typical gesture of the art of theatre.[21]

Audiences know *the theatre* (of their epoch and frequently in reincarnation) and Barker's work relies on this knowledge for the impact of his refusal to 'know the theatre'. In short, our response is predicated upon the upending of conventional expectations. Barker here expresses behaviour in terms of demarcations of space, of gestures, and of looking (to gaze). The spectator reads *through* habits formed in and by *the theatre* to a more vigorous recognition of *the art of theatre*. *Dead Hands* performs its self-consciousness of theatrical constructs, relishing the ways that, in theatre, co-incidence is never coincidental. Barker explores the temporal and representational capacity of theatre for coincidence. Invented stories arise from the paranoia surrounding (potential) intimacy and then come to fruition. The realisation of predictions and desires is emphasised through repetition and inter-subjective reiteration. However, and consequential upon his own impeccable self-construction, Barker objects strongly to the invocation of such conventions, for example, when asked to consider the causal relationship Eff manufactures between himself and the 'offstage' spaces:

> I have said so often that my idea of theatre has nothing to do with the representation of the world, and this more or less entirely separates it from all contemporary method, which is persistently evocative (i.e. evoking what we know already…). In a way – to answer the last question – I have a certain feeling of bad faith about 'going offstage' as if to another place…a sort of realistic fallacy…[22]

TAKING THE PATHETIC OUT OF FALLACY

Upon arriving to visit a relative, it is a common habit to instigate conversation by describing the journey. It is not, however, perceived as usual to maintain this habit of beginning 'with things of little or no consequence' (p 7) when that relative lies in 'an open coffin on a table' (opening stage direction). As, 'strictly speaking the living and the dead cannot be said to meet' (p 14), Eff's opening speech in *Dead Hands* sets up a particular and self-conscious dramatic friction as it is *almost* a monologue, or even an extended aside, because of socialised perceptions of death as nothingness. Barker's programme note to *Dead Hands* identifies that 'the heir beholds the cadaver…through loss, a growing sense of freedom… or has the character of the dead man merely migrated into the heir?'.[23] In production, this concern impacted upon the dynamics of the stage as picture plane and the relation of stage furniture to bodies. The priorities of the stage space shifted from their habitual dialogic focus and the depth of field was modified: both of the other protagonists enter and cross the room to the corpse rather than acknowledging the living presence of Eff. In Sopron's case *marching / stalking / striding* (stage directions) works against the tendency of stilettos to restrict the wearer to small steps. It performs a disruption which persists in the determined

foregrounding of heels as (unsuitable and yet stubbornly maintained) all-terrain wear in
The Fence.

It is from 'the most shocking of the many paradoxes of Death' namely 'the eruption
of a reckless *joie de vivre* created by the spectacle of the cadaver…an exhortation to live
while you can' [24] that *Dead Hands* stages a narrative of tragic experience as compulsion to
action (to seduce the grieving widow).[25] In *Death, The One and the Art of Theatre* Barker
describes how the art of theatre 'draws death back into life, and consequently *alters life*' [26]
because it transforms it into action beyond grieving. Indeed, Sopron's mode of grieving
matches entirely Eff's fantasies of action. His 'incorrigible speculation' that Sopron might
come 'marching in here naked but for shoes' (p 9) is realised moments later when '*A
woman enters, naked beneath a coat. She walks to the coffin. She leans across it as if stricken
with grief. The coat slips from her shoulders.*' (p 11). As the play progresses, this sequence is
replicated twice more. Sopron bending over the corpse appears as an exercise in *déjà vu*
and physical discipline in its choreography: a kind of mirage or ghost that treads a habitual
path reminding its audience of other performing women, of other women in haute couture
with heels, perhaps of other Barker productions. Sopron manifests as a living/surrogate
ghost of Eff's father, raising the spectre of Hamlet's father.[27]

Her appearance, mocking-by-invoking pathetic fallacy to achieve a performative
foregrouding of Eff's paranoia, materialises the notion of sympathetic landscape evoked
by his description of how the vile weather on his journey remitted 'the very moment
she flung up her skirt' for his brother and 'the road began to steam in glaring sunshine
birds became vociferous' (p 31). Similarly, in feverishly talking himself into perceiving
a relationship between Istvan and Sopron, Eff knocks over the chair and this possibility
is immediately assimilated into his narrative (p 30). As there is only one chair onstage
throughout, it maintains tension through the dynamic triangulation of relationships in
various combinations between the three characters and the corpse. If the triangulated energy
of the stage comes from the dynamic between Eff, Sopron, and the corpse, it also comes
from the triangulation of Eff, Istvan, and Sopron – and, to a lesser extent, a third triangle
constituted by Eff, Istvan, and the corpse. *Dead Hands* is occupied with the circulations
of desire in a particular and heightened moment. Eff's perception of co-incidence is the
theatre he creates of the situation which engulfs him even as it seems of his own making.
The extension of the 'house' into the wings and the energetic presence of the offstage
performers accessed through his descriptions of their audacity are experientially real for
Eff and for the audience, as 'here but not here' (p 14). Eff's desire for Sopron causes him
to assert that 'the room is all that matters' (p 57) thus materialising the theatrical world as

predicated on the sphere of his feelings, but also causing the spaces above and below the room to make him paranoid and insecure. The demarcation of that space is verbal. It both is and is not a figment of his imagination. The suspension of the corpse's bed, which hung on near-invisible wires, was extended as a scenographic feature to the frequent practice of flying in props and setting in *The Fence* (2005), the emergence of which as a Barkerian stylistic trope can be traced back to his productions of *Ursula* (1998) and *Und* (1999). Objects are staged not touching the floor, not grounded, but trembling and temporary in the black box space. Eff is 'stretched on imagination'. His ego locates him at what Barbara Freedman has described in theatrical manifestations as 'a delusory centric point'.[28] The play's complex compulsive energies centre upon his (theatricalising) gaze and this is a touchstone / foil / landmine for audience response.

TAKING IT ALL IN HER STRIDE

Barker stages Sopron's nakedness for Eff, having framed it already through Eff's speculation. This strategy has a significant impact upon the way that the audience perceive her nakedness, and a similar effect is achieved by the theatrical quotation marks placed around Eff's desire. Throughout *Dead Hands* this is expressed through a repeated verbal motif, a wish to take 'her whole cunt in my mouth the flesh the fluid and the hair stiff hair I imagine and if she pissed so much the better'. This line is spoken twenty times during the course of the play, and at different points is voiced by all three characters. Its blatancy renders somewhat extraneous (or perhaps potently blatant) the Freudian symbolism commonly relating the shoe and female genitalia, the shoe as the resting place of a (boy) child's eyes averted from the absence of a penis. Eff is fixated by cunnilingus and his fantasy is to bring Sopron to orgasm. The phrasing becomes recognised as currency in the circulations of desire and the transfer of agency, encapsulating the paradoxes, struggles, and reversals that the characters express in their (shared) spoken discourse and in the responses provoked. The audience cannot help but memorise and predict it. Whilst the phrase is repeated, it also shifts, drawing attention to the newness of each theatrical moment, the precise and yet imprecise re-citation that (after Austin, Derrida and Butler) has come to be called performativity. Self-consciousness is a performative shift, a cleavage (to employ Josette Feral's evocative figuration of theatricality).[29] The ambiguities activated by this displacement disrupt the objectifying gaze. They expose the complex construct of subjectivity. Barker uses reflexivity, an aspect of theatricality, to reveal social theatricalisation and thus raises questions of authentic behaviour and socialised (self-) perception. His play acknowledges, and then rearranges, socio-cultural practices and prejudices.

The twenty repetitions of the 'cunt' line draw the audience's attention to its own spectatorship, which can be mapped by the different directions in which the repetitions are pointed – the phrases functioning as metonyms for sexual impulses which are not dispersed by gender or social role, though Eff has already acknowledged imbalances in the sexual economy: 'is it not the tragedy of women that they are obliged to weigh the pleasures of an inspiration against the mounting sarcasm of a contemptuous world' (p 9). A woman 'naked but for her shoes' is perhaps the ultimate in achieving the body eroticised for the so-called male gaze, the ultimate in objectification: her body so utterly stripped and yet still so clearly framed as and for display; in a state to be interpreted as a clear invitation to (think) sexual acts, though the act thought and realised in *Dead Hands* is her pleasure. In *The New Feminism* (1998) Natasha Walter fingers the pulse of a twenty-first century attitude that separates its gender politics from its Jimmy Choo's. Walter perceives reactions against a breed of feminism that 'over-determined our private lives'. She asserts that the new feminism is, instead, located 'in the political rather than the cultural and personal arenas' and allows for 'the subtleties of culture and art'.[30]

So it is perhaps, that now more than ever, stiletto heels are super-charged with ambiguity. Culturally, they carry multiple connotations: as fetish objects, as the weapon of the dominatrix, as sluttish, as glamorous, as alluring and dangerous, as submissive, inviting, as liberation from domestic drudgery, as restrictive and painful and constraining, as desiring and objects of desire. The parameters shift through time. The high heel has a long history, and has enjoyed a recent and massive resurgence of popularity as more and more women buy into designer footwear without perceiving it to be a betrayal of their right to equality. This complexity makes ideological objections to Barker's representation of women, perhaps from the lobbying feminist, even more difficult to sustain. It also renders the notion of auteur-couturier all the more apt.

In discussing films which feature designs by couturiers, Stella Bruzzi describes how 'a result of having arrived at the distinction between costume and couture design is the belief that clothes can function independently of the body, character and narrative' and that in this manner 'alternative discursive strategies can be evolved that, in turn, question existing assumptions about the relationship between spectator and image, not necessarily problematised through the use of conventional costumes'.[31] She is talking here about the work of such designers as Gaultier, Chanel, and Armani, when used in feature films. But the distinction that Bruzzi goes on to make seems important in relation to Barker's refusal of the casual/circumstantial in favour of the causal. This relates the playwright's strategies once again to theatricality, which Josette Feral perceives to emerge 'when the decoding of signs and processes is revealed as insufficient to determine meaning'.[32] Bruzzi asserts that 'the creation of clothes as spectacle is the prerogative of the couturier; the overriding ethos of the costume designer is conversely to fabricate clothes which serve the purpose of the narrative', indeed, the couturier's designs may well 'function as devices for intervention' and that 'even the least extravagant item of clothing is spectacular because it can be recognised as exclusive'.[33] Barker's exclusivity and ambiguity create a stylish displacement in *Dead Hands*. Such displacement functions in raising experience out of the 'common life' by means of palimpsests – in the sense that their actions are parasitic upon, even as they erase, the common (domestic realist) life. This is a redemptive activation of theatrical conventions in much the same manner that Barker's women seek to redeem female archetypes.

There is a photograph by the fashion photographer Helmut Newton of his wife, her face swathed in cigarette smoke. He has been described as '*the* photographer of women' and his signature images are nudes in high heels; images which fast became so iconic as to have 'shaped and crystallised the erotic fantasies of our time'.[34] Newton's work in general, framing models as sexually powerful fetishists, and this photograph in particular, is invoked by Sopron in *Dead Hands*. In the first lines we hear her speak she tells:

> All my gestures
> Every one
> Hang in the air
> Like smoke he said he called smoke perfect and when he smoked he smoked only to
> make smoke dust also he found beautiful its drifting its disintegration in the breeze

adding:

> be smoke always he said to me by which he meant take on the shape of others surely
> be formed by them concede to be moved as smoke is by the air (p 12)

The resonance of Sopron's comment is deepened by what has preceded this speech: Eff has apparently 'formed' her shape and gestures in a moment of fantasy, via the 'incorrigible speculation' that she will enter naked but for her shoes. When this happens, and when it is repeated, Eff is mesmerised by her immobility. Both the stillness and the reiteration shift the way the theatrical image is received. It seems pertinent to return to Helmut Newton on this point, who observes that 'the beauty of photography is that there is a mystery about it – you are just dealing with that one moment'.[35]

TAKING THE ELEVATOR BETWEEN THE FATAL FLOORS

> The old photograph. What is behind the tree? Something was behind the tree. To turn the photograph on its edge. To scratch away the surface of the tree. The land behind the tree continues. A field, leading to a road. The road leads to a city [...] This is both contained in and excluded from the photograph. The essential *agony* of all photography [...] the photograph has the status of a wound, which smarts with its *irresolution*...[36]

In *Dead Hands* moments are heavy with possibility precisely because they are chased by extinction, for 'beauty is a thing seized on the landing when ugliness is halfway up the stairs' (p 45). A sense of constant (literal and metaphorical) movement and provocation is enhanced by the striking pose of momentary stillness. The Dionysian is glimpsed through and because of the Apollonian. Poise here is a kind of teetering, an anticipatory space balanced precariously between liberation and constraint, power and vulnerability: a potent ambiguity recognised in the stiletto as symbol,[37] and enhanced by the profound duplicity of theatricality that manifests so impressively in its capacity for metaphor. In theatrical terms this is presented as a heightening: of the sexual allure of the legs through tension, of the way the body presents as prone. In Barker's recent plays this multi-dimensional capacity is foregrounded in a manner that demonstrates the self-conscious use of one element of the theatrical *mise-en-scène* to frame another, with the extravagance of heightened style but without the need for exaggeration.

Stilettos were once tagged 'limousine shoes' because they were not designed for walking. Barker observes ruefully that the way life is lived these days we do not really have time for seduction.[38] Theatre and stilettos are a (temporary but enduring) lift out of the common life. On the production website a warning that the play contains 'moral speculation' is published alongside the fact that it contains nudity. The woman 'marching in naked but for her shoes' recognises that this performance has a temporal specificity and that there comes a moment when it is ridiculous (see p 9). In his binarisation of 'the theatre' and 'the art of theatre' Barker sets the 'domestic' against 'the hazardous'. After all these years, stilettos are still potent in their dangerous and appealing ambiguity. They are potentially hazardous both to the wearer and to those whose path she crosses. Eff's sense that he will be destroyed by Sopron culminates, as Barker remarks, in 'the final image – not in the text – where he places his hand on her face only to powerfully reject it'. He then observes how the closing image of *Dead Hands* stages 'the oscillations that accompany great sexual encounters – the desire to escape the enslavement of them, followed by the discovery that one cannot breathe without the presence of the loved one.'[39] Stilettos have for good reason been called 'killer heels'. Pitching beauty against agony, poised between sex and death, they have grown into the provocative bedfellows of Barker's theatre.

NOTES

1. H Barker, *Dead Hands* (London, Oberon, 2004), p 14. Subsequent page numbers indicate references to this edition except where otherwise indicated.

2. H Barker, programme note, *Dead Hands* (The Wrestling School production), 2004

3. Quotation from the blurb on the back cover of *Dead Hands*

4. Quotation from the blurb on the back cover of *Gertrude – The Cry / Knowledge and a Girl* (London, Calder, 2002)

5. In the programme note for *Dead Hands* Howard Barker describes the book (i.e. *Death, The One and the Art of Theatre*) as being 'published to coincide' with the opening of the play.

6. From personal correspondence from Barker [undated] in response to author's letter, 20 July 2005. It is worth noting on the point of social status that, once her servant has left, Gertrude cannot dress because she does not know where her clothes are kept.

7. H Barker quoted in C Lamb, *The Theatre of Howard Barker* (London, Routledge, 2005 [1997]), p 200

8. H Barker, *Gertrude – The Cry* in *Gertrude – The Cry / Knowledge and a Girl* (London, Calder, 2002), p 8

9. H Barker, *Knowledge and a Girl* in *Gertrude – The Cry / Knowledge and a Girl* (London, Calder, 2002), p 128

10. H Barker, personal correspondence [undated]

11. Thanks to David Ian Rabey for reminding me of this element of the design.

12. Barker, *Gertrude – The Cry*, p 35

13. *Ibid.*, pp 75–6

14. H Barker, personal correspondence, 29 April 2005

15. Barker, personal correspondence [undated]

16. C Paglia, *Sexual Personae: Art and Decadence from Nefertiti to Emily Dickinson* (London, Penguin, 1992 [1990]), p 36

17. *Ibid.*, p 9

18. H Barker, *Death, The One and the Art of Theatre* (London, Routledge, 2005), p 8

19. See P Thomson, 'Humanism and Catastrophe: a note on Howard Barker's polarities', *Studies in Theatre Production* 10 (December 1994), p 39

20. H Barker, *Arguments for a Theatre*, 3rd edn (Manchester, Manchester University Press, 1997), p 20

21. Barker, personal correspondence, 29 April 2005

22. *Ibid.*

23. From Barker's programme note for *Dead Hands*

24. *Ibid.*

25. Barker, *Death, The One and the Art of Theatre*, p 74

26. *Ibid.*, p 94

27. With thanks to David Ian Rabey for his observations on this point.

28. B Freedman, *Staging the Gaze: Postmodernism, Psychoanalysis and Shakespearean Comedy* (Ithaca and London, Cornell University Press, 1991), p 30

29. J Feral, 'Foreword' in *Substance* 31, 2 & 3 (2002), pp 3–13

30. N Walter, *The New Feminism* (London, Little, Brown, 1998), pp 6, 9, 6

31. S Bruzzi, *Undressing Cinema: Clothing and Identity in the Movies* (London, Routledge, 1997), p 3. In Barker's *The Twelfth Battle of Isonzo*, Isonzo commands Tenna to undress but specifies 'Shoes last', adding 'I've seen the films… It is obligatory'.

32. Feral, 'Foreword' in *Substance* 31, p 7

33. Bruzzi, *Undressing Cinema*, p 25. Bruzzi describes fetishisation as a 'story masquerading as an object', p 38

34. From Adrian Maben and Helmut Newton in Maben's film *Frames from the Edge* (London, Phaidon/ R M Arts, 1988)

35. *Ibid.*

36. Barker, *Death, The One and the Art of Theatre*, p 13

37. For further discussion on this point, see C Cox, *Stiletto* (New York, Harper Design International, 2004); N Friday, 'Of Feet and Fetishes', in *The Power of Beauty* (London, Hutchinson, 1996), pp 461–9.

38. Barker, personal correspondence [undated]

39. Barker, personal correspondence, 29 April 2005.

TOWARDS AN AESTHETIC OF THE SUBLIME

in Howard Barker's Theatre

KAROLINE GRITZNER

In Howard Barker's 'art of theatre' the dramatic characters are anxious inhabitants of unstable territories, passionate travellers through fluid spaces, who often experience their selfhood as contradictory and straying. Traditional aesthetic theory has developed a discourse of the sublime to designate such contradictory feelings (of pleasure and pain, fear and ecstasy, repulsion and attraction), most notably in the work of Edmund Burke (*Philosophical Inquiry into the Origin of our Ideas of the Sublime and Beautiful*, 1757) and Immanuel Kant (*Observations on the Feelings of the Beautiful and Sublime*, 1764; *Critique of Judgement*, 1790). Burke identified the sensual affects of the sublime as sensations of pain, anxiety, terror and awe, whereas Kant, who developed his aesthetics of the sublime in opposition to a theory of beauty, was particularly interested in the startling effects of the sublime on our capacity for reason. According to Kant the beautiful aesthetic object is devoid of any interest (*interesselos*), it exists autonomously, for itself, and awakes in the viewer 'purposeless' feelings of pleasure (*Lust*). Kant's theory of the beautiful in art is for this reason called formalistic (one derives pleasure from one's reflection on the *form* of the work of art). The sublime, by contrast, is characterised in terms of a transcendence of form – a boundlessness and formlessness – which provokes in us awe and terror but also a kind of cognitive resistance. While our awareness of an object's beauty emerges from the effect of sensuous forms on consciousness, the sublime 'object' transcends the level of sensuality (form) and confronts the spectator with the limits of imagination while simultaneously giving us a sense of 'what is not limited in ourselves'.[1] The sublime stretches the ego's sensibilities to breaking point while simultaneously strengthening the power of imagination. Burke's empirical account conceives of the sublime as an 'idea of power' and a 'force which nothing can withstand'[2] which we respond to on a purely instinctual level with anxiety, whereas Kant focuses on the effects of the sublime on subjectivity and reason. Kant is interested in the sublime's concern with what is formless, boundless, unrepresentable, limitless, and in the effects such an experience has on subjective consciousness. The sublime highlights the inadequacy of the ego's attempts to represent ideas sensually and consequently it destabilises our sense of a direct, finite or unambiguous relationship with the world. Kant's analysis of the sublime, with its radical questioning of the notion of representation, provided important impulses for Theodor W Adorno's discourse on the aesthetics of autonomous art – his conception of art's opposition to society. As Andrew Bowie argues,

> [t]he notion of the unrepresentability of the most essential aspect of our existence compels one to ask whether art can ultimately only sustain itself at the expense of any substantial relationship to the empirical content of social life, because the truth it can convey could otherwise be equally well or better communicated in other forms.[3]

Based on this brief overview of some of the key issues in the discussion of the sublime, I would like to argue that Howard Barker's Theatre of Catastrophe (a theatre that 'prefers darkness, if only to separate the audience from itself, and oblige the *individual* to confront the pain on the stage in isolation' [4]) puts forward a discourse of subjectivity which can be termed 'sublime' due to its emphasis on indeterminacy, contradiction and (aesthetic) autonomy. The sublime's presence as an idea and feeling of boundless power (of the Other outside or within) becomes the source of an incomprehensible, terrifying yet fascinating *jouissance* (an enigmatic and ecstatic, heightened form of pleasure) for many of Barker's tragic protagonists. Moments of intense pain and fear are often described as 'beautiful' by his characters, and erotic encounters promise an ecstasy which, far from relieving the characters of their angst or granting them pleasure (understood in the conventional sense as gratification), often deepens their tragic sensibilities by moving them closer to the orbit of death. In *Gertrude – The Cry* the servant Cascan says of Gertrude: 'Her life is such a seeking and so beautiful is her pain' [5] and the Queen in *Knowledge and a Girl*, who is literally being made to suffer for her beauty (she performs a dance of death in hot iron shoes), considers death to be her destiny: 'Death yes / Death I ran towards / Death in every cupboard / Death on every stair'.[6] Such moments of the sublime may be called irrational because the extreme emotional responses they elicit cannot be understood in any ordinary sense. The characters compulsively perform their own individual and in many cases solitary discourses about experiences that are beyond representation and confront consciousness with the limits of language. The destabilising effects of the sublime are consequently felt not only physically but also linguistically – in fragmentations of the body as well as of language. For example, Helen's 'Sliced. Minimal. Reduced. Hacked' body in *The Bite of the Night* is a beautiful and necessary 'monument to pain' for successive generations of Trojans.[7] She embodies the contradictions of the mind's passionate yet self-destructive search for absolute knowledge. Linguistic fragmentation and self-consciousness are characteristic features of all of Barker's work but the experience of a collapse of language is nowhere more intense than when characters are absorbed in erotic encounters: for example, Placida's bewildered attempts at utterance: 'Some accident befell my voice – (*He lifts her skirt over her knees...*) It – (*Her speech falters...*) It – (*She swallows...*) Failed – (*Her breath is uneven...*) Me'.[8]

Barker's work seems to articulate the contradictions of Western culture, especially those of his plays which engage (mostly indirectly and imaginatively and without regard for the enlightenment objective to provide moral certainty or critical clarity) with the catastrophes of European history (for example, Fascism/the Holocaust in *Found in the Ground* and *Und*, or Communism/Stalinism in *The Power of the Dog* and *Hated Nightfall*). In doing this he deploys aesthetic strategies of subversion, transgression and fragmentation which resonate with the philosophical and aesthetic questions that preoccupied Theodor W Adorno (1903–69) who was a leading member of the Frankfurt School. Both men's projects of cultural criticism (the one theatrical/poetic; the other philosophical/aesthetic) interrogate the fate of individuality (the possibility of individual experience), which Adorno conceives as being in a state of regression in the repressively homogeneous 'culture industry' of the post-Auschwitz world.

Barker's *Arguments for a Theatre* sketches the opposition of his Theatre of Catastrophe to the dominant cultural mode of late-capitalist consumer society. Barker, very much like Adorno before him, defines the contemporary cultural mode as authoritarian and reactionary in its false humanistic ideals and its hostility towards individualism. The conventional theatre of today is a form of entertainment and its use value is entirely determined by the criteria of economic viability. Quite willingly the mainstream theatre in this 'age of populism'[9] submits to the laws of the culture industry which 'impresses the same stamp on everything';[10] in fact, theatre itself has been turned into an 'industry' which churns out aesthetic 'products' and disseminates them on the cultural market for general, more or less effortless consumption. Barker's theory and practice do not engage in any kind of artistic 'militarism'. His art of theatre is Adornian in the sense that it places emphasis on the notion of aesthetic autonomy and its interrelated concept of subjective freedom. Precisely because it does not accommodate to the conventional tastes of the majority and refuses to communicate unambiguous moral messages, Barker's theatre can be considered as political *and* subversive.

This dark, enclosed space, detached from the world, is a laboratory of human possibility. It has religious connotations, but whereas religion affirms disciplines, restrictions, theatre explodes them.[11]

Barker proposes his theory and practice of tragedy as an essentially individualising experience which 'complicates life', confronts the subject with unbearable pain and ecstatic pleasure, and thus 'return[s] the individual to himself'.[12] The experience of suffering is important to Barker whose dangerously infatuated protagonists feel compelled to 'suffer' one another (for example, the agonizing love of Claudius and Albert for Gertrude), and it is essential to Adorno for whom the significance of art and philosophy 'after Auschwitz' lies in their expression of a consciousness of suffering. 'Only in the lingering awareness of the ancient wound […] lies hope of a better future'.[13] The 'ancient wound' is a metaphor for the indeterminate, irreconcilable and irrational aspects of subjectivity, those manifestations of the 'nonidentical', which is Adorno's term for the socially impossible contradictions and unresolved tensions that constitute human consciousness. The nonidentical struggles to resist the totalising force of rationality that offers definitions of identity which, for political and social reasons, suppress difference. But an awareness of the nonidentical's abject existence in the abyss of the self can somehow be reached in the aesthetic experience, and most significantly, in the experience of the sublime.

Barker and Adorno's insistence on the transformation of subjective experience in and through art involves the notion of the aesthetic as resistance, not least to the conformist pressures of the administered world. Barker's ostensible celebration of self-expression and self-definition – many of his characters are engaged in 'compulsive process[es] of self-discovery' [14] – seems to be peculiarly logocentric in its espousal of the surface-depth model of Western thought and its search for the (authentic) self. However, self-discovery in Barker's tragedies does not imply a search for wholeness or origin, it is not an attempt to unify the fragments of the self but, on the contrary, to become painfully aware of one's contradictions because contradiction can also mean 'exquisite tension' and 'tender ecstasy'.[15]

Barker's explorations of self-consciousness and self-reflexivity ('self-laceration self-examination self-intoxication self self self I am so tired of self I am so sick with I this I my I' [16]) reveal a certain neo-Romantic sensibility as far as his protagonists' desires to imagine an 'other' world is concerned. The crisis of self can develop into the ego's retreat from the world and other people, implying a renunciation of interpersonal communication and even a withdrawal from meaning, which is for example the case in *Und* where the female protagonist Und, an aristocratic Jew, performs a hysterical monologue while waiting for the arrival of her lover who 'gathers Jews'.[17] The duration of her stage presence equals her solitary action of waiting, her dreaded yet nervously desired anticipation of the appearance of the one who might hold the 'final solution' to her crisis of identity.

Suggestions of a crisis of selfhood also appear in scenographic details, such as in the use of tarnished mirrors in the Wrestling School production of *Dead Hands* (Birmingham Rep and on tour, 2004), which produced the effect of heightening Eff's existentialist (self-) questioning in the presence of death. The image of mirrors is evoked in *Ursula* as a metaphor for the condition of marriage as a series of oppressive reflections of the self back to itself. And in *Knowledge and a Girl*, the mirror-fixated Queen experiences her beauty solely in terms of the effects she has on others: she needs the mirrors not as a confirmation of unified selfhood, but so that she may 'contemplate the shape of pain' of 'whoever beholds' her.[18] A preoccupation with physicality (shape, flesh, physical beauty) is also essential in *(Uncle) Vanya* where Helena's confrontation with her own 'UNDEMOCRATIC BEAUTY' in the reflection in the mirror gives rise to an articulation of self as body ('all things lead to my body').[19]

Barker's tragic theatre repudiates the consolations of 'hope', which is discernible in the characters' refusal to participate in any ideological projects of social and political transformation – as suggested for example in Dancer's rejection of the socialist idea of commitment in *Hated Nightfall*, or in Ilona and Victor's skilful evasions of the power of history in *The Power of the Dog*. But this does not mean that the 'hopeless' tragic protagonists in Barker's theatre are despairing and passively submit to the status quo of the empirical world, this 'nausea of existence'.[20] They are without hope yet they are driven by a kind of instinct, a 'need' which escapes rationalisation (Burgteata: 'I so need / I so / I so need / So / So / So / Need / So'[21]). Adorno says that '[t]he need is what we think from, even where we disdain wishful thinking'.[22] In Barker the need is not only something from which we think but also something from which we intuitively, instinctively act. Language is such an instinctive action, filled with a need, the exact content and purpose of which remain undisclosed. This need can also be construed as the longing for a kind of transcendence, for a means of transgressing the limits of mundane existence – a desire for freedom, which ultimately can only be approached on an individual level and consequently pushes the self into the realm of solitude. In Barker's work the dialectic of hopelessness and nervous anticipation of difference remains unresolved and the introduction of the notion of death pushes it into the regions of the sublime:

> Whereas the tragic protagonist has abolished hope in himself, he is not without *inspiration*. This inspiration is born out of the last remnant of his naïveté – the conviction that at least death cannot be the world repeated... [23]

What energises Barker's characters is a sense that glimpses of an authentic life (as opposed to the ideological prescriptions of a morally 'truthful' life) can only be gained from exaggerated actions in extreme situations. What 'motivates' them is their perceived dissatisfaction with the world ('If you hate the world... You must invent another...' [24]), which drives them into anguished solitude but remains the sole guarantor for a sense of individuality and subjective freedom. An unsentimental recognition of the inadequacy of the world and poverty of existence, which Barker identifies as a defining mark of tragedy, does not rule out the possibility of faith in a substantially *altered* state. They have no hope, meaning they lack an ideological programme for salvation in the utopia of another life, but they nevertheless have faith in the power of the contradictions of their inner selves, in the irrationality of their abject identities, in the anguish they experience when love strikes them. Their faith in contradiction and uncertainty (indeterminacy) instinctively draws them towards the mystery of sex and death, in the proximity of which they continue their (sublimated and sublime) struggle with the real.

The subject in a state of fear becomes aware of his or her closeness to death, but it is the sublime's evocation of death which also becomes an unfathomable source of intense pleasure or beauty. Burke describes the 'delight' that one feels in the presence of the sublime as rapturous and violent and this strong sensuous affect of the sublime can be experienced in the realm of the erotic (Greek *eros* meaning destructive, painful love). As one commentator says, 'whatever excites in the sublime is the presence – the evocation – not only of death but of an *eroticised* death. Thanatos has transformed itself into Eros.' [25] The interrelationship between *eros* and death in the sublime indicates a reversal of both categories, which goes beyond Freud's definition of the death drives (*thanatos*) and the life drives (*eros*). According to Freud, who considered both drives as essential psychological forces, *eros* promotes coherence, harmony, creation and productivity, whereas the death drives aim at destruction and imbalance. Barker's aesthetic repudiates any sense of an opposition of *eros* and *thanatos* and reveals that *eros* as such (the erotic, sexual force elicited and yearned for by dramatic characters in sublime situations) is deathly. 'And if the love destroys me I don't care.' [26] The Freudian emphasis on the unifying tendency of the life drive (*eros*) is challenged in Barker's theatre.

The dialectic of *eros* and death, which produces the dramatic energy in plays such as *Dead Hands* and *Gertrude – The Cry*, seems to respond to the contradictory nature of the sublime, which as we have seen places emphasis on the sensual affect of the sublime (a recognition of beauty in pain, for example) and also provokes self-reflexivity in the individual – which, paradoxically, can lead to the simultaneous experience of self-dissolution and self-definition.

It seems that Barker is in agreement with Bataille's concept of eroticism as transgression, as I have discussed elsewhere,[27] especially in the ways in which erotic passion is construed as an experience of extremes which quite literally causes effects of 'being beside oneself' (the meaning of ecstasy) in plays such as *Gertrude – The Cry*, *Knowledge and a Girl*, and *Ursula*, to name but a few. In 'Sanctity, Eroticism and Solitude' Georges Bataille emphasises the direction of erotic desire as leading to the solitude or otherworldliness of the saint (the tragic hero) – his or her wilful separation from 'the mob, [...] the rest of humanity'.[28] Such a creation of distance from mundane life is a characteristic of Barker's protagonists as well, whose self-conscious articulations of desire make them exiles, positioning them outside of ordinary life. In Barker's work erotic desire not only contributes to the experience of the (tragic) self's alienation from its social and moral Other, it also confronts the individual with the extreme heights and depths of their consciousness.

In *Dead Hands* Eff's encounter with his father's death, which immediately transforms into a sublime passion for his father's mistress Sopron, is an example of the tendency of uncontrollable, transgressive desire to attack the very cognitive foundations of the individual who finds himself in ecstasy, on the border to madness. Eff's confrontation with the mysteries of death and sexuality triggers self-conscious flights of the imagination – he is both fascinated and horrified by speculations on his brother's sexual encounter with Sopron which may have caused his father's death, a death by vision as is also established at the beginning of *Gertrude – The Cry*. Moreover, Eff believes his own sexual attraction to Sopron to be his father's supreme legacy, a Derridean 'gift of death' [29] which he cannot refuse. According to Derrida, the presence of death affirms the individual's experience of singularity and irreplaceability. 'One has to *give it* [death] *to oneself by taking it upon oneself*, for it can only be mine alone, irreplaceably.' [30] By proclaiming that 'tragedy makes death its exclusive concern' and that tragedy's 'proximity to the greatness of death [is] our final expression of anguish',[31] Barker, too, offers a model of self-description or self-definition via the individualising experience of a confrontation with that which cannot be known. Adorno, similarly concerned with the possibility of the experience of individuation in the reified world, conceives of suffering as an authentic individualising experience.

In *Dead Hands* the movement of the imagination, its neurotic (mis)interpretation of theatrical signifiers (the single chair as a place of copulation?; the mystery of Sopron's body parts – her 'infantile but aged hands' (p 7), 'the flesh the fluid and the hair stiff hair' (p 8)), far from delivering the protagonist from his doubt and confusion, is not a movement of structuring, making sense of, or ordering of chaos. On the contrary, in the spirit of Blanchot's conception of writing as effacement and as an aesthetic disintegration of subjectivity,[32] the articulations (the writing) of Eff's speculative and feverish mind catapult him deeper and deeper into a solitude of the imagination which destabilises his sense of self: 'I'm alone / In the world and in my imagination' (p 10) and 'I long to be compromised I long to be corrupted humiliated smeared and soiled by my own appetites yes I am hardly recognizable' (p 32).

The sublime in Barker's theatre can thus be described as an aesthetic experience of indeterminacy in an encounter with *eros* and death – aesthetic in the sense that it is an experience conscious of itself, therefore not spontaneous but deferred [33] – and is tied to a recognition of one's autonomy (solitude and freedom) from the restrictive moral terms of social existence. The Barkerian sublime, the animating and dramatic energy of which is named *desire*, remains a feeling of terror and beauty (tragedy makes pain beautiful) and also approaches Lyotard's (post-modern) re-definition of the term as the paradoxical presentation of what cannot be represented. In 'The Sublime and the Avant-Garde' [34] Lyotard, following Burke's definition of the feeling of the sublime as a combination of terror and pleasure, foregrounds the notion of indeterminacy in his discussion of the characteristic features of twentieth-century avant-garde art. Having dispensed with the idea of faithful representation of nature/the world in art (avant-garde's anti-mimetic project), modern art embraces the idea of disruption, destabilisation, disharmony, and negation, which amounts to modern art's critique of its own foundations, its relentless questioning of the possibility of its existence. Here Lyotard agrees with Adorno's definition of modern art as radical self-critique. Avant-garde art bears 'expressive witness to the inexpressible',[35] it seeks to represent the unrepresentable, to speak the unspeakable. The attraction of the indeterminate, the 'monstrous and the formless' [36] as suggested in the sublime, tends to trigger overwhelming feelings of not-knowing which Barker's characters find exhilarating, frustrating yet inevitable.[37] Moments of indeterminacy occur on all levels of theatrical presentation, for example on the level of poetic speech, which in its fragmented, fractured form points simultaneously to the construction and deconstruction of consciousness.

The use of indeterminate sounds and visual effects in Barker's (as yet unperformed) play *Found in the Ground* (published 2001) also contributes to the effect of the sublime.

The play contains sounds of infinite distance; the imagery of burning books with its suggestion of burning bodies; the metaphors of mud and soil to suggest the dead and the frailty of human life. The sublime effect of these very particular and in a theatrical sense highly determinate performance images and movements nevertheless lies in the ensuing incommensurability between what is physically presented and what is imaginatively suggested.

Adorno draws on the traditional aesthetic concept of semblance (sensuous appearance and illusion, *Schein*) in order to suggest that art's difference from the empirical (the semblance of art makes apparent its otherness from that which is known) nevertheless can only be a result of the immediate, sensuous, material elements of its construction. Adorno says that the semblance of art (its formal and structural appearance) is 'a promise of nonsemblance' [38] and applying Lyotard's reading of the aesthetics of the sublime, one could argue that this nonsemblance (the formless and boundless, the opposite of appearance) is indicated in the indeterminacy of the sublime. In Barker's terms the sublime is a theatrical 'promise written in the air',[39] as Isonzo says. A promise points to the future, indeed it implies and invites the idea of fulfilment or resolution, but in Barker's tragic sublime the promise is also, and crucially, an expression of liminality, a state between present and future, a mingling of the temporal spheres – a threshold. Barker's characters experience the abyss of their selves most intensely when they approach the agonising 'THRESHOLD OF OBLIVION' (Isonzo)[40] – that fragile temporal space in which desire approaches its realisation. But in most cases oblivion (sought in the solitary encounter with sex or death) remains deferred, suspended, painfully real in the imagination yet (necessarily) out of reach.

In *Found in the Ground* the historical signifiers of Nazi crimes (the names of perpetrators, the burning pyres) collide in a theatrical space that is filled with the memories of a judge at the Nuremberg Trials, the painful yet ecstatic collisions of lovers, and Hitler's discourse on walking and art. Burgteata's desperate articulations of a 'need' and the heroism of a physically degenerating librarian (Denmark: 'FROM ME WILL COME NEW DISPENSATIONS'[41]) are perhaps the most forceful enunciations of a promise which is not a promise of reconciliation but its opposite: friction, contradiction, and indefinition. Burgteata feels compelled to sleep with the dying – the proximity to death constitutes her ecstasy – and Denmark's love for Burgteata causes physical and mental degeneration which he is startled by but which he ultimately accepts as the necessary prelude to their extended departure from the stage (to where? – another secret, another promise). Engulfed by the sublime – 'a pleasure mixed with pain, a pleasure that comes from pain'[42] – the characters find themselves on a threshold, in an indeterminate space (between the past and the future) which relates problematically and insufficiently to historical fact. Their threshold is the imagination, and anguished pleasure resides in the experience of suspense in an 'agitated zone between life and death'[43] – the realm of the sublime.

The sublime is evoked in this fundamental struggle to articulate what cannot be articulated, to say what must remain unsaid (a painful secret), to signify what remains outside the symbolic order – according to Lacan this would allude to the *impossible* experiences of *jouissance* and death. Barker's characters are drawn into these two realms of excess, perhaps because the theatrical (aesthetic) appearance of indeterminacy in the sublime contains a promise of *what is not the case* (non-identity, difference). 'Semblance is a promise of nonsemblance'[44] – the aesthetic appearance of the sublime, its presence in the unfathomable experiences of excess and non-meaning (or too-much-meaning), provides a challenge to representation, form and the limitations of social existence, yet at the same time it can perhaps 'bear witness to [...] non-identity'.[45] In Barker's tragic aesthetics of the sublime the erotic experience and the encounter with death, the anguish of love and ecstasy of pain, provoke an affirmation of autonomous subjectivity (the freedom of the ego) while at the same time implying its fragmentation and dissolution. It positions the subject on the threshold between two worlds. In the poetic words of Kristeva, 'the sublime is a *something added* that expands us, overstrains us, and causes us to be both *here*, as dejects, and *there*, as others and sparkling.'[46]

NOTES

1. A Bowie, *Aesthetics and Subjectivity: from Kant to Nietzsche* 2nd edn (Manchester, Manchester University Press, 2003), p 44. Bowie on the dialectic of freedom and constraint: 'Because we feel our limits of our imagination we must *also* feel what is not limited in ourselves: otherwise we would have no way of being *aware* of a limit.'

2. G Hirshberg, 'Burke, Kant and the Sublime' in *Philosophy Now*, 11 (Winter 1994/95), located at www.philosophynow.org

3. Bowie, *Aesthetics and Subjectivity*, p 45

4. H Barker, *Arguments for a Theatre* 3rd edn (Manchester, Manchester University Press, 1997), p 147

5. H Barker, *Gertrude – The Cry* in *Gertrude – The Cry / Knowledge and A Girl* (London, Calder, 2002), p 64

6. H Barker, *Knowledge and A Girl* in *Gertrude – The Cry / Knowledge and A Girl* (London, Calder, 2002), p 129

7. H Barker, *The Bite of the Night* in *Collected Plays vol 4* (London, Calder, 1998), pp 93, 92

8. H Barker, *Ursula* in *Collected Plays vol 5* (London, Calder, 2001), p 63

9. Barker, *Arguments for a Theatre*, p 106

10. T W Adorno and M Horkheimer, *Dialectic of Enlightenment*, tr. John Cumming (London, Verso, 1997), p 120

11. Barker, *Arguments for a Theatre*, p 221

12. *Ibid.*, pp 97, 23

13. T W Adorno, *Minima Moralia: Reflections from Damaged Life*, tr. E F N Jephcott (London, NLB, 1974), p 66

14. D I Rabey, *Howard Barker: Politics and Desire. An Expository Study of his Drama and Poetry*, 1969–87 (London, Macmillan, 1989), p 5

15. Barker, *Gertrude – The Cry*, p 58

16. Istvan in *Dead Hands*; H Barker, *Dead Hands* (London, Oberon, 2004), p 19

17. H Barker, *Und* in *Collected Plays vol 5* (London, Calder, 2001)

18. Barker, *Knowledge and A Girl*, p 102

19. H Barker, *(Uncle) Vanya* in *Collected Plays vol 2* (London, Calder, 1993), p 336

20. H Barker, *Death, The One and the Art of Theatre* (London, Routledge, 2005), p 99

21. H Barker, *Found in the Ground* in *Collected Plays vol 5* (London, Calder, 2001), p 287

22. T W Adorno, *Negative Dialectics* tr. E B Ashton (London, Routledge, 2000 [1973]), p 408

23. Barker, *Death, The One and the Art of Theatre*, pp 60–1

24. Poussin in *Ego in Arcadia*; H Barker, *Ego in Arcadia* in *Collected Plays vol 3* (London, Calder, 1996), p 321

25. G Sertoli in M Groden and M Kreiswirth (eds) *The Johns Hopkins Guide to Literary Theory and Criticism* (The Johns Hopkins University Press, 1997) www.press.jhu.edu/books/hopkins_guide_to_literary_theory/edmund_burke.html

26. Eff in *Dead Hands*, p 36. Subsequent page numbers indicate references to this edition until otherwise indicated.

27. See K Gritzner, 'Catastrophic Sexualities in Howard Barker's Theatre of Transgression' in M S Breen and F Peters (eds) *Genealogies of Identity: Interdisciplinary Readings on Sex and Sexuality* (Amsterdam and New York, Rodopi, 2005)

28. G Bataille, 'Sanctity, Eroticism and Solitude' in C Cazeaux, *The Continental Aesthetics Reader* (London, Routledge, 2000), p 390

29. J Derrida, *The Gift of Death* tr. David Wills (Chicago and London, The University of Chicago Press, 1995)

30. *Ibid.*, p 45

31. Barker, *Death, The One and the Art of Theatre*, pp 48, 59

32. 'Do not hope, if there lies your hope – and one must suspect it – to unify your existence, to introduce into it, in the past, some coherence, by way of the writing that disunifies.' M Blanchot, *The Step Not Beyond* tr. L Nelson (State University of New York Press, 1992), p 2

33. Christoph Menke's definition of aesthetic pleasure, which is derived from Adorno, states that 'aesthetic pleasure should never be thought of as a direct or unmediated response or reaction'; C Menke, *The Sovereignty of Art: Aesthetic Negativity in Adorno and Derrida*, tr. N Solomon (Cambridge MA, MIT Press, 1999), p 13. Despite Barker's emphasis on instinct ('Instinct lies at the heart of the tragic

experience', *Death, The One and the Art of Theatre*, p 62) he rejects the fetishisation of spontaneity and immediacy in modern culture.

34. J-F Lyotard, 'The Sublime and the Avant-Garde' (1984) in C Cazeaux, *The Continental Aesthetics Reader* (London and New York, Routledge, 2000), pp 453–64

35. *Ibid.*, p 455

36. *Ibid.*, p 458

37. KING: […] I never know with you
    QUEEN: How good that is
       How good you never know with me (Barker, *Knowledge and a Girl*, p 104)

38. Adorno, *Negative Dialectics*, p 405

39. H Barker, *The Twelfth Battle of Isonzo* in *Collected Plays vol 5* (London, Calder, 2001), p 276

40. *Ibid.*, p 283

41. Barker, *Found in the Ground*, p 362

42. Lyotard, 'The Sublime and the Avant-Garde' in Cazeaux, *The Continental Aesthetics Reader*, p 458

43. *Ibid.*, p 459

44. Adorno, *Negative Dialectics*, p 405

45. T W Adorno, 'The Essay as Form' in *Notes to Literature 1*, tr. S Weber Nicholsen (New York, Columbia University Press, 1992), p 11

46. J Kristeva, *Powers of Horror: An Essay on Abjection*, tr. L S Roudiez (New York, Columbia University Press, 1982), p 12

THE BODY IN EXTREMIS

Exercises in Self-Creation and Citizenship

MARY KAREN DAHL

> To write tragedy, to paint calamity, is to know the ambiguity that lies behind
> the witnessing of pain, the possibility of beauty in suffering – not as a
> political fetish, but within the privileged and illusory space of theatre, where
> theatre is emphatically not the world but a speculation upon it.
>
> *Howard Barker, 'Goya's Grin'* [1]

In his work for theatre, Howard Barker scripts violent acts either to be staged or to be
imagined by spectators as a result of his poetic provocations.[2] He articulates connections
between the body, power and political systems through images that violate boundaries,
dislocate expectations and transgress sensibilities. The effect is to instigate relationships
between spectators and the performed act that undermine current institutionalised power
relations by creating disturbances at the deepest, most individual and private levels. At its
best, the technique unmoors us from the known, opening up possibilities to defy normative
calls to be 'good citizens, good subjects'.

Tying Barker's name to terms like citizenship might seem odd, especially if one
considers usages that link that term to ideologically laden notions of the nation or
nationalism. Yet in a historical moment when national security concerns may lead to
expanding the limits of state power while the test of loyalty is compliance or silence,
excavating freedom and rehearsing its practice is a matter of necessity. The challenge is
not new. In the West, citizenship status has dictated the relationship between individual
and state since the earliest days of democracy in ancient Athens.[3] That relationship sets
limits to what acts official government agents can perform on individual minds and bodies.
For example, in a contemporary democracy, the state legislates a range of issues – from
reproductive rights and the right to die to health and security measures. The state decides
the degree of citizenship one can acquire and, related to that status, how much access

one will have to public resources or to legal protection of one's human rights. Regarding torture, the state can redraw the lines that limit the kinds of interrogation techniques to be applied to whom under what circumstances. Agents of the state define the levels of pain or physical damage that will constitute torture. Even in liberal democracies such as the United States, the United Kingdom and Israel, official violence exercised on individual bodies manifests and maintains state power.[4] When the actual practice of torture is not at issue, the threat of being subjected to the state's superior power potentially exists for every individual living within its grasp.

With this in mind, I propose that the practice of theatre is inextricably bound up with the practice of citizenship in contemporary democratic societies. We engage in public acts when we craft scripts, stage them, view them or discuss them in print. Howard Barker in particular fully exploits the public nature of theatre to involve spectators in facing the violence at the heart of the state's authority over its citizens and our collusion in that violence. This essay considers how Barker uses corporealised images of the body to entice us to think the forbidden. At the same time, he demands ethical thought by questioning the complicity of artists and spectators alike in appropriating the pain of others to their own ends, whether those ends be the creation of art, of new kinds of knowing, or even the creation of differently constituted, ever changing citizen-subjects. To generate disturbances that contribute to undermining institutionalised power relations and enable citizens to experience and rehearse their freedom differently, Barker stages deeply painful acts. His choice troubles at the same time that it exploits the unique nature of theatre: Holocaust survivor Jean Améry provides a fundamental insight into why this might be so. In *At the Mind's Limits: Contemplations by a Survivor on Auschwitz and its Realities*,[5] Améry explains that the experience of being tortured taught him that mind and body are inextricably interconnected: touch me – touch my very being. If that is the case, then the materiality of staged performance – its reliance on the body as the source of imagistic resonance for the perceiving public – is fundamental to theatre's intervention in our experience of being and acting in the world. Barker consistently puts that perception to work. This essay attempts to come to terms with his dramaturgical tactics by approaching selected moments in *The Castle* and *Terrible Mouth* with the aid of Améry and other writers on the body *in extremis*, Page duBois and Edward Peters.

1. '...THE WITNESSING OF PAIN': THE CASTLE

Live performance calls us to remember that bodies are material – flesh, bone and nerve. Bodies also are the means we have of representing ideas, whether onstage as part of an artistic vision or in the actual pursuit of political missions in the world. As the literal and figurative means of representing ideas, however, bodies inevitably pay a price. Indeed, theories of all kinds, whether aesthetic, political or theological, can cost flesh and blood. That cost may be counted not only in terms of the loss of life and limb. When ideas justify and materialise in the practice of torture, for example, the price of the connection between mind and body becomes all too apparent. As Jean Améry explains in his appropriately titled *At the Mind's Limits*, no matter how profound our intellectual development, when the body is under attack, subjected to torture, our ability to use language or exercise philosophical remedies simply dissolves. The experience of the first blow, he reports, changes us. We lose what he calls 'trust in the world'. The most significant aspect of this trust Améry describes as 'the certainty that by reason of written or unwritten social contracts the other person will spare me – more precisely stated, that he will respect my physical, and with it also my metaphysical, being'. This linkage between the physical and metaphysical is fundamental to his experience. He goes on: 'The boundaries of my body are also the boundaries of my self. My skin surface shields me against the external world. If I am to have trust, I must feel on it only what I *want* to feel' (p 28). He likens the first blow (whether in a police beating or a prelude to torture) to a rape and by linking the acts penetrates to the core of regimes that encourage rape as part of genocidal military policies.

The clarity with which Améry articulates the join between self and body points to the disruptive potential of actions Barker places at the centre of *The Castle* and *Terrible Mouth*. Both plays turn on a sexualised violation of a woman by men functioning as agents of military or state power.[6] In both, men control the means that force individual compliance to the rule of law or conquest. In both, women undergo violation, but elude male control, resisting and reversing efforts to contain or constrain their feelings and choices. Here the body under attack forces the subject beyond philosophical remedies into densely imaged moments of painfully achieved freedom. As a female spectator and critic, I mark these events as particularly problematic and therefore potentially productive for moving beyond language to other forms of knowing, a move that is critical to the moral inquiry that drives citizenship when it is understood as the radical practice of individuals seeking to unmake and remake the *demos*. To this way of thinking, engaging with these moments is a civic act, a challenge to what I know and thus to the boundaries of my self.

In *The Castle*, the witch Skinner is subjected to torture. The play, first staged by the RSC at the Barbican Pit in 1985, deploys complexly schematised images of male and female ways of ruling to depict the struggle between authoritarian state power and citizen-subject. The play represents state power as male and patriarchal, alternatives to the state as female and matriarchal. Stucley, a young knight, returns from the crusades. While he was away, his wife Ann, her lover (the witch Skinner) and the other women redefined the law of the land. They dismantled fences, abandoned the church to pigeons, kept an old man for stud service and redefined intimacy as that which occurs between women; they 'Freed the ground, freed religion, freed the body'.[7] Stucley moves to re-conquer his domain. He succeeds and causes an immense fortress to be built, the castle of the play's title. Skinner, in defiant rebellion against the restoration, seduces and kills the chief builder. She is caught, tortured and condemned to live with his decaying corpse attached to her body. At the play's conclusion, however, it is she and another outsider, the captive Arab engineer (Krak) who designed the castle, who are left to undo the structure and its effects.

Barker has observed that 'States are mechanisms of discipline, and perpetually involved in re-writing and re-ordering experience, annexing it and abolishing it in the interests of proclaimed moral certitudes'.[8] *The Castle* gives the disembodied, all-powerful entity, the state, both physical and symbolic expression. The structure covers the open, fertile fields the women freed (p 33). Its high circular walls allow constant surveillance of its people (p 17). Its dungeons conceal both malcontent citizens and the rooms where they are disciplined into obedience (pp 19, 31–2, 36). As head of state, Stucley eliminates fundamental democratic institutions including jury trials and the right to assemble. State controls extend to each individual's most secret recesses – houses can be searched with impunity, a woman's womb can be destroyed (pp 32–3). The violence which the castle does to its own domain, human and territorial, is replicated in the violence it projects into the world. Krak celebrates his ingenious design: the castle inevitably both initiates and invites conquest. 'It resembles a defence but is really an attack. […] It will make enemies where there are none – […] It makes war necessary' (p 14). Barker populates the stage with male agents of the state – feudal lord, warriors, judge, priest, builder and engineer – and demonstrates that the state requires war to maintain itself.

The playtext encapsulates the state's monopoly of force in an *agon* – literally a contest – between state and subject played out on the field of Skinner's womb. In attacking the builder of the fortress, the murderess has threatened the very fabric of the state. She killed under cover of the sex act. The torture inflicted upon her in reprisal is aimed at her sexual organs, actual site of procreative power and gendered difference, and notional site of desire. The torture is not staged. As a prisoner before a court convened by Stucley, Skinner provides the only details: 'they have done awful things to me down there' (p 31). The most concrete cue to the spectator in his or her work of imagining the torture follows. Skinner asks for a stool to sit on, then flinches and cries out, 'NOT ONE WITH A SPIKE IN THE MIDDLE' (p 32).

The text follows the imagined torture with a vivid staged image of the state's continuing control over its subjects. Sentenced to live with the skeleton of the castle builder she murdered 'strapped' to her in a 'grotesque parody of pregnancy' (p 35), Skinner becomes an ambulatory icon of absence and sterility. The skeleton imprisons Skinner – 'his organ butts against mine' (p 36) – framing her and her invisible wound. The effect is to create a complex figure of the absences created by: A, the castle's devastation of free and fertile fields; B, the potential control exerted by the state's agents over the bodies and minds of citizen-subjects; C, the operation of politics on the field of human intimacy.

But Skinner does not submit. As a prisoner, she takes the stage raging at Ann, in full possession of herself and her pain – both emotional and physical. The torture could not exceed the pain caused by her loss of Ann's love; indeed, she claims that she welcomed the excruciating torment (p 31). The absence of love reciprocated in fact prepares her for politics,[9] although the exchange of politics for desire is neither welcome nor equal. As the action continues, the builder's skeleton shapes Skinner's postures as she traverses the land the state has covered over with its physical and institutional structures, but the corpse of the builder shrinks. It is eaten by birds and rots away. The action likewise shifts power from the state's agents to her: If the authoritarian state is to disappear, it will be because this survivor of torture has agreed to collaborate in dismantling it.

Never subdued, Skinner is wrenchingly active. Page duBois writes in *Torture and Truth* that, while Nazi torture aimed at exterminating their subjects, in other cases

> torturers torture to punish, to offer examples of the pain to be suffered as a consequence of certain actions. They torture to send back out into the world people broken, destroyed, to serve as living warnings. They torture […] to offer for themselves the spectacle of conversion, the body of the other so abused that the tortured gives up a belief and thus comforts the torturer who can then himself believe that he has triumphed, that his cause will triumph over resistance.[10]

Here instead, against the spectacle of conversion, the broken and physically damaged character Skinner unequivocally offers defiance. Ultimately, agents of the state, warrior and priest – and implicitly, the torturers they employ – submit to her. As a composite image, then, the tortured Skinner provides us with a dramaturgically constructed act of wish fulfillment that speaks the outrage that Jean Améry testifies cannot even be thought in the moment of pain.

Because Skinner changes in the course of the action, there is a risk that her transformation will be interpreted as suggesting that suffering torture earns the victim communal respect and/or personal salvation and thus has redeeming aspects. Skinner rebuffs attempts to account for or contain her suffering through such explanatory stratagems. When approached to head up the state after Stucley's death, she at first wants power in order to exact retribution – 'EXECUTE THE EXECUTIONERS!' (p 42) – but refuses that authority because she will be 'too cruel' (p 43). She will be no beatified martyr or stoic hero: 'Oh she is not dignified, she is not charitable, the act of kindness from the victim to the murderer, grey eyes serene in pain absorbed, […] NO! GREAT UGLY STICK OF TEMPER, RATHER' (pp 42–3). Refusing to suffer graciously, she rejects those who seek to appropriate her pain and again subject her to the state's government by charging her with responsibility for the institutions that construct and sustain its power. Only Krak's offer to plan the castle's demolition tempts her to change her mind. The play ends before her decision is clear.

2. '…BEAUTY IN SUFFERING': TERRIBLE MOUTH

Like Barker's agents of the state, scholars who study violence risk doubling the violation of the victims by appropriating their pain and putting it to their own uses. Page duBois sums up concerns expressed by many others: 'I have tried to resist lyricizing the tortured body, offering a baroque description of the body on the rack, of the pains of the slave. […] I have not wanted to sensationalize and exoticise and create desire for torture'.[11] If this is a difficult issue for scholars who can strip lyricism from their rhetorical formulations, how much more challenging might it be for a dramatist like Barker whose objective is a theatre of moral speculation? He lays bare the dilemma at the core of the creative act in an intricate meditation on the artist Francisco de Goya called *Terrible Mouth*, an opera with music by contemporary British composer Nigel Osborne that was staged by David Pountney and premiered as part of the Almeida Opera season in London on 10 July 1992.

The ninety-minute opera is set in 1792; the action takes place against the background of violence sparked by the French Revolution.[12] Travelling with his patroness and mistress, the Duchess of Alba, the Spanish painter Francisco de Goya arrives at a nobleman's country house during the Peninsular War.[13] The house has been commandeered for a hospital; it is gradually filling with victims of the fighting, represented by a six-member chorus of the maimed who seem to have been operated on by another character, an army Surgeon. The amputated limbs of the wounded are the distressingly messy objects that must be disposed of because (as a Nurse carrying one to 'the House of Legs' tells us) the Surgeon believes that 'the sight of limbs detached is not conducive to [the victim's] recovery' (p 3). As this action unfolds, the owner of the house, the nobleman who is known in the play as the Man Without a Conscience, has a sexual liaison with Alba, literally under Goya's nose. A Captain in the revolutionary army takes over the house. He rapes Alba then requires her continued sexual services. She wins his admiration and his escort back to Madrid, leaving Goya behind. The opera concludes with the Man Without a Conscience asking Goya to paint his portrait: 'make me immortal' (p 19). The libretto takes full advantage of opera's formal incompatibility with the conventions of theatrical realism. For example, the figure Goya is split in two, with one actor/singer taking the part of Goya's Voice and another speaking the part of the old, deaf artist.

As this synopsis indicates, *Terrible Mouth*, like *The Castle* and many other Barker texts, places characters in extreme emotional states in the context of extreme political/ historical situations. The opera sets out the problem of the artist's relationship to his or her subject matter, most specifically to the bodies they represent through their art whether on canvas or onstage. Likewise, the play provokes questions about the relationship of spectators to performers and performance. In his essay 'The audience, the soul, and the stage', Barker proposes that his theatre 'addresses itself to those who suffer the maiming of the imagination'. He goes on, 'All mechanical art, all ideological art, (the entertaining, the informative) intensifies the pain but simultaneously heightens the unarticulated desire for the restitution of moral speculation, which is the business of theatre.' [14] *Terrible Mouth* seeks out such sufferers and presents us with a situation that draws us into a troubling inquiry into our collusion in the art we witness.

By his own account, this particular moral speculation arose from Barker's perception that images of Goya were oddly contradictory. Barker notes that, on the one hand, popular imagination sees Goya as 'the responsible artist, the heroic critic and conscience of his age'; on the other hand, an infrequently reproduced self-portrait shows Goya looking sidelong out of the frame, eyebrow arched ironically, mouth curved in a knowing smile; 'Goya's Grin', in Barker's eyes, 'is the repudiation of the enlightenment, a rebuke to reputation, a treachery.' [15] The contrast between interpretations of the painter's point of view led the playwright to question the assumption that 'showing' the horrors of war (as Goya does in the series of drawings called the *Caprichos*) is a simple pacifist act; he suggests instead that the 'psychology of witnessing is more contradictory than this'; accordingly, Barker's Goya is 'a man as much fascinated as repelled by disorder and sudden death'.[16] This mixture of fascination and revulsion ties the painter to Barker the playwright. He observes, 'Only in the hinge of conscience and collusion can be discovered the profound unease that is the real resource of tragedy'.[17] By implication, spectators, too, may enter into what for Barker is a productive state of profound unease. *Terrible Mouth* presents Goya's concentrated exploration of the psychology of witnessing through the sexual violation of his beloved Alba. The dramaturgical choice is not unusual – figuring philosophical questions through violent actions aimed at female characters is a staple in the western tradition. Here the text deploys the act to create the uneasiness Barker requires of tragedy.

The rape occurs within the context of an ongoing relationship between Alba and Goya. Their love has passed through many stages of physical intimacy. They have entered a state of love/hunger that cannot be satiated, a contest between desiring individuals that cannot be won, cannot be resolved. When the Captain rapes Alba, Goya sketches the action; the event enables the lovers' exploration of the terrifying depths of their emotions. Earlier Alba had offered to die with Goya (pp 7, 10). She is his equal and will rise to whatever actions, whatever experiences, no matter how terrible, he can imagine. After the rape, Goya's Voice comments: 'How well I drew! My pencil flew to its target.' The character Goya says: 'Oh my dear one, I am so afraid of my wishes'. Alba herself asserts: 'YOU CAN BE MATCHED BY ME' (p 14). He is the perfect artist, literally able to render, that is, draw, any subject; but whatever actions he dreams, Alba can both undergo and overcome them, using each one to demonstrate her mastery of, her agency in, each situation.

The extended contest between Alba and Goya is tightly interwoven with the problem the text sets out: it is a device constructed to render ideas material. The libretto translates the abstract problem of the relationship of the artist to his or her subject matter into the grossest physical terms. First Goya is forced to grapple with a freshly amputated leg that the Nurse drops. Although he is initially shocked, he adjusts his perspective. Goya's Voice sings, '…all things of horror can be turned to subjects of an academic study'. The character Goya poses with the limb and labels the tableau vivant 'Goya / With / Atrocity' (p 4). Moments later he raises Alba's skirt to examine her leg. Faced with its exteriority, he longs to penetrate the physical surfaces of his beloved. Goya's Voice urges, 'Must love the meat, must love the blood' and Goya confirms his desire to be 'rinsed in some extremity' (pp 4–5). Two scenes later, watching the Surgeon probe the bowels of a wounded man, Goya discovers in himself a need 'to see [his] love in pain' (p 8).

The vehicle for Alba's pain arrives: the Captain is the advance force of a regime that promises to institutionalise egalitarian enlightenment ideas. He hates the aristocracy, especially women such as Alba. As he defines the quality that most enrages him, it seems to be her ability to speak. His adherence to liberal ideology does not extend to the protection of independently articulate females (p 11). His solution is rape, the sheer exercise of physical power. Alba, however, like Skinner in *The Castle*, maintains control over self and situation. She submits physically, but neither intellectually nor emotionally. She controls interpretation even of the act of exposing her body: she insists on undressing herself, saying that she will 'pose the same flesh' the artist has so often drawn, now displaying herself 'not nude but naked'. She refuses to take on an attitude of passive suffering, rejects the Captain's 'little puddle of apology' after the fact and dismisses him as a 'Pathetic / Revolutionary / Man'. For the artist Goya, she simply has a question: 'And am I perfect?' Has she achieved perfect beauty even in the moment of suffering the atrocity of rape? (pp 12–14).

Although I am impatient with, indeed repelled by, the decision to use the depiction of rape as a solution to the problem of probing the artist's complicity in the atrocity he depicts, Barker uses the event to extend the question of complicity far beyond the artist. He scripts attitudes for the characters that suggest diverse positions within the scene from which to view the rape. Each character's stance offers the spectator a moment of recognition and assessment. A: As Goya prepares to draw the scene, Goya's Voice sings his deepest, most forbidden need as an artist and lover. He hungers to explore the 'shape' Alba will assume as the object of violence 'Under the hand of hate' (p 12). B: The Man Without a Conscience earns his name in this scene. The aristocrat enacts impotent complicity. He wants to live, so instead of defending the Duchess, he follows the Captain's orders and attempts to undress her in preparation for the sexual assault (p 12). C: The Surgeon provides the sole voice of conscience. Because he heals the wounded, he prides himself on serving 'the universal good'. At first he refuses to watch the rape, but even he cannot resist. He admits he 'looked' then utters a philosophical meditation on the absurdity of healing those who then use the gift of life to kill and maim (pp 12–13). This multiplicity of positions articulated and enacted by the characters encourages spectators to consider their own role in the performance. Indeed, the dramaturgy sharpened awareness of my own evaluative processes initially as a spectator and now as a scholar and critic.[18] The Captain's hatred of class privilege seduces, while his misogyny repels. The Man Without a Conscience invites comparisons with figures that bemoan disaster, but refuse to put their own assets at risk. The Surgeon wins admiration for his humanitarian efforts, but he capitulates to voyeuristic curiosity. Goya self-indulgently explores his complicity in an atrocity desired by him. Only the victim of atrocity creates herself as admirable. Alba is indeed 'perfect' in the situation – perfectly self-possessed and filled with the quality that Skinner termed 'TEMPER'.

These scripted prompts trigger discomfiting views of self as well as of the characters. In addition, the original staging threw spectators into a position that was distinctly their own, exploiting the fact that the audience comprised a group of individuals who were temporarily occupying a common space.[19] According to the published libretto, the rape takes place during a blackout. Director David Pountney instead staged the scene centre stage as a series of tableaux lit to resemble the historical Goya's use of line, light and color while the character Goya sketched to one side. As a spectator who had moments before impatiently dismissed the use of sexualised violence as a tactic to explore the male artist's psyche, I abruptly was in collusion with the artist, taking pleasure in the aesthetically presented rape and fully conscious that my recognition of the tableaux and their points of reference in the world of 'fine art' was part of the pleasure. Occurring as it did in the midst of the multiplicity of attitudes presented by the characters, the device interrupted aesthetic enjoyment and forced me into self-conscious awareness of the problematic nature of my response to the beauty of the unfolding spectacle.

Having acknowledged my complicity in the act represented, what comes next? Does the provocation to imagine atrocity release me into greater fullness of imagination? Into acts of individual speculation? Is imagining *in extremis* the route to escaping bondage and achieving greater individual agency? If so, what is the action? Do I perform agency by rejecting the image the production stages? By colluding with the character's resistance? By imagining a reciprocal act of vengeance? Or is agency simply found in willing myself to experience and investigate horrific acts transformed 'within the privileged and illusory space of theatre'? How do these possibilities compare with the more obvious agency involved in controlling the text and production through the act of scholarly analysis?

3. '...WHERE THEATRE IS EMPHATICALLY NOT THE WORLD, BUT A SPECULATION UPON IT.'

What is true within the opera is also true of the playwright. Barker explores his own complicity in atrocity, dreaming the horrors of imagination unfettered, using the body of the female performer. He puts pen to paper, scripts the pain to be presented, then invites spectators, individually and together, to become complicit, like Goya inviting the pain of his beloved mistress. Staging the scripted act presents spectators with the profoundly uneasy experience of taking aesthetic pleasure in atrocity. The tactic teeters on a knife's edge between enforcing misogynistic violence and exposing the scandal at the heart of aesthetic delight. As a spectator I experience the double consciousness of colluding with playwright and painter in finding beauty in pain while desiring to take my place beside Alba as she resists subjugation whether by the revolutionary Captain, Goya or Barker. At the same time, the play forces me to admit my own involvement in the atrocity I study. As a scholar, like Goya under Barker's pen: 'I am in the deed itself' (p 15). Goya is in the atrocity he draws. There is no distance between him and what he translates into art, no safe space from which to moralise. As the female voice of Atrocity sings, 'There / is / no / love / like / yours / for / me' (p 17).

In his comments on 'Goya's Grin' quoted at the outset, Barker rejects the use of beauty in suffering as a political fetish. It seems to me that his rejection stems from an observation that theatre often is used to set out ideas that have specific political implications. In such cases, a spectator or scholar may make an interpretive gesture towards unpacking, supporting or critiquing the message. A staged act of violence and the suffering it entails in the victim, for example, might be understood as a condensation of the meanings the playtext is intended to render. In this way, both suffering and violence serve the meaning rather than deliberately operating to provoke complex responses that exceed attempts to explain them. It is the latter that Barker attempts. As Goya walks among the chorus of the maimed, Goya's Voice disclaims belief in any 'theory of the higher cause' that would justify their suffering (p 7). Such suffering is beyond explanation, beyond words.

Barker uses staged violence, even terrible scenes of beauty in suffering, to bring us to the recognition that theories cost flesh and blood when they go to work in the world. So, in *Terrible Mouth*, revolutionary violence fed by liberal enlightenment thought spills from France onto the Peninsula. That thought's consequences are embodied in the chorus of the maimed and enacted in the victor's seizure of the spoils of war, a woman from the aristocracy. In *The Castle*, Skinner's torture punishes her refusal to submit to male authority as articulated in elaborate rationales by the state's agents, both priest and warrior. Although horrific to contemplate, Barker's dramatic evocations of maiming, rape and torture pale in comparison to actual acts performed by agents of the institutions that have governed society in the West. Robert Held tells us in the programme for an exhibition of instruments of the Inquisition that

> The archives of Europe […] tend to show that, owing to the witch-hunts of three and a
> half centuries, perhaps as many as eighty-five percent of the victims of torture and death

by fire were women. Estimates vary, but from about 1450 to 1800 somewhere between two and four million women went to the stake in both Catholic and Protestant Europe.[20]

The exhibition included examples of devices such as breast rippers, shrew's violins and scold's bridles, some of which Held reports were in use as late as the 1870s. It also included examples of oral and vaginal 'pears', contraptions that operate in even more gruesome ways than those that the spiked chair of Skinner's experience prompts us to imagine. The use of rape as a tactic in the ethnic warfare that erupted in the former Yugoslavia in the 1990s was simply one instance of the institutionalisation of a longstanding military practice.

Yet rather than engaging us in a campaign against specific abuses or arguing that mere shifts in political programme can correct the course of human history, Barker invites us into the deepest recesses of that history, a place beyond words where one recognises one's complicity (even as an observer) in the pain of others. In a way, his dramaturgy resonates with, but revises Jean Améry's perception that the first blow of the torturer dissolves philosophy. That is, Barker seeks strategies for undoing the systems and ways of thinking that justify the commission of rape, torture and other atrocities. In the first part of a complex double movement that relies on the fact that 'theatre is emphatically not the world but a speculation upon it', he brings spectators face-to-face with human violence. On one hand, by prompting us to experience 'the ambiguity that lies behind the witnessing of pain', he calls into question assumptions about beauty, perturbs the values that anchor us in the world and urges us towards ongoing, profound restructurings of self. In this, as in depicting the tortured Skinner, he seeks to loosen our reliance on official explanations, formulas and institutions – especially insofar as they justify authoritarian rule or oppression. On the other hand, Barker presents us with victims who defy suffering, who reject rationales that sustain either war or state, and who refuse the dissolution of self even in the grip of pain. This double movement tends towards the much larger effort willed by historian Edward Peters at the end of his survey of the legal definitions and practice of torture from ancient Greece to the late twentieth century.

After reviewing the evidence that torture continues to be employed around the world as a matter of state policy in liberal democracies as well as in repressive or militaristic regimes, Peters assigns responsibility for that continuation not to the regimes, but to the 'civil society that tortures or authorizes torture or is indifferent to those wielding it on civil society's behalf'.[21] In an echo of Améry's recognition that trust in the world is lost when another human violates the boundary of his body, Peters argues that the practice of torture irrevocably distorts the humanity of both victim and torturer.[22] To perform torture, like undergoing it, denies human dignity. Torture both depends on and perpetuates a concept of human characteristics, culture and social institutions grounded in that denial. We therefore must address the crisis in the notion of human dignity that torture – and, I would add, everyday atrocities including rape – reveals.[23] Going beyond Peters, who implies that shifts in doctrine can shift concepts of human dignity,[24] Barker's stage practice prompts spectators to confront the materiality of the body itself and face the fact that rupturing the body puts the self at risk. It violates the bonds of trust in the world that make it possible to live. No doctrine can justify such a rupture.

If Améry clarifies the body-mind join, Barker recognises that conjunction and turns it to his own purposes in his theatre of moral speculation. I use both to clarify my response to violence in the world. As Barker asserts, his imagined and staged acts of overcoming, of resistance to violence, are just that – imagined. They exercise the faculty for moral speculation while potentially strengthening the will to acts of TEMPER in times of duress. Thus Skinner and Alba give form to my desire to break free of authoritarian structures, resist repression and act in my role as a citizen-subject to reinforce what Peters calls 'an operative concept of human dignity' that would make choosing to be either a victim or torturer unnecessary.[25] 'Under the hand of hate' in actuality, of course, it is difficult to know what shape we might assume or (like the Man Without a Conscience) what acts we might perform. Like the playwright's Goya who 'experiences the ambiguities of watching', a spectator may effectively collaborate in violence enacted onstage – or in real life.[26] The body, however, enforces limits. Onstage, the other characters 'compel Goya to transform his voyeuristic appreciation of flesh and blood into tactile confrontation'.[27] The artist masters his aversion to the body parts foisted upon him and treats them as subjects for analysis, yet when the tools of the Surgeon are brought to him instead of his brushes, the action halts. The libretto specifies 'A small succession of dissonant, contemplative sounds' before Goya discards the scalpel he has picked up (p 18). Even he cannot operate on flesh. Body and mind rebel. In the world, this is the reflex I seek: Goya encounters a limit to his collusion in violence, a limit that halts his transgression of the body's boundary: touch me – touch my very being.

NOTES

1. H Barker, *Arguments for a Theatre* 3rd edn (Manchester, Manchester University Press, 1997), p 142

2. This essay celebrates my longstanding engagement with Barker's works and incorporates observations first offered in conference papers in 1990 and 1992.

3. E Peters, *Torture* (New York and Oxford, Basil Blackwell, 1985), *passim*

4. J Conroy, *Unspeakable Acts, Ordinary People: The Dynamics of Torture* (Berkeley, Los Angeles and London, University of California Press, 2000). Further described on the title page as 'An Examination of the Practice of Torture in Three Democracies'.

5. J Améry, *At the Mind's Limits: Contemplations by a Survivor on Auschwitz and its Realities* tr. S Rosenfeld and S P Rosenfeld (Bloomington, Indiana University Press, 1980). Subsequent page numbers indicate references from this edition until otherwise indicated.

6. David Ian Rabey rightly notes the parallel with Barker's *Women Beware Women*.

7. H Barker, *The Castle* in *Collected Plays vol 1* (London, Calder, 1990), p 6. Subsequent page numbers indicate references from this edition until otherwise indicated.

8. 'A Dialogue with David Ian Rabey' in *Arguments for a Theatre*, p 203

9. A reference to the play's epigraph, 'What is Politics, but the absence of Desire...?'

10. P duBois, *Torture and Truth* (New York, Routledge, 1991), pp 146–8

11. *Ibid.*, p 141

12. Programme note, Almeida Opera, 2 July 1992

13. H Barker, *Terrible Mouth* (London, Universal Editions, 1992). See Barker's prefatory note to the libretto, 'Barker on *Terrible Mouth*'. Further references to the libretto will be in the text by page number until otherwise indicated.

14. H Barker, 'The audience, the soul and the stage' in *Arguments for a Theatre*, p 69

15. Barker, 'Goya's Grin', *Arguments for a Theatre*, p 141

16. *Ibid.*

17. *Ibid.*, p 142

18. I attended one of the original performances at the Almeida in 1992.

19. In the provocative conversation 'A Dialogue with David Ian Rabey', Barker noted: 'I am against the solidarity of the audience [...] The best moments in the theatre for me are those in which solitary movements can be discerned, in which a sense of contest can be registered between the stage and the disjointed audience. These solitary contests are of course determined by the fact of the existence of others, they would be harder to achieve in isolation.'; *Arguments for a Theatre*, p 205

20. R Held, *Inquisition: A Bilingual Guide to the Exhibition of Torture Instruments from the Middle Ages to the Industrial Era* (Florence, Qua d'Arno, 1985), pp 21–2

21. E Peters, *Torture*, p 176

22. Peters argues that deliberate training procedures create and sustain the torturer, pp 178–84.

23. Peters: 'Societies that do not recognize the dignity of the human person, or profess to recognize it and fail to do so in practice, or recognize it only in highly selective circumstances, become, not simply societies with torture, but societies in which the presence of torture transforms human dignity itself, and therefore all individual and social life.'; *Ibid.*, p 187

24. *Ibid.*, p 163

25. *Ibid.*, p 187

26. Author's prefatory note to *Terrible Mouth*

27. *Ibid.*

A NEW TREMENDOUS ARISTOCRACY

Tragedy and the Meta-Tragic in Barker's Theatre of Catastrophe

LIZ TOMLIN

Howard Barker's 'Forty-nine Asides for a Tragic Theatre' was first published in the *Guardian* in 1986.[1] The article consisted of a polemical list of instructions and propositions designed to define, or re-define, the tragic form, and, as such, served as an introduction to Barker's own Theatre of Catastrophe, explored at length in *Arguments for a Theatre*.[2] In this, and all successive accounts of his work, it is the tragic properties of his theatre which have been most consistently highlighted. In *Arguments* Charles Lamb identified the quantity of common ground Barker's drama shares with the classical Greek tragedies:

> where one finds the opposition of collectivity and individualism formalized in the division between tragic protagonists and the choruses: the former demonstrating hubris by overstepping the bounds, the latter tending to present conventional social wisdom.[3]

At the heart of Barker's identification with the tragic tradition lies not only his emphasis on the opposition between the individual and the collective, but his refusal to justify or sanction the actions of the individual by recourse to the wider sociological or political environment. To blame such an environment, Barker argues, is to remove the tragic dimension from the work:

> The source of the humanist's resentment of the tragic character – she is no one's *victim*. Humanist art thrives on the *victim*, for in the absence of victims there is no *shame*…[4]

Rather, Barker would argue along with Hegel that

> to genuine tragic action it is essential that the principle of individual freedom and independence, or at least that of self-determination, the will to find in the self the free cause and source of the personal act and its consequences, should already have been aroused.[5]

Barker's imperatives of self-determination, his use of the choric form and the emphasis his theatre places on the conflict between conventional moral wisdom and the protagonist's amoral desire for forbidden knowledge, clearly position his theatre in the tragic genre. However, his particular perspective on a number of tragic conventions, which he uses as often to subvert as to uphold the genre, deserves a more detailed analysis.

His argument that 'the greatest tragedy...makes of death a necessity, even a perfection',[6] proposes a different truth than conventional interpretations based on 'hubris', 'fatal flaws' or 'catharsis', whereby the death of the one is seen as a sacrifice to the divine will to ensure the moral equilibrium of the many. All such interpretations, of course, arise from a humanist perspective on tragedy, the vantage point of the 'still living', which, as Barker elucidates in *Death, The One and the Art of Theatre*, may be utterly incomprehensible from the vantage point of the dead.[7] Instead, he argues that the tragic protagonist is far from being the victim of hubris, or the religious or social conventions which restrict him or her, but rather that death is the protagonist's own logical, necessary and desired conclusion. On behalf of such a protagonist Barker writes:

> If the consequence of my act had not been death I should never have undertaken it...if you gave me more life I should throw it back in your face. Do you think I did this to be forgiven?[8]

In this way Barker reinterprets the conventions of the tragic tradition to place the perspective of the protagonist, rather than the 'still living' society, at its core. In so doing it raises the question as to whether Barker's tragic vision should, more accurately, be defined as meta-tragic; a critique and re-reading of the tragic forms which have preceded his work. By tracing the influences of the tragic tradition through Barker's theatre, this chapter hopes to arrive at a more precise definition of his tragic vision, and the implications of such a vision on our understanding of the genre as a whole.

TRAGIC LEGACIES

In his thesis on Romantic Tragic Drama, Jeffrey Neal Cox accepts the definition of tragedy put forward by George Steiner:

> A hierarchical world order defines the hero, for it defines as heroic those who occupy the summit of that order, it reveals the significance of their fall from such a height, and it ensures that this fall will have a public significance.[9]

Thus, when that hierarchical order was seen to collapse, the protagonist, who had formerly represented man's struggle to oppose, first the Greek gods, then the 'Divine Order' of Elizabethan England, no longer had a providential structure against which to pit his individualistic endeavours. For this reason the romantic drama which followed the breakdown of the traditional hierarchies was, for some critics, a non-tragic form. As Cox explains:

> Romanticism celebrates the liberated individual, not the man trapped within the closed world of tragedy. Romantic art arises to a large extent in response to the French Revolution and its destruction of the hierarchies, immutable laws, and mythic repetitions that defined that closed world.[10]

However, Cox goes on to argue that it was precisely the loss of such a structure which resulted in the hostile and chaotic environment which was to engender the new form of tragic romanticism:

> With the loss of a providential plan for the world, society's hierarchical organization also ceases to provide a meaningful structure for human life. The romantic protagonist, feeling the loss of a divine presence, finds his society to be merely a limit upon his quest for order.[11]

Despite the classical form borrowed by Barker's numerous choruses, the 'conventional morality' contained in their warnings to the tragic protagonist is more (socio-) political than religious, placing the work firmly within the tradition of tragic romanticism in which, as Raymond Williams confirms, 'society is identified as convention, and convention as the enemy of desire'.[12]

The earliest significant dramatic inheritor of romanticism was the realist movement which culminated in the work of Chekhov. Faced with a world which was devoid of pattern or meaning for the humans who inhabited it, Chekhov's characters consistently fail in their quest to impose an oppositional narrative against the hostility and pointlessness of human existence. This is the pessimism which Barker attacks through his own re-working of Chekhov's *Uncle Vanya*. In the programme notes for the Wrestling School's 1996 production he writes:

> We love Vanya but it is a love born of contempt. It is Chekhov's bad faith to induce in his audience an adoration of the broken will. In this he invites us to collude in our own despair.[13]

Chekhov's refusal to allow his protagonists to determine anything of their desires, coupled with the strong implication that it was the social environment which was to blame for their apathy, negates, in purist terms, the tragic dimension of his work. The significance of his theatre lies rather in its philosophical signposting of the tragic form which was inevitably to succeed it. Williams distinguishes between the condition which is the definitive feature of Chekhov's drama and the condition of the absurdist drama which was to follow:

> In a deadlock, there is still effort and struggle, but no possibility of winning: the wrestler with life dies as he gives his last strength. In a stalemate, there is no possibility of movement, or even the effort at movement; every willed action is self-cancelling.[14]

In Samuel Beckett's *Waiting for Godot*, the seminal play of the modern tragi-comic tradition, the condition of stalemate reaches its apotheosis. The wider social and political environment which threatened to 'corrupt' the purity of Chekhovian tragedy has been well and truly eradicated; in this desolate landscape waiting – the definition of non-action – has become the pinnacle of human endeavour. In Barker's *The Last Supper*, Lvov references Beckett's play to identify the absurd condition which will be the inevitable consequence of the annihilation of his own divine presence:

> LVOV: …When I'm gone you'll simply –
> ARNOLD: Gone? Gone where?
> LVOV: Simply degenerate into wit and banter
> ARNOLD: Gone where?
> LVOV: Sit at the road side gibbering [15]

Although the desolate landscapes of absurdism can be found throughout Barker's later work, most notably in *The Bite of the Night*, *The Last Supper* and *A House of Correction*, his theatre refuses the inherent nihilism of a tragic form which extends the hopelessness and apathy of Chekhov's pessimism even deeper. In *A House of Correction* Barker brings together Chekhov's *Three Sisters*, and Beckett's *Waiting for Godot*, in a piece which ultimately refuses to accept the deadlock or stalemate of the tragic legacies which have informed it.

In *A House of Correction* three sisters and Hebbel, a bed-ridden poet (later identified somewhat ambiguously as their father), inhabit an unspecified institution which stands isolated and set back from the road. The potentially Chekhovian domesticity of the setting is undermined by Barker's refusal to clarify the function or location of the house, and the unsettling and vicarious relationships between the three women and the old man.

Thus, the house becomes a symbolic and mythical entity set in no-man's land between two unspecified borders. The post-providential landscape is barren of moral purpose and beyond human comprehension, characterised by symbolic, but ultimately meaningless, routines, like the sisters' continuous folding and unfolding of bed linen to pass the time while they wait for the unspecified, but expected, 'crisis' to break. Far from being feared, this 'crisis' is longed for as it will force catastrophic disruption to the conventions of their lives. Death, Shardlo explains, is 'the very low habit of the morning…and the very low habit of the night'.[16] Such a disruption, she anticipates, will enable her to discover what she believes herself to be capable of. 'I do want to triumph' she confesses to Lindsay, 'I do so want to discover the extent of my magnificence'.[17]

In the worlds of Chekhov and Beckett the waiting would continue and the crisis never come, but in Barker's world Godot arrives, in the barely disguised form of Godansk, a courier who stops at the house in search of some water for his horse. Far from carrying the message that will end the crisis, as Shardlo fears, Godansk, himself, is gradually revealed as the catalyst for change which is to activate the latent desires of the three sisters. The initial antagonism he invokes makes her, she declares, 'unfamiliar to myself',[18] and after his subsequent failed attempts to leave them, Lindsay is both inspired by, and fearful of, Shardlo's impending self-discovery:

> LINDSAY: I want to see you…I want to witness you…in full possession of yourself…
>
>   I always have…
>
> SHARDLO: Have you…? I'm touched…
>
>   […]
>
> LINDSAY: But not at some appalling cost…to me…
>
>   *Pause…*
>
> SHARDLO: Too bad…
>
>   …AM I SUPPOSED TO CEASE BECOMING ME FOR YOUR
>
>   She's gone.[19]

On his inevitable third return, Godansk locates a previously undiscovered well shaft, and casts Hebbel into its depths. This manifestation of the crisis inspires Shardlo to embrace the re-birth hitherto denied to her by Hebbel's determination of her actions, as Vistula explains:

> she is magnificent, and the man who both created and subsequently maimed her
> character, paddling at this moment in a pitch black well from which he can never

emerge, has already shrunk to occupy an infinitely obscure corner of her memory, a well itself, down which no bucket of recollection will ever plunge [20]

But Hebbel refuses to die, calling out insistently for Shardlo from the depths of the well, pushing her journey of self-discovery to further limits. Speaking to the servants she instructs them in the rules of the new order:

> He cannot be recovered from the well, he is profoundly altered and so are we.
> The world is, furthermore, no longer what it was. All this makes it impossible to
> even contemplate the restoration of the conditions that originally prevailed. On the
> contrary, we must move with the current of events… You transport the bricks and I
> will drop them in.[21]

If, as Cox writes, 'tragedy teaches man that there is no final order to life, that any order he creates is a human illusion created in violence against the chaos that is reality',[22] then Barker's response to the absurd condition is not nihilistic, but romantic. His protagonists are charged with transforming the illusion of order into their own subjective and autonomous reality, whereby society's moral conventions can be subjugated to the individual's drive for self-determination. Furthermore, this self-determination bestows on his protagonists a stamp of authorship which enables them to refuse the humanist or nihilist consequences of the death of God, to become, instead, the creator and manipulator of their own self-determined narrative and, in so doing, to reclaim and reconstitute the divine.

SUPREME CONJURORS OF THINGS

In *The Birth of Tragedy* Nietzsche introduces the oppositional structure of Greek Tragedy which he identifies as the clash between the deities Apollo and Dionysus. For brevity I will borrow from Keith Ansell-Pearson who writes that:

> The two deities, Apollo and Dionysus, reveal for Nietzsche the deep tension in which
> the Greeks existed as creatures who could only overcome nihilism by cultivating an
> aesthetic appreciation of the spectacle of life – life as primordial pain, suffering and self-
> contradiction. Through art the Greeks gained a Dionysian sense of the primordial unity
> of nature and of man, and, at the same time, were redeemed from its intoxicating effects
> through the pleasurable illusion afforded by the Apollonian.[23]

Thus tragedy is identified as the perfect medium through which the misery of the human condition can be transformed into a human ideal of the artist's own design. In conclusion to *Death, The One and the Art of Theatre* Barker reflects:

> It is impossible – now, at this point in the long journey of human culture – to avoid the sense that pain is necessity, that it is neither accident, nor malformation, nor malice, nor misunderstanding, that it is integral to the human character both in its inflicting and its suffering. This terrible sense tragedy alone has articulated, and will continue to articulate, and in so doing, make *beautiful*...[24]

This philosophy underpins the self-determination of his protagonists, whose desires to redesign themselves and their worlds force them to write, rewrite and overwrite their own tragedies, stamping their desired identities like a series of ever changing brand marks onto the world of their creation. For this reason Barker defines his tragic protagonist as a liar, a 'supreme conjuror of things' who 'in his impatience to evade the actual...resembles a dancer and like a dancer...is susceptible to mortal exhaustion, for the *actual* will insist upon itself, leaning hard on his shoulders'.[25]

The protagonist Dancer is, unsurprisingly, one of Barker's master conjurors, a tutor-turned-revolutionary ordered to murder the Russian Imperial Family he serves. In *Hated Nightfall* we see how his obsession with narrative construction marks him out as the uncontested author of his own history and the role which he has chosen to play within it. In a previous article I have analysed at length the details of Dancer's rhetorical skills and semantic strategies,[26] but of particular significance to this essay is the fact that, even when facing certain death, his delivery is rhetorically and aesthetically structured for effect:

> I have been ordered to place myself under arrest
> *Pause.*
> I've done so, obviously.
> *Pause.*
> ...Privacy
> Idiosyncrasy.
> Call it what you like.
> Must be extinguished like a cigarette.
> His words, not mine.
> *Pause.*

The personality is no longer the exotic garden of indulgence but the park of the
people.

Pause.

His words, not mine.

Pause.

Gates down. Walls down. The squeals of dirty infants in the summer house...

Pause.

My words, not his...

Pause. [27]

Here the words of the revolutionary mouthpiece are utilised by Dancer to construct a
sardonic critique of their original ideological intention. In this way all Barker's protagonists
use language to regain creative mastery over the manner of their departing, even if the
departing itself has moved beyond their control. As Barker himself observes:

> In the fall of the tragic protagonist we witness therefore the *exhaustion of the conjuror*...in
> the spectacle we are privileged to know the supreme law of limitations but simultaneously
> to be *ecstatically uneducated by it*...[28]

The creation of such spectacles, as the word suggests, requires an artistry which goes
above and beyond linguistic and rhetorical skills, vital though these undoubtedly are. For
Barker's protagonists are not only writers of their scripts and performers of their identities,
but artistic directors of their intricately imagined *mises-en-scène*. In *Hated Nightfall* we see
Dancer transforming the space he controls into one such spectacle, and the people he
controls into performers, in the narrative-turned-theatre of his own vision of history:

> GRISELDA: (*Staring at the banquet.*) What is this for? If they are going to murder us, what
>   is this for?
> HELEN: I think they want to make us foolish. I think it is grotesque and horrible and –
> GRISELDA: The food *is* poisoned, I suppose
> HELEN: ALTOGETHER TYPICAL OF MR DANCER.
>   ...I can see exactly what they want. They want us to sit here in a parody of plenty and
>   then possibly on film, certainly with photographs, to suffer an agonizing death, falling
>   across the table, choking on the silverware –
> CAROLINE: (*Who has not moved.*) IT'S A WEDDING.[29]

The *mise-en-scène* for the second act, the intended murder of the Romanoffs, has been set up by Dancer in such a way as to avoid 'the mundane practice of all revolutions' which 'fails to grasp THE / SYMBOLISM / OF / THE / SACRIFICE.'[30] In this way he mirrors Barker's own mastery of visual symbolism, in which the mute child of the Romanoffs periodically traverses the stage with a watering can; a sequence which concludes in his silently pouring a red-black liquid over the tiered travesty of Dancer's wedding cake to symbolise, among other things, Dancer's decision to marry death.

This ability to artistically arrange death, to 'dance' even on the verge of mortal exhaustion, is one of the seminal characteristics of Barker's tragic protagonists who must 'not yield to death, as it were to a physician', but 'shake [...] death with what he demands of it'.[31] For tragedy, Barker elucidates, 'assures us that if Man cannot overcome the fatuous terms of his own existence he might overcome the fatuous apprehensiveness of its demise...'.[32] In his analysis of the role death plays in Barker's work, Charles Lamb observes how Doja, the world famous anatomist and tragic protagonist of *He Stumbled*, performs for an audience a final dissection on himself, 'seizing back the possession of his own death'.[33] Lamb then goes on to draw significant comparisons with *The Last Supper*, in which the prophet Lvov instructs his disciple Judith to oversee the consumption of his own body by his followers after they have murdered him. It is through symbolic acts such as these that Barker's tragic protagonists seek to rise above the mundane conventions of death to ensure that their narrative control does not die with them; to ensure that in the memory of the 'still living' they can attain some kind of divine immortality.

MASTERS OF HUMANITY

In *Thus Spoke Zarathustra* Nietzsche's prophet rejects the compensations of a limited humanity and calls for an *Übermensch* who will take on the task of challenging the barriers of conventional morality and move beyond a mortal concept of good and evil to create a heroic self whose will to power will raise himself and mankind to a divine greatness. Keith Ansell-Pearson refers to a note written by Nietzsche at the time of writing *Beyond Good and Evil* in which he 'speaks of a master race which will constitute the future masters of the earth':

> It will form a 'new tremendous aristocracy, based on the severest self-legislation'... He looks forward to the masters of humanity in terms of a group of 'artist-tyrants' who look upon man as a sculptor works upon his stone.[34]

In conclusion this chapter will argue that Nietzsche's 'artist-tyrants' are fully realised in the protagonists of Barker's tragic theatre; artists who work first and foremost on shaping themselves; yet also, inevitably, tyrants who will coerce others to bend to the shape of their created world. In *The Theatre of Howard Barker* Charles Lamb argues that, despite the central importance of power relations within the plays, Barker's protagonists avoid the authoritarian tendencies of the classical logocentric tradition which 'has been concerned with power, comprehension, "grasping" – above all, the reduction of the Other to the Same'.[35] He argues, instead, that Barker's relationships are based on an ethics of desire proposed by Levinas and expounded by Derrida whereby, 'desire…permits itself to be appealed to by the absolutely irreducible exteriority of the other to which it must remain infinitely inadequate'.[36] Such a reading does elucidate the power relations played out between Barker's protagonists which, as Lamb describes, become 'a vertiginous and unrelenting duel';[37] a game of seduction and counter seduction which continues until one, or often both, are dead. The nature of these power relations, as exemplified by Lvov and Judith in *The Last Supper*, Savage and Helen in *The Bite of the Night* and Godansk and Shardlo in *A House of Correction*, are paramount to Barker's tragic vision, but a full analysis of the tragic aspect of his work also needs to address distinct, but comparably significant, power relations which sit far less comfortably within Lamb's thesis of seduction.

If Barker's sparring protagonists can be read as dramatic embodiments of Nietzsche's 'new aristocracy', rising above the restrictions of determined humanity and aspiring to the self-authorship of the divine, then how might we read those 'others' who get drawn unwittingly into their grand design? Ansell-Pearson describes Nietzsche's 'new aristocracy' as 'conquerors who love danger, war, who refuse to be reconciled to, or compromised or castrated by the present, and who, above all, realise that every enhancement of "man" requires a new kind of enslavement'.[38] In *Beyond Good and Evil* Nietzsche writes:

> The essential thing in a good and healthy aristocracy is, however, that it does *not* feel itself to be a function (of the monarchy or the commonwealth) but as their *meaning* and supreme justification – that is it accepts with a good conscience the sacrifice of innumerable men who *for its sake* have to be suppressed and reduced to imperfect men, to slaves and instruments. Its fundamental faith must be that society should *not* exist for the sake of society but only as foundation and scaffolding upon which a select species of being is able to raise itself to its higher task and in general to a higher *existence*.[39]

Thus, in Nietzsche's philosophy, does the mass of humanity become no more than the raw material on which the privileged 'artist-tyrant' draws in the creation of his or her own desired reality. This particular subject/object dialectic occurs in Barker's work when the tragic protagonist seeks to determine the making of a world which requires particular contributions from the characters who refuse or are unable to countenance such aspirations of their own.

In Barker's *Ten Dilemmas in the Life of a God* the protagonist is Draper, a land-owner who craves a sustained separation from Becker, the woman he worships, to prolong the impotence she inspires in him, thus preventing the consummation of his idealised desire. It is, he pronounces, 'more beautiful...to rot in celibacy' [40] than to accede to mundane sexual comfort, and he achieves this desired separation through his random and arbitrary murder of a visiting musicologist, a guest of Becker's:

PLAYDEN: ...Why me?

DRAPER: (*Taking him gently in an embrace.*) Why not you? By the same token, why not?

PLAYDEN: I DID NO WRONG TO YOU

DRAPER: Oh, the irrelevance of that! The pathos of such a calculation, as if murder could follow only on offence! You do offend me, but how innocently, no, nothing can attach to that, you were chosen by her beauty, as I was. Her beauty sank your life, as your death will sink mine...

PLAYDEN: I refuse to be an element of your degenerate life...

DRAPER: Yes...

PLAYDEN: I refuse...!

DRAPER: Yes, and how appalling it is nobody knows but me I REQUIRE NO PITY and you are petulant to quarrel like this, isn't he, when my mind is I MUST BE LOCKED AWAY AND YOU'RE THE MEANS.[41]

Sharp, the solider who has provided Becker with sexual fulfilment in the absence of Draper, highlights, on the latter's return from prison, what he sees as the artificiality of the union which Becker and Draper have constructed between them:

SHARP: I RENOUNCE NOTHING I YIELD NOTHING EVERYTHING BEFORE I CAME WAS ARTIFICIAL –

DRAPER: Where did you come from exactly –

SHARP: AND MACABRE –

DRAPER: When I left I shut the gate

SHARP: AND DISEASED –

DRAPER: Who opened it again?

SHARP: AND I CAME LIKE A WIND OF HEALTH –

BECKER: For God's sake –

SHARP: AND HYGIENE TO THIS WOMAN

BECKER: SHUT UP –

SHARP: AND FUCKED HER YES.[42]

But as Sharp later attempts to re-assert his own narrative of uncomplicated sexual potency by taking Becker from behind, she hands the narrative control and protagonist status back to Draper, as the crowd applaud:

BECKER: (*To DRAPER.*) That was for you!

DRAPER: His fluid… travels…down your thigh…

　　Pause.

BECKER: Your fluid… (*She looks boldly at SHARP, then to DRAPER.*) Yours.[43]

As Sharp's sexual effort is appropriated and presented as an aesthetic symbol of Draper's desire, we can glimpse the Nietzschean implications of Barker's tragic vision. Such moments suggest that the self-construction of the tragic protagonists may well be achieved through the oppression, appropriation or manipulation of the raw material at their disposal; their privilege as artists, in other words, may be bought by their tyranny.

This is not to suggest that Barker is advocating a systematic application of Nietzschean philosophy, or that the power relations exemplified in the above references to *Ten Dilemmas* constitute a definitive, or complete, analysis of the piece, but rather to highlight the real challenges to our own moral preconceptions that his work proposes. Barker himself is clear about the unpalatable implications of a tragic vision which 'deems all acts both *possible* and *justified*, thereby countering the humanist slogan '*we are all human*' with the terrible riposte '*this is human also…*'.[44] Attempts to analyse Barker's work solely through readings based on Lamb's thesis of seduction risk evading the most challenging implications of Barker's tragedy by focusing only on the power relations between his protagonists. This, in turn, places emphasis on the harm to Self, or harm to a consenting 'Other', while occluding any mention of the harm done to the unwitting subjects throughout his plays who have been drawn unwillingly into one, or more, protagonist's designs. If the Nietzschean implications of Barker's tragedy are obscured by applications to a Derridean ethics of 'Desire', it can too easily lead to readings which propose an ethical rationalisation of the cruelty of Barker's philosophy, or a denial of the political consequences of his protagonists' amoral drive for self-determination. It is true that Barker himself has argued that such self-determination is not synonymous with a need or desire to control the narratives of others, writing of the tragic protagonist that 'where he remains *profoundly* human is in his instinct for domination – not of others, which would render him merely *political* – but of self'.[45] However, I would argue that while the *instinct* of Barker's protagonist is absolutely driven by the need to dominate or determine his or herself, the *consequence* of such an instinct, that is, the determination or objectification of others, while not explicitly looked for, remains, in its inevitability, a fundamental property of the instinct for determination of self. Such a reading would challenge the limits of Lamb's argument, as outlined above, that the power relations in Barker's work refuse 'the reduction of the Other to the Same', and would rather suggest that the authorship sought by the tragic protagonist can too easily assert its own authoritarian impulse over the subject-objects which become caught up in the protagonist's narrative of self-determination.

An acceptance of the Nietzschean dimensions of Barker's tragic vision is essential to an understanding of his re-interpretation of the tragic form. Readings of the classical tragic protagonist, to return to Steiner, have conventionally focused on the 'fall' of the hero; the hubris that led to death, the choric wisdom that should have been heeded, the cathartic lessons to be learned by the 'still living'. On the contrary Barker argues that death is not a fall or a punishment, but a 'mystery to be violated'.[46] He proposes:

> Death as an object of desire (not death as an undesired consequence of a desire for another thing, e.g. power, another man's wife, a price reluctantly paid…) [47]

Barker's tragic vision, then, suggests a reinterpretation of the tragic narrative: principally that the will to knowledge is not an act of hubris from which the 'still living' must be discouraged, but an invitation from the protagonist to follow where he or she has led, despite any of the consequences to self or other which may follow:

> The failure of even the tragic character to overcome the gravitational pull of all things, the impossibility of sustaining his conjuring of values, does not educate us against his arts. Let us repeat: *Tragedy is not a warning.*[48]

Consequently Barker's theatre is much more than a reworking of the tragic form, it is a meta-theatrical critique and radical reinterpretation of tragedy's conventions. It is a theatre which draws heavily on Nietzsche's vision to reveal, with neither approbation nor condemnation, that cruelty has always been a necessary consequence of the tragic will to self-knowledge and that death has always been its desired outcome. Such revelations pose uncomfortable challenges in the contemporary cultural climate, but the resulting discomfort or offence is intended to provoke the beginnings of a re-evaluation of the moral landscape of tragedy itself.

NOTES

1. H Barker, *Arguments for a Theatre* 2nd edn (Manchester, Manchester University Press, 1993), p 17

2. *Ibid.*

3. *Ibid.*, p 166

4. H Barker, *Death, The One and the Art of Theatre* (London, Routledge, 2005) p 96

5. G W F Hegel (original source not referenced) cited in R Williams, *Modern Tragedy* (London, Chatto & Windus, 1966) p 33

6. Barker, *Death, The One and the Art of Theatre*, p 44

7. *Ibid.*, p 1

8. *Ibid.*, p 78

9. J N Cox, *The Vision of Romantic Tragic Drama in England, France and Germany* (Ann Arbor MI, University Microfilms International, 1985) p 5

10. *Ibid.*, p 2

11. *Ibid.*, p 26

12. Williams, *Modern Tragedy*, p 94

13. H Barker, programme note for the Wrestling School's 1996 tour of *(Uncle) Vanya*

14. Williams, *Modern Tragedy*, p 142

15. H Barker, *The Last Supper* (London, Calder, 1988) p11

16. Barker, *A House of Correction*, p 353

17. *Ibid.*, p 323

18. *Ibid.*, p 330

19. *Ibid.*, p 352

20. *Ibid.*, p 372

21. *Ibid.*, p 385

22. Cox, *The Vision of Romantic Tragic Drama*, p 48

23. K Ansell-Pearson, *An Introduction to Nietzsche as Political Thinker* (Cambridge, Cambridge University Press, 1994) p 67

24. Barker, *Death, The One and the Art of Theatre*, p 105

25. *Ibid.*, p 40

26. L Tomlin, 'The Politics of Catastrophe' in *Modern Drama* XLIII, 1 (2000), pp 66–77

27. Barker, *Hated Nightfall*, pp 39–40

28. Barker, *Death, The One and the Art of Theatre*, p 93

29. Barker, *Hated Nightfall*, p 25

30. *Ibid.*, p 26

31. Barker, *Death, The One and the Art of Theatre*, p 83

32. *Ibid.*, p 40

33. C Lamb, *The Theatre of Howard Barker* (London, Routledge, 2005) p 195

34. Ansell-Pearson, *An Introduction to Nietzsche as Political Thinker*, p 149

35. C Lamb, *The Theatre of Howard Barker*, p 47

36. J Derrida, *Writing and Difference* tr. A Bass (London, Routledge, 1978) p 93; cited in Lamb, *The Theatre of Howard Barker*, p 47

37. Lamb, *The Theatre of Howard Barker*, p 63

38. Ansell-Pearson, *An Introduction to Nietzsche as Political Thinker*, p 150

39. Nietzsche, *Beyond Good and Evil*, p 174

40. *Ibid.*, p 358

41. *Ibid.*, p 363

42. *Ibid.*, p 353

43. *Ibid.*, pp 381–2

44. Barker, *Death, The One and the Art of Theatre*, p 35

45. *Ibid.*, p 98

46. *Ibid.*, p 75

47. *Ibid.*, p 75

48. *Ibid.*, p 93

'ENGLAND BRINGS YOU DOWN AT LAST'

Politics and Passion in Barker's 'State of England' Drama

CHRIS MEGSON

> A friend in the theatre emailed to describe how, while leader of Sheffield council in 1983, Mr [David] Blunkett went to the Crucible to see *A Passion in Six Days*, a play by Howard Barker about the decline of the Labour party. He walked out, not at the theme, but at a nude scene.
>
> *Simon Hoggart* [1]

> I think, taken as a body, my 'English' plays amount to an indictment and a compulsive collection of writing.
>
> *Howard Barker* [2]

It is difficult to resist attaching wider significance to the abrupt departure of David Blunkett, one of the future architects of New Labour and latter-day senior Cabinet Minister under Tony Blair, from Sheffield's Crucible Theatre in the Autumn of 1983. The compelling symbolism of this incident arises both from the timing and wider context of its occurrence. Only a few months earlier, in June of that year, the Labour Party had suffered a cataclysmic electoral meltdown at the hands of the seemingly unassailable Conservative Prime Minister, Margaret Thatcher. This defeat triggered ideological guerrilla warfare in the Labour Party culminating in a leadership contest that had far-reaching and unsettling ramifications for the British Left. The contest was eventually won by Neil Kinnock who was declared victorious at the party's annual conference in October; under Kinnock's leadership, the Labour Party commenced its irrevocable and controversial long march rightwards, proceeding throughout the next decade to jettison many totemic left-wing policies that the new hegemony saw as a liability in its indefatigable quest for wider electoral appeal. The premiere of Howard Barker's *A Passion in Six Days*, in October

1983, coincided precisely with the inception of the 'modernising' project that paved the way for what would become, with Blair and Blunkett in the vanguard, 'New Labour' – indeed, the production opened on the Friday of that historic conference week.

'AGE OF THE NEW PURITANISM'

To be sure, the then leader of Sheffield Council was not the only audience member to leave the Crucible in disgust – theatre critics at the time reported a small army of disgruntled spectators, many perceived to be Labour supporters, heading for the exit doors before the play's conclusion.[3] For many, the production seemed particularly audacious for having been commissioned and staged by the Sheffield Crucible, a theatre located squarely within what the *Guardian* wryly described as 'the celebrated Socialist Republic of South Yorkshire'.[4] Yet the wider significance of Blunkett's decision to walk out derives from the insight it gives not only into the unexpectedly delicate sensibilities of a future hard-line Home Secretary but also into the nascent preoccupations of Barker's playwriting at this time. According to Hoggart's report, Blunkett's discontent did not stem from the play's political content nor from its perceived topicality, not from its caustic depiction of a divided Labour conference, nor, for that matter, from its ferocious and ferociously eloquent analysis of a party increasingly soldered to pragmatism and cynical expediency – not even from its finger-on-the-pulse portrayal of a calculating, youthful and charismatic new leader-in-waiting, Brian Glint. Instead, far more intriguingly, the tough-talking council leader from Labour's industrial heartlands walked out because he was offended by the very occasional nakedness of the actors in one or two scenes of the play, a reaction that seems particularly bewildering given the fact that Blunkett is blind.

It is reasonable to conclude, however, that this offence at nudity on stage amounts to much more than a mere dislike of the play or a rejection of the staging choices evident in the 1983 production. It is symptomatic of a wider consternation, evident in the reaction of critics and indeed some commissioning theatres, to Barker's treatment of political subject matter in the late 1970s and early 1980s. Nakedness and exposure, both physical and emotional, are key thematic motifs in *A Passion in Six Days* that shape its visual and rhetorical registers, and the nature of its meditation on the contemporary political climate. Blunkett's departure, in this context, attains resonance because it exemplifies something of the Labour Party's dogged puritanical streak, its ongoing resistance to 'passion' at the very moment of the modern(ised) party's inception. It is telling in this respect that the most pronounced characteristic of the play is its defiant opposition to what one theatre critic heralded presciently as 'the age of the new puritanism' – a puritanism shared by Left and Right alike that would intensify as the Thatcherite hegemony tightened its grip in the aftermath of its election victory.[5] Barker's strategy in this play, as in others of this period, is to orchestrate the elements of theatrical performance so as to bestow on the audience an experience directly counter to puritanism – that of compelling *excess*. In *A Passion in Six Days*, he achieves this by combining sweeping rhetorical devices – the use of music, the chorus, the electrifying conference speeches, the scabrous but poetic dialogue – with scenes that reveal the desired and desiring body in its nakedness, its materiality and sensuality. 'For me,' states Barker in a revealing formulation, 'the sexual is the ungovernable.'[6]

This tension between an ascendant political puritanism and the 'ungovernable' passion of Barker's theatre of excess establishes the terms for an analysis of his 'State of England' playwriting. It is this body of work, written and produced over a ten-year period, from *Claw* in 1975 to *Downchild* in 1985, which provides a focus for this essay. With some notable exceptions, the plays remain neglected by scholars and are rarely performed even though they were widely reviewed when first produced, were often staged in major subsidised theatres including the Royal Court and the Royal Shakespeare Company's Warehouse Theatre, were frequently lauded by actors, and were instrumental in establishing a foundation for Barker's subsequent explorations in tragic form.[7] Further, these plays register a significant refocusing of his aesthetic priorities – what he has since described as an attempt to develop 'a specific dramatic language for emotions and subjects behind the "issue"'.[8] In terms of Barker's theatrical trajectory, they occupy a strikingly liminal position, drawing on satirical and often topical frames of reference while marking an intensification of his interest in the inability of humanist political systems to confront the radically destabilising force of sexual desire. In their movement away from orthodox creeds of realism to more metaphoric and poetic performance registers – paralleling what Lamb rightly describes as a concurrent gravitation in his work from 'the political to the personal, from stereotype to the individual' – these 'State of England' dramas co-opt the satirical impulses of his early pieces while prefiguring in important ways the moral and imaginative speculation that lies at the heart of his Theatre of Catastrophe.[9]

BARKER AND SOCIAL REALISM

Barker's plays of the 1970s, including landmark works such as *Claw* (1975), *That Good Between Us* (1977), *The Love of a Good Man* (1978), *The Hang of the Gaol* (1978) and *Downchild* (written in 1977 but not performed until 1985), are freighted with disappointment at the failures and squandered opportunities of the British Left, particularly as manifested in the canny pragmatism of Harold Wilson and the disastrous managerialism of his successor as premier, James Callaghan. Barker's procedure in these plays is to elaborate a scenario for the dramatic action that renders the hermetic and parochial nature of English society in terms of the suffocating effects of its stagnant institutions on individual subjects, who are themselves often trapped within opposing polarities of the class system. In this respect, his work is responsive to widespread anxieties at this time about the inefficacy and decline of Britain's institutional structures.[10] As Rabey puts it: 'Barker's plays of the 1970s reflect the contemporary political climate in their fundamental sense of the disjunction between the social institutions and the ideals which they ostensibly embody, of the individual's alienation from the real and severance from the possibility of the ideal.'[11] He articulates this sulphuric sense of corruption within the machinery of state in a series of bizarre, disturbing and often darkly satirical sequences that are studded throughout these plays. A primary example is the murder of Noel Biledew, the eponymous anti-hero of *Claw*, whose death is the price he pays for entertaining fantasies about his possible accession to the ruling elite; his bathtub execution in a mental asylum stands as one of the most scorching and affecting dénouements in Barker's entire canon. Clapcott, the Home Secretary responsible for his death, explains away Biledew's murder to the House of Commons with all the breezy disinterest of a polished political operator: 'I would take this opportunity to remind the House that accidental deaths in mental institutions are running currently at slightly under 20 a year, and that what at first sight may appear a high accidental death rate at Spencer Park is not in any way exceptional [...]'.[12] Another of Barker's laconic Home Secretaries, Stagg in *The Hang of the Gaol*, instructs his civil servant Jardine to cover up the arson scandal in Middenhurst prison in order to save the party's face at the upcoming election. He advises, with a directness that is at once convivial and threatening: 'There comes a time you 'ave to stop polishing yer conscience. Yer end up hypnotized by it.'[13] The more unforgiving view of Jardine's acquiescence is set out by Matheson, his colleague and former lover, in a brittle but poignant exchange towards the end of the play. Her comment resonates outwards beyond the context of its utterance, establishing a leitmotif for Barker's preoccupations in this period: 'England,' she says, 'brings you down at last...'.[14]

Barker's 'Two Plays for the Right', both performed in 1980, share similar thematic concerns but here the focus is on the complex demagogic and atavistic impulses that drive the extreme Right. The disorienting impact of these two plays in performance hinges, first, on Barker's careful construction of visually dynamic sequences suffused with bitter irony and, second, on the strategic juxtaposition of scenes that solicit contrary effects: the concentrated and atmospheric opening sequence of *Birth on a Hard Shoulder*, for example, is off-set by Scene Two when the audience is exposed to the surreal spectacle of a manic group of senior police officers clustered jovially around a ouija board. This penchant for melding the topical with the outlandishly bizarre reaches a conspicuous apotheosis in *The Loud Boy's Life*. This fractured, compelling play opens with Ezra Fricker's guest appearance at a meeting of the Ancient Order of Savages as his bid for political power gathers momentum. Set deep within the City of London, the sequences in the banqueting hall attain theatrical force not so much from Fricker's urbane address to this patrician sect of misogynistic 'loud boys', but from the gratuitous homosocial rituals that are played out as part of their antiquated ceremonial: a formal exercise in breast-feeling opens their meeting and, later, Fricker himself is coerced into performing a partial striptease in one of the many grotesque parodies of female sexuality that dominate the testosterone-fuelled etiquette of this right-wing cabal.

'It is the institutional life of England which is so fundamentally rotten,' Barker commented in 1981, 'and that's why parliamentary change has been so grotesquely irrelevant.' [15] In its engagement with the travails and failures of liberal democracy, and in its deeply-rooted sense of the collapse of parliamentary politics as a meaningful instrument of social and individual transformation, Barker's playwriting of the 1970s shares, at least notionally, certain points of contact with that of his left-wing contemporaries. The most obvious comparison to be made in this respect is with the large-scale 'state of the nation' plays that came to prominence in the major subsidised theatres during this decade. Epic in scale and social realist in their stylistic orientation, plays such as David Edgar's *Destiny* (1976) and David Hare's *Plenty* (1978) embed the experiences, suffering and imploding ideals of individual protagonists within a broader historical canvas that strives to make sense of burning topical issues by locating them in relation to Britain's industrial and imperial decline. Drawing on Lukács (and Brecht), Edgar sets out the aesthetic principles that inform this approach to political playwriting: 'The characters and situations are [...] not selected solely because that's how things are – but because they represent a significant element in an analysis of a concrete social situation.' [16] *Destiny*, in particular, exemplifies this strategy: the episodic structure of the play works dialectically to clearly identify and historicise a logical chain of cause and effect in the social experiences encountered by its central characters. Hare, in an important lecture delivered in the year that *Plenty* was first performed, offers a more impassioned and polemical defence of the social realist mode:

I would suggest crudely that one of the reasons for the theatre's possible authority, and for its recent general drift towards politics, is its unique suitability to illustrating an age in which men's ideals and men's practice bear no relation to each other; in which the public profession of, for example, socialism has often been reduced by the passage of history to wearying personal fetish, or even chronic personality disorder. The theatre is the best way of showing the gap between what is said and what is seen to be done [...] [17]

It is worth pausing at this point to note that critical responses to Barker's drama, although variegated, have often served to denigrate it as the erstwhile twisted sister of the 'state of the nation' play. This can make a clear-eyed assessment of this work problematic. Lamb argues that the tendency of some theatre critics to locate Barker's playwriting in a sole relation to existing paradigms of political drama 'served to obfuscate the plays' principally unique and artistically radical qualities'; Barker himself offers the pointed assertion that critics on both the Left and Right recoiled from his work at this time because it lacked optimism – the staple ingredient of propagandist drama.[18] Yet, reflecting back on Edgar and Hare, it is the particular emphases that are brought to bear in social realist playwriting – on the studied exposure and explication of the political and historical realities confronting Britain, on the illumination of social processes through carefully-conceived representative characters and situations, on the encouragement of audiences to adopt a position of collective judgement on the central action – that account in large part, I argue, for the negative and even vituperative critical hostility visited upon Barker's work in the 1970s and beyond.

'THE CURSE OF DEBATE'

To argue that contemporary critics merely misunderstood Barker's 'State of England' plays is to elide the privileged status they habitually accord to the constitutive discourses of theatrical realism. Occasional expressions of admiration for his signature skills as a playwright – typically, his unrivalled facility for visceral stage poetry – tend to be sharply undercut by a presiding sense of incomprehension at Barker's apparently wayward approach to structure and dramatic meaning. These concerns, of course, belie an unambiguous and rather brutal attempt to correlate how far his plays fall short of the preferred social realist or documentary mode. 'The problem is Mr Barker offers us [in *The Loud Boy's Life*] superior melodrama,' opined Michael Billington of the *Guardian* in a particularly strenuous assertion of his predilection for empiricism, 'when we hunger for tangible fact'.[19] Robert Cushman of the *Observer*, although commenting that 'the play contains some of Mr Barker's best writing', nonetheless complains that it 'lasts nearly three hours and that is a long time not to be told things'.[20] Frank Marcus's review, for the *Sunday Telegraph*, of Barker's much earlier play *Stripwell* (1975) is equally revealing: 'unless we can believe in the protagonists as human beings, there will be no illumination or therapy'.[21] Aside from the expressed 'hunger' for facts, information and therapy, a related trope in reviewers' discourse is the rather obsessive attempt to explain Barker's work in terms of its perceived documentary authenticity. Fricker in *The Loud Boy's Life* is often adiscussed unproblematically as a straightforward dramatic reincarnation of Enoch Powell.[22] The eponymous Downchild, too, is heralded as a version of Tom Driberg, with Roy Scadding an approximate Lord Lucan.[23] Michael Coveney's review of *A Passion in Six Days*, with its scattergun references to contemporary public figures, takes this preoccupation to outlandish proportions:

> Raymond Toynbee is projected by Christopher Wilkinson as a cunning amalgam of Michael Foot and Peter Shore. Another actor looks like Eric Heffer but says surprisingly little. Another looks like Gerald Kaufman but is, in fact, a pale carbon of Sir Robin Day. [...] The implication that Mr Kinnock either carries on like this or was already plotting for the leadership at last year's conference is surely delicate ground.[24]

Hoggart, as we have seen from his remarks earlier, reduces *A Passion in Six Days* to the status of reportage: for him, it is 'a play about the decline of the Labour Party'. Barker's original title for *A Passion in Six Days* – *The Curse of Debate* – conveys more accurately his sense of the futility and banality of contemporary political culture. It also, however, expresses in pithy shorthand Barker's summary estimation of social realism and its limitations. To attempt, in the manner of these reviewers, to bring these plays too closely into the orbit of social realist or documentary theatre practice is to overlook the very qualities that make them stylistically unique and challenging: the vertiginous and quixotic moments of self consciousness that emerge when desire collides with conscience, the brazen scatological humour, the eviscerating poetic dialogue far removed from the measured cadences of 'everyday' speech, the contradictory attitudes they build to leading protagonists. These elements in combination establish a trenchant poetics of despair that stands irrevocably counter to the social realist project.

'TESTAMENT OF DESPAIR'

> The exercise of power – presumed or real – had a natural appeal to me before I had
> uncovered an urge to write tragedy, for which no social democratic political figure could
> be an appropriate protagonist. When I moved towards plays like *Victory* or *The Power of
> the Dog* I had discerned that what I required was a narrative about the *evasion* of authority
> and not the exercise of authority. Until then, English political types figured extensively in
> my work because the failure to be heroic – surely what characterized all English politics
> in the 1970s – brought these individuals into the scope of satire. I was a satirist because I
> was trying to evade social realism. I had not found an aesthetic that would edge me beyond
> satire, and when I found it, the objects of the satire disappeared with it.[25]

These important observations underline two central tenets of Barker's 'State of England'
playwriting: the status accorded to 'evasion' in his theatrical negotiation of authority and
its effects on the individual, and his related struggle to shape an aesthetic that ruptures
the familiar perspectives of political theatre practice. Indeed, these plays deploy a range of
structural and stylistic devices that work from within to explode the theatrical apparatus
of social realism. Barker has noted elsewhere a deliberate attempt in his work from the
mid-1970s to engage with more complex psychology.[26] This manifests itself in a number
of ways, not least in the focus of these plays on individual characters who execute actions
that offend the shibboleths of humanist sensibility. Old Gocher in *Fair Slaughter* (1977)
retains his electrifying commitment to ideology regardless of its bloodied legacy, while
the beleaguered murderer Finney in *Birth on a Hard Shoulder* is compelled repeatedly
to review the terms by which he evaluates 'wrong' action. Fricker's hot-headed shooting
of the German bomber in an early scene of *The Loud Boy's Life* constitutes, for him, a
supreme epiphany: from this moment on, he identifies himself as the man who by force
of will transforms the context. It is in Barker's later plays, however, that sexual desire is
foregrounded as the principal catalysing agent of transformation. *A Passion in Six Days*
is comprised of various scenes at a Labour Party conference set against the haunting
backdrop of the sea. The action of the play works cumulatively to set the utopian promise
of a politics that can accommodate new forms of living, which can give fullest expression
to the imaginative possibilities of desire, against the stark reality of a political system that
has become increasingly anaemic and ethically redundant. The collision between utopian
possibility and the restrictive pragmatism of *realpolitik* finds a dramatic articulation in
the set-piece orations made by individual delegates to the conference. In one of these,

the idealist John Axt offers an emotional but ultimately ineffective onstage address that desperately attempts, against a background of heckling and interruption, to detach the institution of marriage from property relations: 'Comrades – the Labour Party forgets it is the party of personal liberty, and that means sexual liberty, and we must free ourselves from our own capitalism, the capitalism in our hearts'.[27] Axt intimates this freedom as a possibility but the play is in part focused on his debilitating struggle to act on it.

Barker's use of unorthodox and defiantly non-domestic settings adumbrates the sense of existential crisis and despair confronted by his protagonists. As he puts it: 'The room can't any longer be the place where serious social collision occurs, in which social alienation is properly represented.'[28] Often, the decrepit scenic environments function metaphorically to instantiate the stultifying decay of bankrupt institutions and repressive social structures: a hospital ward in Wandsworth prison (*Fair Slaughter*), a burned out prison (*The Hang of the Gaol*), a partly built cemetery (*The Love of a Good Man*), an isolation hospital or docklands warehouse (*Birth on a Hard Shoulder*). 'There is despair in all this,' Barker has remarked, 'the plays seem to me a testament of despair.'[29] As important, however, is the fact that the audience's confrontation with pessimism, far from debilitating, presents possibilities for radical transformation in perception. To an extent, this derives from the inclusion of set-piece sequences that require the audience to set new terms for its engagement with the action: examples include Tovarish's heavenly train ride at the end of *Fair Slaughter*, the sudden appearance of the grumpy spectre in *Birth on a Hard Shoulder*, and Natley's devouring of Fricker's ashes in a ritual of homage to his deceased icon in *The Loud Boy's Life*. More than any other dramatist of his generation, Barker has restored to theatrical dialogue a sensual poetic force that surfaces even in the most unlikely situations: 'Gee Gee, after all the filth I've been with, no one can twist my womb like you,' confesses Angie to her husband Clapcott in *Claw*, 'You freeze my blood'.[30] The comment is almost throwaway, a coquettish colloquial aside, but such is the economy of the writing that it conveys both the carnal properties and the unfathomable dimensions of her desire. The fact that she delivers her statement immediately after Clapcott has approved the murder of Noel Biledew adds a further layer of complex sexuality to her remarks.

Reflecting on his plays of this period, Barker detects a 'rudimentary tragic consciousness' at work.[31] It finds an expression, sometimes fleetingly, in certain images and utterances but primarily in the existential weariness with which his protagonists arbitrate their relationship to forms of institutionalised authority. It is a sensibility reflected in Staveley's moribund comment on politics in *Fair Slaughter*: 'All opinions, only wavelets, but the river carries on'.[32] His observation has an exact counterpart in *Birth on a Hard*

Shoulder when Hilary deploys a kaleidoscope metaphor to express a similar sentiment: 'You shake it and the coloured bits move but the ingredients are the same. That is why we reject politics.' [33] In the same play, the coup-plotting Croydon offers an altogether more ebullient summation of the politician's art: 'It's shit and trickery, Brian, and you have filled your guts with it!' [34] Perhaps most memorably, there is Fricker's disintegration in *The Loud Boy's Life*: in the grounds of St Clare's mental hospital, as guest of honour at the tepid annual summer fête, the loquacious politician attempts to contrive an anodyne speech for the gathered crowd in the assured expectation that the phone in front of him will ring inviting him to take high office. The call, in a desolating *coup-de-théâtre*, never arrives; history has moved on. These amount to theatrical moments of profound melancholy that precipitate a tangible dislocation of identity, a sense of loss that attends an individual's willed or else serendipitous alienation from hegemonic structures of power. In these instances, Barker's protagonists are exposed to the possibility of the Catastrophic – that is, the point at which the necessity for radical transformation and self-reconstruction countermands the prohibitions of the socialised conscience.

In 1981, Barker revealed his 'sense of overcoming [...] the stirrings of some change in form'.[35] The remark signals his restlessness with overtly political subject matter, a fatigue with the vestiges of realist form, an instinct to escape the clutter of the topical. With the benefit of hindsight, it is tempting to position his 'State of England' plays in too close a proximity to the work that preceded and followed it – in a word, to allow it to lie neglected in the long shadow cast by Barker's dazzling masterpieces of modern tragedy. What is certain, however, is that these plays, on their own terms, merit attention, reassessment and revival. Barker:

> Perhaps in time they will be [revived], but only when the 'issue' elements are rinsed out of them, when they seem to be about the melancholy of defused ambitions rather than any rage that might attach to them. I think *Fair Slaughter* could stand this now...the pity of Old Gocher's blind defence of dead and – indeed – cruel ideology, Downchild's sexual servitude, Scadding's faith in sexual love when all else has been betrayed...things like that...[36]

NOTES

1.   S Hoggart, *Guardian*, 8 December 2001

2.   Quoted in M Hay and S Trussler, 'Energy – and the Small Discovery of Dignity', *Theatre Quarterly*, 10, 40 (1981), p 12

3.   See Irene McManus's review in the *Guardian* and Michael Coveney's in the *Financial Times* in *London Theatre Record*, 24 September 1983, pp 866–7

4.   I McManus, *Guardian* in *London Theatre Record*, 24 September 1983, p 866

5.   P Allen, *New Statesman* in *London Theatre Record*, 24 September 1983, p 867

6.   Quoted in C Lamb, *The Theatre of Howard Barker* (London, Routledge, 2005), p 197

7.   The following offer particularly important assessments of Barker's work in this period: C Lamb, *The Theatre of Howard Barker* (London, Routledge, 2005), D I Rabey, *Howard Barker: Politics and Desire: An Expository Study of His Drama and Poetry, 1969–87* (Basingstoke, Macmillan, 1989). Lamb also discusses the neglect of Barker's work by major theatres, p 3.

8.   Quoted in C Megson, 'Interview with Howard Barker' in 'Martyr, Misfit, Monster: the Staging of the Politician in British Theatre Since 1968' (PhD thesis, University of London, 2001), p 471

9.   Lamb, *The Theatre of Howard Barker*, p 6

10. In his contemporaneous study of the nation state, published in 1980, Kenneth H F Dyson reaches a damning conclusion: 'In Britain an attempt is made to avoid a fundamental reappraisal of institutions [...] in two ways: by an almost excessive tinkering with the formal working arrangements of discrete institutions (as in "machinery of government" reform); and, particularly, by taking institutions less seriously, by assuming that informal, fluid processes of élite consensus-seeking [...] will provide a satisfactory [...] way of accommodating problems and that personal moral virtues of the individuals who take part in institutions are the foundation of good government.'; Kenneth H F Dyson, *The State Tradition in Western Europe – A Study of an Idea and Institution* (Oxford, Martin Robertson, 1980), p 280

11. D I Rabey, *Howard Barker: Politics and Desire: An Expository Study of His Drama and Poetry, 1969–87* (Basingstoke, Macmillan, 1989), p 42

12. H Barker, *Claw* in *Collected Plays vol 1* (London, Calder, 1990), p 71

13. H Barker, *The Hang of the Gaol* and *Heaven* (London, Calder, 1982), p 77

14. *Ibid.*, p 82

15. Quoted in Hay and Trussler, 'Energy – and the Small Discovery of Dignity', *Theatre Quarterly*, p 10

16. D Edgar, *Plays One* (London, Methuen, 1987), p viii

17. D Hare, 'The Play is in the Air' in *Obedience, Struggle and Revolt – Lectures on Theatre* (London, Faber and Faber, 2005), pp 114–15

18. Lamb, *The Theatre of Howard Barker*, pp 6, 196

19. M Billington, *Guardian*, 28 February 1980

20. R Cushman, *Observer*, 2 March 1980

21. F Marcus, *Sunday Telegraph*, 19 October 1975

22. I Wardle, *The Times*, 28 February 1980

23. G Gordon, *Punch*, 6 November 1985; I Wardle, *The Times*, 25 October 1985

24. M Coveney, *Financial Times* in *London Theatre Record*, 24 September 1983, p 867

25. Quoted in Megson, 'Interview with Howard Barker' in 'Martyr, Misfit, Monster', p 471

26. Hay and Trussler, 'Energy – and the Small Discovery of Dignity', *Theatre Quarterly*, p 6

27. H Barker, *A Passion in Six Days / Downchild* (London, Calder, 1985), p 31

28. Quoted in T Dunn (ed) *Gambit: International Theatre Review* (Howard Barker Special Issue) 11, 41 (London, Calder, 1984), p 38

29. Quoted in Megson, 'Interview with Howard Barker' in 'Martyr, Misfit, Monster', p 472

30. Barker, *Claw*, p 58

31. Quoted in Lamb, *The Theatre of Howard Barker*, p 196

32. H Barker, *Crimes in Hot Countries* and *Fair Slaughter* (London, Calder, 1984), p 77

33. H Barker, *Two Plays for the Right: The Loud Boy's Life* and *Birth on a Hard Shoulder* (London, Calder, 1982), p 104

34. Barker, *Two Plays for the Right*, p 90

35. Quoted in Hay and Trussler, 'Energy – and the Small Discovery of Dignity', *Theatre Quarterly*, p 14

36. Quoted in Megson, 'Interview with Howard Barker' in 'Martyr, Misfit, Monster', p 473

FACING DEFACEMENT

Barker and Levinas

ELISABETH ANGEL-PEREZ

Slaves are faceless

The Dying of Today [1]

When Shakespeare turns Edgar into Poor Tom, he strips him of his social garments but emphasises his humanity; when King Lear himself proceeds to the 'unbuttoning' of his shirt and is left almost naked on the moor, he similarly acquires a sense of humanity of which he was previously unaware. Howard Barker, like all genuine tragic authors, is concerned with what it is that makes mankind human. The issue is however complicated by the fact that Barker's century, unlike Shakespeare's, is a century that has witnessed the industrialisation of death. Adorno, whom Barker quotes at the beginning of *Found in the Ground*,[2] turns Auschwitz into the symbol of the historical rupture that enables man to discover his intrinsic inhumanity. This philosophical aporia opens the gate to the postmodernist crisis that affects all arts.

Barker's Theatre of Catastrophe advocates a new sort of theatre, brutal and lyrical, intellectual and visceral ('I go from my belly', says painter Galactia in *Scenes from an Execution* [3]), a theatre whose central preoccupation is to stage the human in all its complexity. Barker's dramaturgy therefore consists in finding a necessary language that would allow us to in-scribe/de-scribe the unnameable – and Barker, like Paul Celan, is determined to persist in the artistic obligation to confront the 'barbarous'.[4] The numerous artists that people Barker's plays set themselves to engaging with and embodying the ethical and aesthetic aporia, and stepping out of its confinements: Galactia claims she has 'to find a new red for all that blood. A red that smells',[5] while the Weaver of *The Possibilities* wonders: 'Look, as soon as this is dry, we shall have a different red. I feel certain this is a different red.' [6]

Representing the face, and staging the face, is a major stake in contemporary art (from Penrose's butterfly-eyed Valentine to Bacon's screaming popes). From the biblical interdiction to Deleuze's 'faciality' (*visagéité*) via Levinas's ethical face and Merleau-Ponty's theory on the visible and the invisible, the face also ranks among the main questions that philosophy inescapably tries to address. In the main plays of the Theatre of Catastrophe, the face (or the non-face for that matter) is central. Barker literalises the phrase 'to lose face' so as 'to give a face to our faceless world' (Dürrenmatt).[7] Emmanuel Levinas considers the face[8] as the place of encounter with the Other, the ethical place. Barker's plays read in many respects as enactments of Levinas's philosophy of the face: they stage the 'experience of the face', which gives Levinas's ethics its contours. It will be my contention here to show that Barker stages a post-traumatic, defaced humanity as a first step towards the opening of an ethical stage.

DEFACING HUMANITY: POST-TRAUMATIC THEATRE

Barker's theatre is the theatre of a moral activist who paradoxically discards all set morals: it shapes a new language that exposes the inhumanity of man without trying to collapse the oxymoron, a new language that reveals that humanity builds itself out of inhumanity ('the humanity in inhumanity', as Barker puts it[9]), what Auschwitz has horrendously compelled us to realise and which is confirmed by the genocidal episodes of recent history. The humanistic vision of man can no longer be defended: 'The whole place stinks of corpse', Beckett writes in *Endgame*. If Barker's plays very frequently focus on the motif of the cadaver (*Gertrude – The Cry*, *Dead Hands*, *He Stumbled*), the eradication of humanity, which is itself constitutive of humanity,[10] is equally foregrounded through the process of defacement.

Brutalism: Maiming the Face

The face and its representation are indeed responsible for an abundant philosophical literature; yet the non-representation of the face poses a bigger problem.[11] Destroying the face onstage might constitute the most disturbing effect of an artistic medium which so far has been devoted to multiplying the faces (masks) and to masquerading: Deleuze and Guattari refer to the 'dismantling' of the face as 'no small business' and describe it as a political action that commands the entrance into the clandestine,[12] what Barker would glorify as 'the secret'.

Face mutilation is one of the topoi of most of Barker's plays at the end of the 1980s and early 1990s. Barbarity disfigures humanity: Barker gives a stage version of this assertion through a systematic attack against the face. In a ritualised tradition that dates back to Seneca-influenced Elizabethan and Jacobean dramatists (with the expected profusion of torn off tongues and of plucked out eyes), Barker systematically tortures, negates and wipes out the face. He therefore shows the actor first gifted with, and then deprived of, the extraordinary instrument of meaning which the human face constitutes. The character is therefore amputated of his/her signifying tools: eyesight, voice, facial mimicry. In *The Bite of the Night*, Homer keeps airing his blind face, Helen's husband has his tongue cut off, Helen herself is submitted to a highly codified 'pruning'. In what may be a proposition of the intrinsically destructive nature of language,[13] Barker cuts through the faces of his characters: Scrope's lipless face in *Victory*, a resuscitated image of Yorick's lipless skull in *Hamlet* (V: i: 182), provides a resonant image of this effect. In *Victory*, which marks a breakthrough in Barker's concept of the Theatre of Catastrophe, the face occupies a central position in the thematisation of the quest. Milton's blind presence in the play allows us to confirm that Susan Bradshaw's quest serves as a metaphor for the quest for truth. Barker here rewrites, somewhat palimpsestuously, two major hypotexts. Susan Bradshaw, in search of her husband's scattered remains, re-members Isis frantically looking for Osiris' dislocated body. This myth, which sends us back to Ancient Egypt, rewritten by Milton in *Areopagitica*, also stands at the very centre of T S Eliot's 'The Waste Land'. In *Victory*, King Charles II has decreed that Puritan dissident Bradshaw should not be made whole: his body is doomed to rotting out in the open. When she learns this, his widow concentrates her quest on his head as she learns it is to be exposed on a pike before it is to be destroyed by being pelted by balls, in a macabre game of 'Aunt Sally' that characterises Charles's court as a lethal funfair:

> NOD: Oh, I 'it him!
> GLOUSTERSHIRE: He spun! I touched him, he spun!
> CLEVELAND: The eyeballs! The eyeballs are watching us, ugh!
> HAMPSHIRE: Knock him round, then, knock him round!
> DEVONSHIRE: What are we doing exactly?
> NODD: Jaw dropped! Did yer see it?[14]

Bradshaw's quest for her husband's head literalises the Levinassian quest for the face of the other in a faceless world. In a horror-building process, Barker undoes or dismantles the face either step by step, gradually amputating it from its attributes, or radically, as in *Rome*, *(Uncle) Vanya*, *Judith* (where the head is simply cut off) or in *Wounds to the Face* which explicitly presents itself as a series of variations on the expression 'to lose face'. By defacing his characters or maiming their bodies, Barker gets rid of all the attitudes and poses one adopts to screen one's vulnerability: Levinas sees in the face 'a defenseless exposition', 'an essential poverty' that one tries to dissimulate by 'posing or taking up airs'.[15] In *Wounds*, the faceless soldier, whose face is wrapped, mummy-like, in bandages, appears as the paroxysmal representation of the ultimate destruction of humanity. His medicalised blind mask does not come on top of the face (providing an extra or second face, the frequent literal or metaphorical motif and pretext in examples of the Comedy of Manners) but it comes in place of the face. Barker here exploits the negative power of the mask: because it paralyses the expression, the mask is death-like.

Destroying the Face so as to Reveal the Face

To destroy the face for Barker is therefore a means of showing the inhumanity of a world, a world that has tilted over into sheer post-ethicality. In his earliest catastrophist plays such as *The Possibilities*, Barker stages characters that are beyond good and evil: 'Even his breath I longed to breathe. [...] I could not have cared if he dripped with my father's blood, or had my baby's brains around his boot,' Judith asserts boldly in 'The Unforeseen Consequences of a Patriotic Act'; 'and his murders, how they flooded me with desire', says The Woman in 'Not Him'.[16] Barker's characters are both victims and victimisers: there is no innocence in this world. Even the fairy tale universe is perverse: Snow White in *Knowledge and a Girl* does not live in a comfortable pre-lapsarian realm. In contrast to 'Donkey Skin', the Charles Perrault tale of a king who falls in love with a daughter who does her best to escape his incestuous proposals, Barker's Snow White keeps repeating her incestuous invitations in her haste to have access to knowledge: 'Dear Daddy, come and see my garden';[17] and the copulating dwarfs are not maintained by Barker at the pre-oedipal stage in which the Brothers Grimm restrained them.[18]

Emmanuel Levinas elaborates the notion of the ethical encounter through his original conception of the face, which is at the centre of his philosophy. To see the face of the Other ('*le visage d'autrui*') is to discover the vulnerability of the other. This causes a sense of moral responsibility to appear: I can see the vulnerability of the other and therefore I can feel the urge to destroy the other because I know I can do it, yet I also sense this vulnerability as an injunction 'not to kill' (the face in its vulnerability seduces me towards both crime and non-crime). For Levinas, the experience of alterity is that of the vulnerability of the Other. This vulnerability gives me a feeling of responsibility: I perceive this vulnerability and feel responsible. This double evidence is what Levinas calls 'the experience of the face' (*l'expérience du visage*): 'The face of the Other disarms the warrior in me' (*Le visage désarme le guerrier que je suis*); a faceless world is a world where the face no longer retains its 'disarming' effect on the warrior that I am.[19]

Like Levinas, Barker suggests that it is not the visualisation of the face in its entirety that makes one actually see the face and therefore that causes one to sense its ethical implications. To *see* the face of the Other does not mean you can describe it: Levinas proposes that the best way to encounter the Other is not even to notice the colour of his eyes.[20] The proliferation of blind or blinded characters in Barker's plays may very well indicate their keener sensing of the face, compared to other sight-granted characters, as if Barker was somehow re-contextualising the classical topos of the blind prophet (whose figurehead is Tiresias, the haunting presence of T S Eliot's 'The Waste Land'). He who can't see the face is probably more able to transcend conventional perception. Only then does the ethical encounter lie within reach.

ENCOUNTERING THE OTHER: KNOWING AND NOT RECOGNISING

To take place, the ethical encounter must avoid a number of traps and most notably those of recognition, that necessarily reduce the Other to the same: hence Barker proposes a new theatrical language that unteaches and 'decivilises'[21] the spectator. The spectator has to unlearn what he knows.

Escaping the Same: A New Language for the Stage

Barker provides us with a number of situations which represent the difficulty in encountering the Other: like Levinas, Barker shows that there are plenty of ways NEVER to meet the other (the choice of such a title as 'Not Him', in *The Possibilities* is quite meaningful). Power relationships (dialectical situations of dominance and subservience), so frequent in Barker's plays, constitute one of the Levinassian traps: to dominate someone is always to make the other like oneself; it has to do with encompassing the Other in my totality. Needing or missing someone is another way never to meet him: the other only comes in to satisfy a painful hollowness within the self: Und in the eponymous play or Claudius in *Gertrude – The Cry* may be seen as characters embroiled in this pseudo-ethical encounter: theirs is a solipsistic love. Ethical knowing has nothing to do with recognising.

The Other is irreducible to the same. This is precisely the point which Barker develops in 'Recognition as Aesthetic Paralysis in the Theatre'.[22] For both Levinas and Barker, in the act of recognition the self is confined to its own 'totality' since the self does not let the other in, but on the contrary endeavours to find NOTHING but itself: the self wants to engulf and 'totalise' the exterior object, and therefore denies all possible access to infinity. It therefore appears clearly that for Barker all landmarks have to be uprooted so as to avoid the knowing subject's solipsism. Barker therefore insists on the necessity for a stage language that would be drastically new so as to disorient the audience. The audience must be at a 'loss'[23] and only this experience of being at a loss can open the way to the ethical encounter.

For Barker, ethical reflection cannot be dissociated from an aesthetic research: for Barker as for Levinas, face and language are intimately related. Barker, like Levinas, can be seen as a phenomenologist: both Barker and Levinas describe man by what shows: his face, body and his language.

The new stage language Barker invents turns humanism into an obsolete viewpoint[24] and arouses a feeling of 'genuine anxiety' by insisting on man's inhumanity. One of Barker's most revealing images of the paradoxical coexistence of the inhuman at the heart of humanity (strikingly synthesized by George Steiner through the powerful image of the music-loving Nazi[25]) is in *Found in the Ground*: the Piero della Francesca-like virgin-cum-child Burgteata simultaneously breastfeeding Hitler and Nuremberg judge Toonelhuis (in fact her own father), turning them into foster-brothers. To express the man who 'comes after' (in Steiner's sense[26]) Auschwitz, all previously existing forms of art are disqualified: neither comedy, nor political post-Brechtian theatre; neither post-Beckettian theatre of derision nor even codified Aristotelian tragedy seem suitable: 'the Theatre of Catastrophe is more painful than tragedy, since tragedy consoles with restoration, the reassertion of existing moral values'.[27]

Of all the artistic languages that man has at his disposal, those that have already 'worked' are dismissed. The camera of *13 Objects* (as well as the realistic mode it suggests) becomes an 'instrument of terror':

> YOUTH: [...] I dread to contemplate the banal subject matter it has been focused on if one could wash a camera I would wash it yes or fumigate it holidays babies in prams unreturning soldiers football teams some pitiful pornography the uncleanliness of it appals me if he was buying me a camera why not a new one.[28]

Just like this camera, language, jeopardised by its own history, can only convey absence ('Take my absence to him please', p 290). The Idealist is doomed to throwing away the camera, just as the Billionaire burns the canvas. These already used languages are deprived of their functions: they are de-funct. They are languages that no longer speak. Barker, a protean artist, therefore finds himself in the same situation as Galactia or the Weaver: he needs to find 'a new red', a 'red that stinks'. The situation 'calls for a new language / It calls for poetry' (p 259) says the Officer of *13 Objects*. In *Pity in History*, the apprentice Pool exhorts the master mason Gaukroger to find 'New manner for new situation'.[29]

This new language, this poetry of and for the stage, is the very essence of Barker's Catastrophism. Barker's Theatre of Catastrophe is not concerned with the Aristotelian reversal that would take us from good to evil and eventually back to good, it is concerned with a reversal of the generic models: the Theatre of Catastrophe is primarily a theatre that looks like no other, a theatre that builds itself against all the theatre types that exist. The Theatre of Catastrophe therefore teaches the 'catastrophist' spectator to renounce his expectations, to give up all ready-made hermeneutical tools, to repudiate his taste for categories and for ready-made morality so as to be able to live the 'experience of art', an experience that does not leave one intact ('It's an artist's job to be coarse. Preserving coarseness, that's the problem' [30]).

Unteaching the Audience

How is this new language to find its way through to the heart of the theatre, in itself a hyper-codified genre that rests, more perhaps, than any other, on conventions? The pruning of Helen in *The Bite of the Night* metaphorically reflects the treatment Barker inflicts upon the spectator: we are quite brutally amputated of all our landmarks; we are required to eradicate our certainties so as to have 'a right to experience meaninglessness'.[31]

Space is the most immediate and vital paradigm whose conventionality needs to be destroyed: most of Barker's plays take place in a post-cataclysmic universe: battlefield and burial ground (*The Love of a Good Man*), the ruins of a university, the ruins of Troy (*The Bite of the Night*), spaces swept by 'a wind of desolation' (*The Last Supper*). The Spade that opens both *13 Objects* and *Animals in Paradise* is highly emblematic of this world in which gravediggers continuously bury what so far constituted our familiar landscape, structurally, morally, linguistically stable. Norris, the compulsive mother in *Animals*, seems to be planting corpses (in an impetus that recalls Eliot's 'The Waste Land': 'the corpse you planted last year, has it begun to sprout?'[32]).

Time is equally rendered indefinite. Historical landmarks abound but are systematically blurred: the multiple Troys in *The Bite of the Night* show the essentially postdramatic, palimpsest nature of time. *Found in the Ground* discloses the simultaneous presences of Babe Hitler and of a Nuremberg judge: this play locates the spectator simultaneously before, during and after Auschwitz, thanks to some sort of trans-historicity clearly exposed by Macedonia's multiple identity:

MACEDONIA: I am all the Ann Franks

Pause.

All the Ann Franks me

Pause.

The ditches full of

Pause.

The pits of

Pause.

Composers

Violinists

Physicists

Pause.

I am all the Ann Franks

Pause.

All the Ann Franks me [33]

Thanks to its chiasmatic circularity that confesses the impossibity of escape from history, her litany anchors the play in an ever-present Auschwitz.

This systematic blurring of the indicators of time contributes to the deconstruction (in the Derridean sense of destruction + construction) of the character. With Barker, we are in a world where nurses relentlessly deprive orphans of their food, where thinkers never think but sleep, where soldiers kill nobody (*The Last Supper*). The catastrophist characters can be defined by their readiness to be the contrary of what we expect them to be. Helen of Troy, Beautiful Helen, distinguishes herself by her extreme ugliness:

HELEN: I have had nine children, my belly's a pit, or as the poetically-inclined say when they're lapping me, a sandy strand from which the tide receded leaving feathered frontiers. Ugly, but who's deterred? [34]

Similarly, rituals are catastrophically reversed: in *The Last Supper*, the Eucharist is parodically turned into a scene of cannibalism leading to a possible 'ghastly epiphany'.[35] Lvov, the guru whose name refers to one of the most devastated towns of Poland, is eaten by his disciples:[36] the wrathful prophet lucidly proffers himself as their literal food in a parody of Christ's Last Supper. The same perversion of the Christian myth can be found in the repulsive dinner which Toonelhuis relishes: yet, if Toonelhuis eats up the ashes of the war criminals he has condemned, it is less to incorporate them than to eradicate them, in a completely reversed parody of the Eucharist:

> LOBE: We have the usual five here
>   Hoss
>   Funck
>   Delbuch
>   Klysek
>   Rimm
>   *Pause.*
>   Hitler is not on the menu
>   *Pause.*
>   We never serve him here
>   *Pause.* [37]

Deprived of its certainties concerning place and time, the linear fabric of the text ends up being deconstructed in its syntagmatic horizontality: meaning is not revealed by the juxtaposition of words one after the other but remains to be construed vertically thanks to echoes and ricochets: parabolic episodes step in to disrupt the linear unravelling of the fable (*The Last Supper, The Bite of the Night*) and in some plays the text opts for a decidedly a-narrative and poetic development. The verticality of the text on the page makes it clear that the reader-spectator has to construe the text along the vertical paradigmatic line more than along the horizontal linear line.

Halfway between the obstetrician (*Animals in Paradise*) and the anatomist (*He Stumbled*), Barker maieutically dissects the corpse of language. What is exposed is the flesh of language and with it, the crises of language. Aposiopesis – the device of suddenly breaking off in speech – disrupts the flow of language into so many reversed (catastrophist) psychological arias: they stand for the dumb-founded symptoms of the revelation of what it is to be human. In a luminous study of Barker's rhetoric, Michel

Morel describes the aposiopeses in terms of 'afflicted meditation' or of 'halted moments of petrified understanding'.[38] It is only when this stage is reached, when no vestige of a past knowledge can come in to jeopardize the process, that the encounter with the Other can take place and that the ethical space/stage can be opened.

OPENING THE ETHICAL SPACE/STAGE

Moral Suspension

These multiple deconstructions (space, time, character, structure and ultimately linearity) leave the spectator utterly at a loss: one has entered a world whose codes one doesn't master, a world where all one's hermeneutical attempts are doomed to failure. One finds oneself compelled to renounce one's aesthetic, cultural and above all moral expectations. The spectator discovers himself alone in front of his pain. No answer is dictated to him, no message delivered to him. No rationality seems traceable. As Howard Barker makes it clear in the Second Prologue to *The Bite of the Night*, clarity is resented as a fascistic form of oppression:

> Should we not
> I KNOW IT'S IMPOSSIBLE BUT YOU STILL TRY
> Not reach down beyond the known for once
> [...]
> CLARITY
> MEANING
> LOGIC
> AND CONSISTENCY
> None of it
> None [39]

Barker intends for the spectator, faced with the negation of all his landmarks, to experience 'a genuine moral anxiety' and a condition of 'moral suspension':[40]

> The abolition of routine distinction between good and bad actions, the sense that good and evil co-exist within the same psyche, that freedom and kindness may not be compatible, that pity is both a poison and an erotic stimulant, that laughter might be as often oppressing as it is rarely liberating, all these constitute the territory of a new theatrical practice, which

lends its audience the potential of a personal re-assessment in the light of dramatic action. The consequence of this is a modern form of tragedy which I would call Catastrophism.[41]

It is only when the spectator finds himself at a loss, when he has unlearned everything he took for granted, that the process of the encounter can take place. Only then is the spectator ready to meet the other, escaping the traps of solipsism. Only then is the spectator able to see the nudity of the other's face.

The Ethical Stage and Nudity

For Levinas, the face is the metonymical expression of the whole of the Other inasmuch as the other exposes his/herself in his/her 'nudity', in other words, in his/her truth. What Levinas calls the face has in fact a broader application. It refers to the whole of the individual, to the body as a whole and in its nudity. Here again, one can see in Barker's theatre a frequent literalisation of Levinas's concept. Nakedness is a topos of Barker's plays, and works precisely as it does in Levinas's works, as the revealer of the Other's combined vulnerability and strength.

Nudity, in Barker's plays, does not correspond to easy voyeuristic situations and mechanisms.[42] Although the naked body's beauty cannot (and must not) shun the erotic effect it compulsively causes, nudity has more to do with exposing the body both in its dominant and yet utterly vulnerable shape: nudity, such as Gertrude's or Algeria's ('she tosses her head contemptuously'[43]), is used as a strength: 'a director should use nakedness very carefully as it is an instrument of power'.[44] As some sort of concretisation of Bataille's theory, the paradigms of eroticism and death collide in Barker's theatre:[45]

> In every journey to the theatre (we do not talk of visiting the theatre) there lingers a never-extinguished prospect of personal destruction, which is the nature of all supremely erotic encounters also. No one cares to express this, for who dare admit that she aspires to her own catastrophe? It is the erotic secret of tragedy.[46]

These theoretical lines find an onstage mouthpiece in the catastrophic character for whom the spectacle of nakedness is painful: Albert, albeit a comic character in *Gertrude – The Cry*, expresses this Levinassian attitude: 'I AM IN SUCH A TENDER ECSTASY I WOULD NOT CARE IF I WERE DEAD'; and Claudius comments upon his ecstatic attitude in this way: 'YOUR NAKEDNESS WAS MORE INCREDIBLE TO HIM THAN IF GOD STOOD AND PRESSED THE FIRMAMENT AGAINST HIS LIPS'.[47] Ecstasy is etymologically what makes you step out of yourself. Gertrude's nakedness epitomises the Levinassian double bind: it turns the vulnerability which is intrinsically linked to nudity into a weapon that 'disarms the warrior that I am'. The moment of nudity on stage is a moment of utter suspension as well as a moment of revelation; it is a moment of loss as well as an epiphany. As such, it provides a visual echo to the aposiopesis that disrupts the linearity of the text. Barker speaks of such moments as 'moments of immaculate exposure to seduction/destruction – instances of imminent nakedness'.[48]

Furthermore, in keeping with what is explained by Levinas, on Barker's stage the ecstatic revelation is imposed upon us: the ethical demand is something I don't choose: this responsibility falls on me before I have had time to decide. The encounter with the Other enslaves me into not killing. It deprives me of my freedom. The dissymmetrical face to face between me and the Other turns me into some kind of prisoner, a hostage in fact: I have no choice, I am bound to being utterly absorbed by this relation: this ethical demand is the very heart of humanity for Levinas. It is the very binding nature of this stage experience ('the power of staged experience'[49]) that Barker analyses in dramatic terms and images.

Reading Barker through the prism of Levinas's writing highlights the paradox that lies at the heart of Barker's Theatre of Catastrophe: Barker's theatre teaches nothing, delivers no message, gives access to no superior truth. It starts from experience and not from essence. It is concerned with exposing a fundamentally non-Platonic beauty (any consideration as to its being 'good' – therefore allowed – or not, is immaterial) and with revealing the very kernel of desire, the human bind. Because of the inferred sense of loss, Barker's theatre enables the advent of the Other and opens the ethical space: Barker's plays proclaim their amorality so as to ground their ethicality.

NOTES

1. H Barker, *The Dying of Today* (written 2004, unpublished)

2. 'In the innermost recesses of humanism, as its very soul, there rages a frantic prisoner.' H Barker, *Collected Plays vol 5* (London, Calder, 2001), p 285

3. H Barker, *Scenes from an Execution* in *Collected Plays vol 1* (London, Calder, 1990), p 271

4. In 1955, Theodor W Adorno published an essay called 'Kulturkritik und Gesellschaft' (*Prisms*, 1955) where he declared that, 'It is barbarous to write a poem after Auschwitz.' (Later, in *Negative Dialectics*, he amended this highly polemical sentence.) Paul Celan immediately replied with 'Speech-Grille' where he showed that the only way to write a poem after Auschwitz was to write a poem in the terms of Auschwitz.

5. Barker, *Scenes From an Execution*, p 257

6. 'The Weaver's Ecstasy at the Discovery of New Colour', *The Possibilities* in *Collected Plays vol 2* (London, Calder, 1993), p 79

7. 'Le grotesque donne un visage à ce monde sans visage'; F Dürrenmatt, *Ecrits sur le théâtre*, tr. R Barthe et P Pilliod (Paris, Gallimard, 1970), p 136.

8. For Levinas the face does not refer strictly to the face, but to the body in its nudity.

9. H Barker, *Arguments for a Theatre* 3rd edn (Manchester, Manchester University Press, 1997), p 64

10. Giorgio Agamben explains that the human is he who can survive man and that the only genuine human being is that whose humanity has been totally destroyed; G Agamben, *Remnants of Auschwitz: The Witness and the Archive*, tr. D Heller-Roazen (London, Zone Books, 2000)

11. As part of the OuLiPo practices, quite playfully and though deceivingly playfully, George Perec had imagined making a 'lipoprosopean', i.e. faceless film (Signe particulier: NÉANT) that would have been the equivalent of his e-free novel – *La Disparition*. The film, as described by Perec, was to stage actors whose faces could never be shown. See B Magné, quoted in *Vertigo* 11, 12 (1994), p 61

12. G Deleuze, and F Guattari, 'Year Zero: Faciality', in *One Thousand Plateaus*, tr. B Massumi (Minneapolis, University of Minnesota Press, 1987), pp 167–91

13. See G Bataille, *Literature and Evil* (London and New York, Marion Boyars, 1990)

14. H Barker, *Victory* in *Collected Plays vol 1* (London, Calder, 1990), p 145

15. 'Il y a dans le visage une exposition sans défense. Une pauvreté essentielle…la preuve en est qu'on essaie de masquer cette pauvreté en se donnant des poses, une contenance'; in E Levinas, *Ethique et infini* (Paris, Livre de Poche, 1984), p 90; and E Levinas *Ethics and Infinity*, tr. R Cohen (Pittsburg PA, Duquesnes University Press, 1985)

16. Barker, *The Possibilities*, p 127

17. H Barker, *Knowledge and a Girl* (London, Calder, 2002), p 99

18. B Bettelheim, *The Uses of Enchantment: the Meaning and Importance of Fairy Tales* (New York, Vintage, rev. ed. 1989)

19. E Levinas, *Totalité et infini* (Paris, Livre de Poche, 1971), p 217; E Levinas, *Totality and Infinity: An Essay on Exteriority*, tr. A Lingis (Pittsburg PA, Duquesne University Press, 1989)

20. Levinas, *Ethique et infini*, p 79

21. Barker, *Arguments for a Theatre*, p 110

22. *Ibid.*, p 109

23. *Ibid.*, p 110

24. See the frequent oppositions Barker draws between the 'humanist theatre' and 'the catastrophic theatre'; *Arguments for a Theatre*, p 71

25. *Ibid.*, p 8: 'Nous savons désormais qu'un homme peut le soir lire Gœthe ou Rilke, jouer des passages de Bach ou de Schubert, et le lendemain matin vaquer à son travail quotidien, à Auschwitz.'

26. G Steiner, *Language and Silence* (London, Faber, 1967), p 6

27. Barker, *Arguments for a Theatre*, p 70

28. H Barker, *13 Objects* in *Plays Two* (London, Oberon, 2006), p 284. Subsequent references to this edition appear as page numbers, until otherwise indicated.

29. H Barker, *Pity in History* in *Gambit* 41 (London, Calder, 1984), p 31

30. Barker, *Scenes from an Execution*, p 271

31. Barker, *Arguments for a Theatre*, p 79

32. From the performance script of *Animals in Paradise*; not included in published version: H Barker, *Animals in Paradise* in *Plays Two* (London, Oberon, 2006)

33. H Barker, *Found in the Ground* in *Collected Plays vol 5* (London, Calder, 2001), p 310

34. H Barker, *The Bite of the Night* in *Collected Plays vol 4* (London, Calder, 1998), p 22.

35. See G Bas, 'The Cunts, the Knobs and the Corpse: Obscenity and Horror in Howard Barker's *Victory* (1983)' in N Boireau and W Lippke (eds) *Beyond Taboos, Contemporary Theatre Review*, 5, 1 (1996), 33–50: p 41

36. H Barker, *The Last Supper* (London, Calder, 1988), p 50. See E Angel-Perez, 'Pour un théâtre de la barbarie: Peter Barnes et Howard Barker' in *Études Anglaises*, 2 (1999)

37. Barker, *Found in the Ground*, p 325

38. M Morel, 'La Rhétorique du Non Sens' in *Howard Barker et le Théâtre de la Catastrophe* (Paris, Editions Théâtrales, 2006), pp 173–89

39. Barker, *The Bite of the Night*, pp 7–8

40. Barker, *Arguments for a Theatre*, p 101

41. *Ibid.*, p 52

42. C Kiehl, 'Le Corps dans le Théâtre de la Catastrophe de Howard Barker' (Thèse de Doctorat sous la direction de Nicole Boireau, Université de Metz, 2005), 345 sq., p 491

43. H Barker, *The Fence in its Thousandth Year* (London, Oberon, 2006), p 57

44. 'Wrestling with Barker Workshop', quoted in Kiehl, 'Le Corps dans le Théâtre', p 346

45. G Bataille, *Eroticism*, tr. M Dalwood (London and New York, Marion Boyars, 1962)

46. Barker, *Arguments for a Theatre*, p 160

47. H Barker, *Gertrude – The Cry* (London, Calder, 2002), pp 58, 61

48. Barker, Arguments for a Theatre, p 160

49. *Ibid.*, p 160

'APPALLING SOLITUDE'

Reading *The Ecstatic Bible*

CHARLES LAMB

Howard Barker's *The Ecstatic Bible*,[1] with a playing time of over seven hours, 29 scenes and a cast of 84, is, by any reckoning, an extraordinary text. One of the perceived virtues of the dramatic form is its capacity, utilising the *mise-en-scène*, to convey a lot of information in a highly concentrated form within a very short duration. This feature, however, in spite of Barker's admirably laconic and precise stage directions, can make *The Ecstatic Bible* a particularly difficult text to decipher from the printed page. Its sheer complexity would appear deliberately to flout Aristotle's injunction that 'plots must be of a reasonable length, so that they may be easily held in the memory'.[2] Barker, however, has specifically rejected Aristotle's project of identifying a role for tragedy in promoting the successful functioning of the social whole. Indeed, his declared intention is quite the opposite:

In Excess

theatre proclaims its divorce

from

the myth of ordered life

Too many narratives

too many digressions

too many themes

being the condition

of

willing surrender [3]

This 'excess', he identifies as 'Plethora' – a term the connotations of which serve to underline his counter-sanitary purpose. Such admonitions do not preclude critical analysis of the order that exists within the work itself – particularly when this order – which is demonstrably there – constitutes an important element of the work's beauty. What Barker's texts do not do is accommodate themselves to the standardised and increasingly restricted recipes of theatrical consumption. The Barker play, nevertheless, while challenging the categories of 'Clarity / Meaning / Logic / And Consistency',[4] does not exist in a space permanently beyond them; to engage with the work is to struggle (hence the name of his theatre company, The Wrestling School) and, at times, this effort needs to be made in order to establish even the most basic understanding of what is going on. Maurice Merleau-Ponty identifies this disorientation as the most valuable quality of the work of art:

> What is irreplaceable in the work of art? What makes it far more a voice of the spirit whose analogue is found in all productive philosophic or political thought, than a means to pleasure? The fact that it contains, better than ideas, *matrices of ideas* – the fact that it provides us with symbols whose meaning we never stop developing. Precisely because it dwells and makes us dwell in a world we do not have the key to, the work of art teaches us to see and ultimately gives us something to think about as no analytical work can; because when we analyse an object, we find only what we've put into it.[5]

It is possible to appreciate many of the scenes of *The Ecstatic Bible* on the basis of their own dramatic content. This has, of course, been one of the traditional ways of reading the Bible: with illumination, inspiration or even ecstasy being stimulated via the scrutiny of, and reflection on, particular episodes, rather than attempting a consistent 'reading' of the whole work; this focus on the part rather than the totality was a mode of experiencing poetry which was also familiar to the Classical world. It is clearly Barker's intention, however, to dispose these individual adventures within a larger canvas which challenges us to make a more extensive set of connections. I have already argued elsewhere [6] that Barker's plays present his audiences with a 'world' which, while patently artificial, is nevertheless recognisably a consistent 'world'. *The Ecstatic Bible* can be seen as a bold experiment which pushes this conception of an artificial world to its extreme limit. In this essay, I wish to consider – in a necessarily tentative and fragmented way – some of the features of the world of the play.

In referring to the work as a 'Bible', Barker invites comparisons with the Judaeo/ Christian original. While the subtitle, 'A New Testament', would suggest the latter, there are as many, if not more resemblances to the Old Testament. In his preface, Barker states: '*The Ecstatic Bible* is a testament not to the presence of God in the Universe, but to his absence, consequently a testament to the absolute solitude of Man.' (p 7) The reference to the absence of God is particularly reminiscent of Nietzsche whose philosophical project was not dissimilar to that outlined here. In his case, however, *Thus Spoke Zarathustra* is a fictional device which acts as a mouthpiece for its author's thinking. With Barker, characters and action are in the first instance products of his dramatic imagination; the reflections which arise appertain to the characters in situ and should not be construed as endorsed by the dramatist: as he himself has said, he isn't trying to convince us of the correctness or desirability of any political or philosophical programme.

The insertion of 'Ecstatic' is clearly significant both in terms of religion and of its use in Barker's oeuvre as a whole. Here, ecstasy comprises an experience of extreme rapture which, becoming the object of an all-consuming desire, is thereby capable of utterly transforming the subject. In most instances, this involves sexual love but the term is also applicable to heightened states of consciousness traditionally associated with religious experience: the proverbial instance of Paul on the road to Damascus provides a paradigm where a moment of ecstatic revelation leads to a life dedicated to a cause. Ecstasy is very important in the context of Barker's work where it is clearly distinguished from other concepts such as 'happiness' or 'pleasure'.

One feature of the Old Testament that Barker employs to interesting effect is the endowing of particular characters with great longevity. This happens in Genesis with patriarchs such as Abraham who, we are told, attained the age of 175 years. A span of this length allows a character like Gollancz to bear children who, on becoming adults, have children of their own; as Barker says in his preface – 'she peoples the play with her progeny' (p 7). *The Ecstatic Bible*, therefore, encompasses many generations. This wide canvas allows Barker to present inter-generational transmutations of character in a concise and focused manner – one of the principal advantages of an extended form of the drama – for example, Aeschylus's *Oresteia*.

As I have already indicated, the principal dramatic form in use is the scene. Though these have been given titles, through employing them at times obscurely and inconsistently, Barker avoids the potential trap of providing thereby a Brechtian analysis; the title or caption can easily acquire the authority of the pointing finger of the dramatist. Some, as in the case of the second scene, state the obvious – 'A Birth', where Gollancz's birthing of McChief is indeed the central event. With the first scene, the title – 'Paradise, Coercion and Paradise' is altogether less clear: it is perhaps relevant to figure an ironic paralleling of the Old Testament Garden of Eden ('A field in sunshine' p 13). Shaw's seduction of Gollancz and his subsequent murder of her war-maimed husband, precipitate not only her 'expulsion' and wanderings but also those of her lover, Tread, and her aspirant lover – the Priest. Coercion is an issue referred to by Tread and a number of other admirers of Gollancz: they perceive her as deliberately refusing to resist anything that is urged upon her; her strategy with coercion is invariably to acquiesce to it. This applies also to seductions – as happens in this scene. Tread says to the man with the ladle:

> As for the child, what evidence exists for its paternity? It might be yours for all I
> know. And I say that in the full consciousness of her undiscriminating and unresisting
> character... (p 21)

'Coercion' may also be seen as what Tread applies to himself in refusing to pursue Gollancz until she is, in effect, lost to him. The subsequent 'Paradise' could refer to his rather surprising reaction:

> SHE'S GONE AND I AM DELIGHTED
> IT IS NECESSARY TO ME
> MORE THAN MOST MEN I REQUIRE TO SUFFER AN ORDEAL (pp 22–3)

The ordeal in question involves dedicating his life entirely to searching for Gollancz. He is exhilarated at his own self-control in refusing to catch her when he could have done so and he is intoxicated at the sheer magnitude of the task that now faces him.

There is a scene later in the play entitled 'An Animal in Paradise'. The setting is a park – 'an idyll' (p 210). Which of the participants is the animal? The most obvious candidate is Poitier who is trying to possess Gollancz by any underhand means available to him. Later, in a scene where Poitier meets a gruesome death, his son, Lamb, says of him: 'Well, he was an animal so...' (p 286) and he helpfully proceeds to suggest a number of possibilities – bullock, ox, puma, jackal and crow. Titles, therefore, while they do possess a definite relation to the scene, do not provide a reliable and systematic set of signposts to facilitate analysis. They tend to lead to more questions.

What does link the scenes together and provide the play with its overall structure? There are clear allusions to biblical or religious subject matter. Some of these have been suggested already but there are many others: on the scenic level there are 'nativities' and 'last suppers'. In terms of the incidents, the Priest and Shaw are crucified. There is also the phase where Gollancz becomes an anchorite in a church and Poitier, the 'animal', is in fact the Inquisitor. It is in this role of enforcer of religious orthodoxy, that he attempts unsuccessfully to burn Gollancz. Perhaps the clearest link to the religious/biblical is the Priest, known throughout simply by his vocation. With Gollancz this character provides the main unifying factor: they are present in the first scene and are the final figures we see on stage at the end; in all, they each appear in 15 of the 29 scenes – more often than not, together. There are other roles which appear in a number of scenes but none approach the level of these two. Barker's endowing them with longevity, therefore, provides an element of consistency while the mass of other characters come and go.

Before proceeding to consider them and their relationship, I wish simply to point to a third unifying factor which concerns subject matter and to which I will return later. There are a number of thematic issues which frequently focus on particular situations or actions. For instance, I have alluded above to Tread's heroic resistance to a powerful instinct to stop Gollancz from leaving him; this is typical of a number of other situations in the play where characters restrain an overwhelming impulse to act. Another example would be Semele's restraint of her pity by stopping herself from giving water to the Priest in the final scene of the play. A final point worth mentioning here is the background to the action of the scenes. As is often the case with Barker, this comprises war, social breakdown, revolution and general chaos. At the outset, we are told that Mr Gollancz suffered maiming in the war; itinerant vagrants are common since the war; the nurses go to visit the cemetery. War comes to the fore in 'An Impertinence' (p 54) where McChief, one of Gollancz's progeny, commands an army. Later, in 'A Pestilence' (p 91), she is overthrown, tortured and executed by her daughter, Winterhalter. The latter seems to continue her mother's policies and appears in a remote military hospital ward full of the wounded and dying in 'A Postcard' (p 112). After this there seems to follow a period of peace but war rumbles in the distance in 'The Unvisited Shelves of a Library'. In 'The Recollections of a Hairdresser', Conti tells of 'lorries…convoys five miles long…how they laughed, those dead men in the lorries' (p 232). 'Exile' (p 276) involves the overthrow and hanging of the Emperor, Maurice, but Poitier's attempt to supplant him comes to grief at the hands of a howling mob who tear him apart and devour him. In this scene, the Dantonesque Paraffin appears as the dominant revolutionary leader. The following scene, 'The Solitude of the Margins' (p 288), sees him a hunted fugitive seeking refuge amongst the destitute and dreaming of a return to power. That this doesn't come about is attested to by the next scene, 'A Museum', where a widow, Germania, is searching amongst the dead for her husband who was 'taken in the night' (p 303). From this point on, two Thieves who have hitherto shown a passion for poetry and a facility for murder, find new roles for themselves as police. The figure behind this police state would appear to be Poitier's son, Lamb – the 'man of destiny' (p 270).

Gollancz and the Priest drift through this landscape of mayhem – sometimes at the very centre of things and sometimes utterly marginalised. Their initial elopement took place as a result of the murder of Gollancz's maimed husband. She has scandalised the Priest by openly taking a lover, Tread, and becoming pregnant. The Priest is simultaneously outraged and infatuated:

> THEY WILL HANG YOU AND YOU WILL DESERVE IT I SHOULD LIKE NOTHING MORE
> TURN ON THE ROPE YOUR INFANT IN THE COOLING WOMB TURN TO A CHORUS OF
> CONTEMPT ROCKS EARTH VEGETABLES SALIVA VENOM THE URBAN ETCETERA
> *Pause.*
> Certainly that is one thing I want. The other is to wash you head to toe, to plait your
> hair and draw you by the dim light of the morning, little mattress on the dusty floor,
> carts and lorries hooting in the street below... (p 19)

As a purification ritual, this image of washing carries Biblical connotations (Christ washing the feet of his disciples) and occurs in other scenes of the play: McChief washes the Priest's body after his crucifixion (p 79); Germania washes Semele in the final scene (p 320). The Priest believes that Gollancz herself killed her husband and that her tale of a vagrant is a lie. The actual killer, Shaw, did it in gratitude for admitting his advances which is why Gollancz owns that his act of murder 'somehow included' her (p 17). The Priest confesses to stealing her clothes; this, he feels, puts him on a par with her – they are both 'stained', he a thief and she a murderer. The aspect of their elopement he finds hardest is abandoning his flock – some of whom are clearly dependent on him. His flight therefore represents a real ordeal which he is forced to suffer in his encounter with the man offering the ladle. For her part, Gollancz appears – initially at least – to be less interested in the Priest; in a later scene, 'A Wall', she says of him:

> For forty years he has hardly been out of my sight. Which is not to say I know him,
> for to know requires some small investment of curiosity, which with regard to him I
> have never had... (pp 87–8)

She is, in fact, much more interested in Shaw, her husband's killer and the player of seductive music on his violin: she identifies the direction in which he departed as 'Eastwards' (p 20).

As I indicated above, Tread watches Gollancz's departure with the Priest and as soon as they have gone, he commits himself to a quest he will continue for the rest of his life. This action – of channelling the force of intense desire into patterns of ritual or the labouring at a mundane task – is often encountered in *The Ecstatic Bible*: there is Tread's quest which is later bequeathed in an altered form to the Fourth Porter and something similar obtains with Davis in the second scene – 'A Birth'. He is a recluse who inhabits a chateau within which he has built a distillery. This solitude is consciously chosen and reinforced with an ethic which could be summed up as an undertaking not to interfere with others providing they don't interfere with him. Gollancz arrives there just as she is about to give birth. Her companion, the Priest, beats frantically on the door but without immediate effect. It is also obvious that their relationship has not developed. As she goes into labour, it is clear that the Priest has no choice but to empathise with her pain: although she stoically refuses to cry out, he bellows. While Barker asserts that *The Ecstatic Bible* bears witness to the absence of God, it would appear that the Priest does not share this view: his lapse into sin was because he found the sin attractive – presupposing a God and a moralised universe. At one point in this scene, he provides what could almost be a definition of a God in his own idealised image: 'God however / He / Has / Boundless / Sympathy' (p 30).

The reclusive Davis, when he appears, is clearly not a man of boundless sympathy and only becomes involved when Gollancz, in the final throes of childbirth, starts to cry out. He tells the Priest that she is dying, admitting later that this was a fabrication because he found the idea attractive of an infant brought to him 'as it were, on the wind' (p 29). He also says that he loves her. This provokes the Priest to attempt suicide and the childbirth is punctuated with the offstage bangs of his misses – 'deflected / By the hand of God' (p 30). Gollancz is insistent against both men that Davis washes the newborn infant and he disappears with it into the chateau. Immediately, Gollancz attempts to stand up and get on her way, ignoring the blustering of the Priest who is appalled at her perceived lack of maternal feeling. Eventually, she deflates him:

GOLLANCZ: Why are you a Priest?

Pause. He looks helplessly at her.

PRIEST: I don't know… It has brought me such unhappiness…

She looks, moves away.

Mrs Gollancz…

She stops.

I think desire is the most painful thing in the world…

GOLLANCZ: Yes, why shouldn't it be, when it is also the most beautiful? (pp 32–3)

The animus behind this curt rejoinder is striking given the context of Gollancz's general passivity. It certainly alerts the Priest to the possibility that she might have a concealed agenda expressed also in her overriding concern to be on her way.

Returning empty-handed, Davis 'makes trial' of Gollancz by claiming that the child has in fact met with a fatal accident – as the Priest predicted. She receives this information with apparent equanimity, a gesture that shocks but also – contrary to his expectation – enthralls Davis:

> DAVIS: No solitary cloud of pity passed across your gaze…
>
> PRIEST: Pity? The word is not in her vocabulary…
>
> DAVIS: I must marry her. You do it. You are the Priest. (p 34)

This moment constitutes a seductive reversal for Davis as he himself points out – 'I / THE / SOLITARY / MAN / WILL / SACRIFICE / MY / SILENCE / TO' (p 34). Barker's punctuation here is – as always – significant: 'TO' is not followed by a series of dots or by a dash which would indicate either the thought petering out or that his words are cut short by the ensuing speech of the Priest. Davis does not know what he is sacrificing everything for: there is, however, in all such gambles, a sense that the prize will exceed the value of the stake. When it is made clear to him that Gollancz will acquiesce to anything and that she does not reciprocate his enthusiasm, Davis retires slowly behind the portal of his chateau/distillery. Gollancz comments:

> How infinitely – proper – this man is…how perfectly refined his sensibilities…he adores me…and he will never see me again… (p 35)

Davis's gesture here is comparable to Tread's heroic self-control in refusing to pursue Gollancz until she was effectively lost to him. As with Tread whose passion metamorphosed into an exercise in mechanical repetition (his search grids), so Davis, we are informed later by his adopted daughter, transmuted his anguish into ritual:

> McCHIEF: …the man I call my father described her parting not once but a thousand times, frequently tracing her steps as far as the edge of the field. You can see for yourself he walked there every evening from the white track worn in the turf. At the end of this track he invariably wept. As a child I lay in my cot with my window open, hearing his strange sobbing as the sun went down. (p 43)

As Gollancz remarks on the setting sun, the Priest attempts to reassert his dignity: by throwing his lot in with her, he has abandoned his vocation as a guardian of public morals and his efforts at heroic gesture – the suicide attempts – end in humiliating failure.

Nevertheless the Priest insists:

> I must announce – besieged as I am – eroded as I am by love and the servitude that
> must attach to it – I intend to make the necessary effort to hold to my beliefs… (p 36)

The next occasion the audience encounter these characters is after a considerable lapse of time. (Gollancz claims it is fifteen years since the murder of her husband.) The Priest, as Gollancz states, is inclined to 'admire everything now' (p 47) – where once he would have condemned.

> GOLLANCZ: And once you were indignant…
> PRIEST: That was silly. (p 47)

He has apparently abandoned the 'beliefs' he asserted above. In this scene, 'An Escape', Gollancz has tracked down the lover who seduced her and killed her husband in the first scene. The original seduction involved Shaw serenading her with the violin. This included a challenge with him asking her to name a composer. She insists on Proust – which leaves him embarrassed: 'Ah, Proust…! I could play Proust once.' (p 15.) He attempts something 'similar' but Gollancz remains unsatisfied. It is at this point that they couple – after which he cuts her husband's throat and leaves playing 'a snatch of violin music'. He shouts from offstage – 'That's Proust…!' Later in the same scene, the Priest seizes upon this information in order to ridicule Gollancz's story of a vagrant:

> PRIEST: Proust? Proust is a novelist.
> GOLLANCZ: Yes
> PRIEST: (*Triumphant*.) A NOVELIST NOT A COMPOSER. (p 19)

There is perhaps an allusion here to *Swann's Way* and the incident of Vinteuil's Sonata where Proust seeks to analyse, in meticulous detail, the operations of a seduction. In the first instance, Swann is seduced by the music:

> This time he had distinguished quite clearly a phrase which emerged for a few moments
> above the waves of sound. It had at once suggested to him a world of inexpressible delights,
> of whose existence, before hearing it, he had never dreamed, into which he felt that nothing

else could initiate him; and he had been filled with love for it, as with a new and strange desire.[7]

The music sparks Swann's infatuation with Odette – a woman whose charms had hitherto made no impact on him and whom he later considered to be entirely foreign to his tastes and social situation. In *The Ecstatic Bible*, Shaw has acquired all the trappings of success: he is a surgeon, has a beautiful and intelligent wife who was 'the greatest companion' of his life and 'a perfect lover' (p 46). In spite of – or perhaps because of this, he is prepared to abandon it all and go off with Gollancz – whom he no longer finds particularly attractive. Within his perfect life, however, the music had remained for fifteen years an unassimilated and irrational ritual. Shaw says:

> I was expecting you. What other reason could there have been for this compulsive
> playing of the violin? Always with the window open and the same few bars, my wife
> interrogated me, my wife…demanded to know the reason for this monotonous
> behaviour and I was unable to tell her, unable to explain because even as I dredged the
> depths of my unconscious I was simultaneously heaping my secret with obscurity. In
> the end she was satisfied to think of it as my single eccentricity. All she required was
> that I played here in the clinic and never at home. (pp 45–6)

Both Gollancz and Shaw recognise their union as destiny – which means that Shaw must leave his wife, Fashoda. Gollancz is clear that this will kill her but accepts it as necessary. The first time Fashoda appears she pleads with Gollancz to go. The Priest in his new mode of 'admiration' spectates at the confrontation between the two women:

> I do not know I cannot say which of you I most admired which of you most drew my
> sympathy because whilst she was obviously the supplicant your adamantine silence
> was – (p 49)

When Fashoda returns with a gun, however, his sympathies seem more engaged with the injured wife and he encourages her to kill Gollancz. In the event, she is unable to kill either Gollancz or her husband and instead shoots herself offstage – an outcome Gollancz foresaw.

> *A shot from the corridor.*
> *The PRIEST seems to crumble. Tears rush to his eyes.*

PRIEST: I HATE YOU...

OH, I STILL HATE YOU...

His fists open and close...at last his eyes rise to meet GOLLANCZ's... He straightens.

This collapse would suggest that he has not succeeded in ridding himself of his indignation – or of his pity. The scene ends with Shaw passionately kissing Gollancz while the Priest gestures hopelessly towards the corridor where lies – presumably (no one has gone to investigate) – the dead body of Shaw's wife. This prefigures a number of other instances in the play where characters either pursuing or in the throes of an ecstasy ignore the desperate demands of pity: it would seem that, once they have acclimatised themselves to the situation, rather than detracting from their rapture, the other's pain actually enhances it.

This theme – broached in Gollancz's assertion cited above – that desire is the most painful and the most beautiful thing, is pursued in 'A Contract' where she and her two male adherents have resumed their vagrancy. The Priest encounters a 70-year-old woman, Henderson, seated in the garden of her house who tells him that it is perfectly all right to rob her. When he does enter the house, however, all he discovers are boxes containing seven thousand love letters. Inflamed by this reading, he returns and demands to see her naked: he says – 'HIS DESCRIPTION IS / APPALLING / APPALLING NEED / APPALLING PAIN / APPALLING / APPALLING' (p 66). Again, she acquiesces. The Priest asserts: 'I came here to steal and I am stolen!' At this point, he is violently seized by two male adherents of Henderson who proceed to torture him – inexplicably. The Priest protests – up until a sudden insight:

PRIEST: I think I know what I am...I am your pain...

Pause. Distant sounds of voices calling.

HENDERSON: They're looking for you...

Pause.

And you don't reply...

PRIEST: I can't -

I can't –

He shakes his head.

Oh, your life...drowns mine... (p 69)

One has the sense here that the Priest is struggling at the limits of language to express his transformation from rejection to an unqualified acceptance of the suffering. Because

Henderson's life has made his own seem impoverished by comparison, he can only be ennobled by her pain. It is not difficult to see a correspondence between these sentiments and aspects of the conventional Christianity of his vocation.

When Gollancz and Shaw arrive, the Priest berates them as 'profane' and 'desecrators' (p 70). Gollancz realises immediately that he is in love with Henderson and appears to regret the loss of her 'ally' (p 71). The Priest's new worship, however, is devastated when the potent Shaw propositions Henderson – 'Take me to bed…' (p 71) and receives an affirmative response. The Priest finds that his impulse to 'kill the surgeon' is being seconded by Gollancz – 'What's stopping you?' Both have obvious motivations of jealous resentment, but Gollancz seems additionally to be moved by a concern for the Priest's psychological health – 'I cannot bear to see you struggling with the burden of yet another undone act…' As the Priest pointed out previously, Gollancz rarely expresses an opinion, so this comment is worthy of note not merely in terms of demonstrating a concern for the Priest but also as providing evidence of her own attitude to life. Whereas the Priest inhibits his impulses – ostensibly on account of ethical considerations, Gollancz doesn't; she believes that the Priest's sufferings are attributable to these inhibitions – the main 'undone act' being his failure to have sexual relations with her. Other 'undone acts', such as the botched suicide attempts, relate back to this initial smothering of an impulse.

The two of them listen to the sounds of Shaw and Henderson's love-making – providing yet another moment when intense pain is suffused with a profound sense of beauty:

> GOLLANCZ: Shh…! That's her
> *The Priest covers his face. He breathes deeply.*
> How perfect
> How melodious
> I am not immune to beauty
> I experience it rarely, that's all
> *She puts her finger to her lips. They all listen, rapt, pained.* (p 72)

There is a similar juxtaposition in the following scene, 'An Intrusion', where the vagrant trio – Gollancz, Shaw and the Priest – have been apprehended as thieves by the military authority. This authority, stemming ultimately from McChief, is vested in her lover, the Boy. He is under strict instructions to crucify all thieves. While we hear the cries of Shaw and the Priest as they are crucified offstage, a seduction takes place between the Boy and Gollancz.

GOLLANCZ: Let them die…
    I am deaf to them
    You
    Exquisite
    Boy…
    He observes her a long time.
    Cries offstage.
    Her gaze is unfaltering… (p 75)

The affair is tragically short-lived because McChief has the Boy executed. She is, of course, Gollancz's daughter who was abandoned by her mother to the reclusive castellan, Davis, in the second scene, 'A Birth'. It could be argued therefore that the mischief engendered by McChief and her even more atrocious daughter, Winterhalter, could be traced back to Gollancz herself. Another example of this is to be found in Lamb, the philosopher, who ousts Paraffin and runs a police state: he is the reluctant product of Gollancz's liaison with Poitier. This is certainly the conclusion that the Priest comes to in one of the final scenes of the play:

PRIEST: This is all Mrs Gollancz…
    Not only this…
    But everything is Mrs Gollancz…
    And whereas at one time I should have said, so be it, I am neither more nor less than
    the inert or sometimes volcanic substance of Mrs Gollancz, her flora, her fauna,
    her detritus, now I say all that came from her, all consequences of the fact of Mrs
    Gollancz her creation and participation in the world, has been to my detriment and to
    the detriment of others, and I announce this without a trace of bitterness, I announce
    it as one might announce the dawn to a windowless cell of the condemned… (p 297)

While on her part, Gollancz seems to embody a principle of perpetual if amoral and indiscriminate creative renewal, the Priest, described – not without a certain irony – by Barker in the dramatis personae as 'a stable character', evidences a correspondingly limitless capacity for suffering: not only is he subjected to humiliating beatings – by Davis, Henderson, Troop and Season – but he is by turns crucified, strung up by a hook on fish scales, drowned and starved of water. This is not to mention the even greater deluge of psychological trauma inflicted on him – not least on account of his desire for Gollancz herself. There is no indication that he specifically invites this punishment though he does occasionally attempt to use it to gain sympathy and prestige: 'LISTEN I HAVE BEEN CRUCIFIED' (p 108). In this respect he contrasts with the stoically silent Gollancz. In 'The Solitude of the Margins', the Priest becomes the target of violence because he protests in the mildest way at Troop's attempt to strangle his (Troop's) partner, Season. His intervention leads to the 'dysfunctional' couple uniting to vent their rage on him.

Both the Priest and Gollancz are highly conscious of their longevity: in 'The Compelling Attraction of Unrepentant Characters', the Priest, having just encountered Gollancz after thinking she had been incinerated at the abbey, comments –

> OH SHE LOVES ME AND THAT IS WHY SHE CANNOT DIE...
>
> Or the opposite...
>
> We cannot rule it out that my devotion is a steel shutter outside which death is obliged
> to prowl a frustrated burglar angry obviously (p 195)

In the final scene, 'A Little Theatre', the Priest encounters Mrs Gollancz again. She acknowledges her part in keeping him alive: 'It's me, isn't it, that drives the blood through those withered veins...the heart went years ago...' (p 324) For his part, in his state of delirium, he seems to have split Gollancz into two separate entities one of whom is his idealised 'love' and the other a malign witch – a duality consistent with the contradictory attitudes he expresses in the first scene (p 19 – as cited above). Unaware of the identity of his interlocutor, he admits his dread of encountering Gollancz and when she suggests he might avoid this by death, he tells her that death 'shuns' him. (Earlier in the scene Germania tries and fails to kill him.) She responds to this:

> GOLLANCZ: Me also...
>
> *They look into each other.*
>
> The infinite ditch...stopped short of me...
>
> *A mutual fear suspends them in their gaze.*
>
> HOLD MY HAND...!
>
> *She throws out an appealing hand to the Priest, who stares.*
>
> Hold...!
>
> Hold...!
>
> *The Priest emits a long howl.*
>
> HOLD IT I SAID...
>
> *He falls back with a sob.*
>
> Oh, won't you...won't you...comfort this appalling solitude...?

He writhes.

PRIEST: We are immortal…

GOLLANCZ: We are immortal and God knows what we did to deserve it…

PRIEST: IMMORTAL…! Mrs Gollancz…Oh, Mrs Gollancz…

He extends a hand now.

You have been the curse of my existence…!

GOLLANCZ: Yes

I have

With or without intention

Intention being

Such a paltry thing

PRIEST: As if one steered a barge in a torrent by a broken straw… (pp 329–30)

I have quoted this passage in full not only because it constitutes a powerful dramatic climax to the Priest/Gollancz thematic linking the whole play, but additionally, because it raises significant philosophical issues. 'They look into each other' is a stage direction frequently encountered in Barker texts: it denotes a moment of profound emotional contact between individuals – often a moment of seduction. In this instance, their mutual apprehension that they are eternal is suffused with horror; death by comparison appears a blessed relief. This is the 'appalling solitude'. In his essay, 'There is: Existence without Existents', Emmanuel Levinas defines this primal horror by positing a hypothetical universal collapse into nothingness. This nothingness, according to Levinas, even though it would involve the extinction of all existents, could not abolish existence itself:

> Something would happen, if only night and the silence of nothingness… Like the third person pronoun in the impersonal form of a verb, it designates not the uncertainly known author of the action, but the characteristic of the action itself which somehow has no author. This impersonal, anonymous, yet inextinguishable 'consummation' of being which murmurs in the depths of nothingness itself we shall designate by the term *there is*.[8]

Implicit in this thought is the total absence of God. Levinas suggests that night provides an experience of the *there is* – that the silence and the darkness become a presence which submerges the subject, the 'I'. He refers to this as participation:

It is a participation in the *there is*, in the *there is* which returns in the heart of every negation, in the *there is* that has no 'exits'. It is, if we may say so, the impossibility of death, the universality of existence even in its annihilation.[9]

Both Gollancz and the Priest have lived lives of extreme physical and mental suffering; as audiences or readers we have witnessed that and this moment of realisation is rendered dramatically feasible by the extensive action which has preceded it. According to Levinas it is in suffering that we are most directly exposed to being: 'It is the fact of being backed up against life and being. In this sense suffering is the impossibility of nothingness.'[10] Both characters recoil from this chilling apprehension of their destiny, taking refuge in diversionary contact with each other by holding hands. In the seductive world of the play, events come about according to destiny and Gollancz has always had a strong intuition of this. Here she and the priest agree in dismissing the efficacy of human intention in events – a conclusion that is clearly consistent with the epiphany described above where all causality is stifled in the brute fact of existence. It is tempting to see in his response to her laughter at his simile of the broken straw, not a ray of hope but the possibility of a refuge in this spiritual desert:

> I like your laugh… It's a laugh that comes between great doors…or if a gaol
> cracked…and a little sky fell in…a chip of day like ice that skidded on the floor…
> *Pause. They lie, staring at the sky…* (p 330)

In the final coda where Ernitsin arrives in murderous pursuit of his unfaithful lover, the Priest still attempts to behave 'ethically' by misdirecting him. But when he tries to intervene directly by going to the tower, he seems to suffer a huge failure of will – 'his resolution decayed' (p 332) according to the stage directions. Is this because he has – finally – accepted the paltriness of intention? The appearance of the laundresses is marked by 'bright laughter' (p 330) and it is this same laughter heard later from inside the tower that alerts Ernitsin to the whereabouts of his quarry. Laughter, then, features strongly – if ambiguously – in the play's conclusion.

NOTES

1. H Barker, *The Ecstatic Bible* (London, Oberon, 2004). All further references to this text will be referred to by page numbers of this edition.

2. Aristotle, 'On the Art of Poetry', tr. T S Dorsch in *Classical Literary Criticism* (London, Penguin, 1967), p 42

3. H Barker, *Arguments for a Theatre* 3rd edn (Manchester, Manchester University Press, 1997), p 140

4. H Barker, 'Second Prologue' to *The Bite of the Night* in *Collected Plays vol 4* (London, Calder, 1998), p 8

5. M Merleau-Ponty, 'Indirect Language and the Voices of Silence', tr. C McCleary, in *Signs* (Evanston, Northwestern University Press, 1982), p 77

6. C Lamb, *The Theatre of Howard Barker* (London, Routledge, 2005), chapter 6

7. M Proust, *Remembrance of Things Past 1* tr. C K Scott Moncrieff and T Kilmartin (London, Penguin, 1989), p 228

8. E Levinas, 'There is: Existence without Existents' tr. S Hand, in *The Levinas Reader* (Oxford, Blackwell, 1989), p 30

9. *Ibid.*, p 33

10. E Levinas, 'Time and the Other' tr. S Hand, in *The Levinas Reader*, p 40

I HAVE CALLED MY PAIN 'DOG'

Wounding Texts and Artistic Figuration[1]

ELIZABETH SAKELLARIDOU

The content of this essay has been largely inspired by my reflections on a number of cultural, artistic and intellectual events of the past few years. The Turner Prize Exhibition of 2003, at Tate Britain in London, with all the public controversy it rekindled on the issue of art and provocation, was one source of inspiration.[2] A second flashpoint was provided by a huge contemporary art exhibition in Athens (2003), entitled 'Outlook', where uproar followed the removal of two works – one on the grounds of religious offence[3] and another after an act of vandalism committed by an enraged visitor.[4] Another motivation sprang from the meeting of the European Directors Guild in Thessaloniki in April 2002, which closed with Max Stafford-Clark's emphatic remark 'we need more stories' – a verdict that met with the tacit approval of all other participants. 'But what kind of stories?' – one is tempted to ask. It seems to me we have had enough of the small stories that postmodernism has kept feeding us after the presumed demise of all master narratives of the past (possibly also of the future). I also recall a panel on the future of experimental theatre during the ESSE Conference of 2002 in Strasburg, when the fancy term 'in-yer-face theatre' was still a hot critical term, ready-made for academic consumption.[5] Finally I shall mention my visit, in summer 2003, to the island of Samos, which is one of the main sites of archaic art in the world. This trip was followed by my reading of Howard Barker's *Gertrude – The Cry* (2002) – a play I had only seen on video and of which I had, therefore, missed part of the underlying preoccupations, namely its reflections on the notion of the archaic.[6] The mingling of these two experiences has formed the nucleus of this essay.

It is hard to deny that sex, violence, physical decay, pain and death are the major themes highlighted in the visual, performance and literary arts of today. We cannot escape this necessity under the precarious conditions of contemporary life. What can be doubted, however, is the necessity of shallowness and trivialisation in the treatment of these themes: a compulsory narrative dwarfism in artistic creation and, most of all, postmodernism's claim to originality in the blunt representation of shocking reality – an empty posture which has deflected our eyes, in contempt, from an assumed ignorant or prudish past to the celebration of 'new' epiphanies of a sensational surface. Howard Barker's work gives an answer to many of these ailing questions. This is why I intend to place his work within a wider cultural and artistic perspective, both synchronic and diachronic.

One such link is Terry Eagleton's recent book on 'the idea of the tragic', entitled *Sweet Violence* (2003). This publication provides a complete contrast to some cultural resonances of Aleks Sierz's sensational book *In-Yer-Face Theatre*, to which I alluded earlier. I may not fully agree with the political twist that Eagleton gives to the present meaning and function of the tragic but I do share his tenacity in claiming, in his introduction, that 'tragedy is an unfashionable subject these days, which is one good reason for writing about it'. He then proceeds to enumerate the strengths of the tragic art over a variously thin or thinning postmodernism:

> There is an ontological depth and high seriousness about the genre which grates on the postmodern sensibility, with its unbearable lightness of being. As an aristocrat among art forms, its tone is too solemn and portentous for a streetwise, sceptical culture. Indeed the term hardly scrapes into the postmodern lexicon.[7]

Eagleton is a latecomer to the field by comparison to Howard Barker, whose serious engagement with tragedy dates back over 15 years to his hallmark play *The Bite of the Night* (1988) and an accompanying series of essays on the same theme. However, the publication of Eagleton's book is significant in that it coincides with a more general revision, on the part of other scholars, of older traditions of literature and art – a move which renews our interest in values and forms utterly discarded by postmodernism. For instance, the idea of the 'pagan divine' – in the sense of the supernatural, the dark, the irrational and the forbidden – is one of the notions currently revisited. In this domain I must mention Roberto Calasso's book *Literature and the Gods* (2001), in which Calasso describes the return of the pagan gods as 'the fugitive guests of literature', in the mode of 'involuntary parody', a 'sparkling intermezzo', until the time comes when 'the tragedy begins' again.[8] Calasso anticipates a stage in contemporary culture when a deep, firm and creative reconciliation will be achieved with the ancient tragic: a state which he calls 'absolute literature'. In this state of literature:

> The head [i.e. the archetypal poet Orpheus's head] that drifts on the waters sings and bleeds. Every vibration of the word presupposes something violent, a *palaion penthos*, an

'ancient grief'. Was it a murder? Was it a sacrifice? It isn't clear, but the word will never cease to tell of it.[9]

Howard Barker is unique among contemporary British dramatists in reflecting, increasingly, the developments described by Calasso in his quest of the tragic. This is particularly clear in his recent play *Gertrude*, where references to an untraceable divinity and to ancient cries and griefs from a dark beyond become remarkably dense and ominous. The only other name in the contemporary European spectrum with similar visions of the tragic that I can think of is the German dramatist Heiner Müller.[10]

It is from the word 'archaic' that I will start my investigation – a historical and artistic term but also one of the cornerstones of Nietzschean philosophy. The use of this word first struck me in Barker's extraordinary, poetic female monologue, *Und* (1999). After my visit to Samos and the subsequent cross-reading of *Gertrude*, the word gained for me a new cultural and symbolic meaning. Loitering among the ruins of the ancient city of Samos, I came across an astonishing statuary complex, a unique family portrait in marble, initially comprising six figures in different postures, standing, sitting and lying. Of the middle ones the two are missing. From the maimed figures of the remaining four archaeologists have identified on the right the reclining figure of the father, on the left the seated figure of the mother and in the middle the elegant figures of two daughters, gracefully lifting their skirts over a slightly protruding right leg so as to better reveal their attractive femininity, also showing in the shaping of the bust. The original statuary is kept in the museum of Samos. But it was the copy in the ruined city, among dry weeds and possibly creeping reptiles underneath, that gave me the double vision that, under the surface narrative of glamour and felicity, something was at stake, that told of a different *marginal(ised)* story: that of mortality, which vividly contrasted to the narrative of compulsory happiness and the sanitised view of life as depicted in the *institutionalised* archaic monument I had just visited.

When I read *Gertrude* (Barker's revision of *Hamlet*), some time later, I was most surprised to see that the conflicting images and notions of the archaic in this play came to match and illuminate my own misgivings. In *Gertrude* Barker offers a multi-layered reading of an 'archaic' world, a collage of three different views, voiced separately by Hamlet, Claudius and Gertrude. Hamlet's version comes first, as he recalls his mother's austere face during his childhood, a face 'chiselled out of stone'.[11] He then completes the image while dreaming of the puritanical laws that he would like to reinstall as the new king of Denmark:

...now I am king the entire emphasis of government will be upon decorum sitting still
for example
HOW FEW PEOPLE CAN SIT STILL
Pause.
Only you [i.e. Gertrude]
Pause.
Only you sit still
[...]
How they must dream
I have often thought this
Of your still white body [12]

To this image of petrified female beauty Claudius's despairing words at the entrance of
Gertrude, dressed in a white, glove-fitting wedding gown, ready for the matrimonial
ceremony with the much younger Mecklenburg, ring like an equivocal antiphon:

look at us however were two ever better made to thrive in such a landscape me wire
you stone I cannot look at you such polished stone you are and the thin stuff drawn
over you your arse of stone your breasts of stone and the thin stuff clinging [13]

Claudius's words try to dig behind the stiffness, the decorum and the coldness of the white
marble; to activate the hidden body and its desires, speaking under the fine material of the
clinging dress, suggesting such corporeal pleasures as gracefully hinted at by the elegant
lifting of the skirt in the archaic Samian statues I referred to.[14] Claudius darkens this
image of open, scopophilic desire with the harsh, neurotic discourse of much unhappier
times and more repressive social structures than the ones depicted in the playful, teasing
mannerisms of Sapphic poetry – a major representative of archaic art. It is in this feminine
art of elegant dressing and alluring deportment, as reflected in Sappho's lyrics and the two
statues of the Samian Korae, that Gertrude is a real connoisseur: an expert in coquetry
and sophistication.[15] At the same time she is aware of their anachronistic absurdity. Her
provocative haute-couture dressing style is as impressive as it is uncomfortably misplaced
in the grim world of Barker's revision of the Shakespearean play, and it becomes a symbol
of her tragedy.[16] In a monologue, more far-reaching than Claudius's on the same issue, she
ruminates over the possibility of recovery of an ancient sinless conscience, an unspoiled
beauty and gaiety, in an unspecified Mediterranean locale:

Two weeks in a warm climate
Two weeks in a warm climate more is not possible
the business of the government demands his swift
return
Two weeks of too-red flowers
Two weeks of too-blue seas
[…]
The scents at dusk
The casement creaking in warm airs
I'll sleep I'll sleep I'll sleep as simply as a child
And with his child inside me he declares we cannot
leave without an heir *he sinks his mouth into my hair and breathes me* [my emphasis] [17]

But she soon recovers from the absurd reverie only to recapture her harsh and ineluctable reality:

The making of a garden grey this garden everything I plant grey we are northern are
we not great is the
grey stone and the moss grey grey waves and me grey naked I'll stoop even in frost
boots on my feet grey socks
[…]
And he shaving in a so-high window will glance
from the mirror to my arse
Grey garden
Grey garden
Ashes scattered on it
Scattered ashes of burned men
HE'LL RUSH TO FUCK
HE'LL RUSH TO FUCK [18]

And so she appropriately rejoins the cynical discourse of the other characters in the play and she accepts her ruined face ('adored like that' [19]), keeping however the dim memory of a mythic world, with which she can engage in quasi-Nietzschean dialogue. Through her Barker has taken his most advanced step into the darkness of early antiquity and the beginnings of the tragic, while also noting the risks of ridiculous displacements both for his characters and for an authorial re-establishment of the tragic aesthetic as mere unqualified tragic mimesis. As one of the reviews of *Gertrude* rightly argues, Barker's modern tragedy is saved from ridicule 'because it has its own highly developed sense of the ridiculous. High style and absurdity walk together'.[20] Indeed, Barker handles the imagery of the archaic in a dual symbolism: on the one hand, launching a critique against the Christian puritanism that circumscribed the portrayal of Gertrude in Shakespeare's play; on the other, deconstructing the mythology of compulsory innocence and happiness of an early culture, which excluded pain and suffering in order to immortalise in art the frivolous splendours of the material world.[21] However, the volatile and arrogant postures of the pre-archaic and archaic art already received their first serious critique and deconstruction in later antiquity itself: in Athenian philosophy and, in the literary field, in the biting tongue of Aristophanes and the abysmal depths of Euripides' mind – both writing in the midst of an already disillusioned and declining Athenian state, which had to face national humiliation, material loss, war, illness and mortality. What a match for the cracking world of our own times!

As a contemporary tragic writer Barker is unique in transcending the 'amnesia', characteristic of postmodernist attitudes to history and cultural tradition. The more he dips his pen in the domain of the tragic, the more he evokes the transgressive aspects of the above classic writers, as he combines the merciless and unashamed satire of Aristophanes and the unspeakable horrors of Euripides.[22] In an early statement Barker declared that 'the most appropriate art for a culture on the edge of extinction is one that stimulates pain'.[23] In the years that have elapsed between this statement and the present moment there has been so much banal exploitation of this fascinating material that, more than ever, it is necessary to posit again some serious aesthetic questions which the formidable postulations and denials of postmodernism have obliterated for too long. A much revered writer in the field of aesthetic theory, Erich Auerbach, bases his critique of realism on the extensive use of the Latin term 'figura', a dynamic mode of artistic representation in the plastic and visual arts as well as in literature.[24] Auerbach describes the process of figuration as follows:

> the sensory occurrence pales before the power of the figural meaning. What is perceived by the hearer or the reader or even, in the plastic and graphic arts, by the spectator, is weak as a sensory impression, and all one's interest is directed toward the context of meanings.[25]

In an era when 'in-yer-face' or sensational art insists on banging us with shocking (glittering even) but mostly ineffectual images of the literal and the obvious,[26] one feels more and more obliged to return to the effect of 'figura', and to works of art that grow off the picture frame or off the page in order to offer bold insights into the dark territory of the 'as if' or the 'what if'.

There is a memorable image in Howard Barker's *Und*, where the protagonist reflects on the power of words to bounce off the page, to become three-dimensional, to turn into images, themselves growing out of the canvas:

> Oh the terrible power of a single word
> Black
> Scrawl
> On
> White
> *Pause.*
> Which word however
> Which
> Or does the word not matter the word perhaps is immaterial what matters is the
> word's appearance on the page
> Its angled its dishevelled form
> A WORD CAN BE DISHEVELLED

Then she contemplates a number of words, 'dog', 'mat', until she comes up with a word whose imaginative possibilities please her more – 'grass'.

> GRASS SAY
> *She scrawls.*
> Grass at a steeply angled gradient grass leaning violently and so indented so very
> passionately he could not fail to
> *She takes another sheet.*
> Or the opposite
> GRASS FALLING BACKWARDS
> Grass toppling off the page
> Grass
> Yes [27]

In the totality of Barker's work one can trace a number of different strategies, in which ordinary or familiar images, gestures or words become a 'figura', or – to adopt another striking Latin term – attain a 'punctum'. Observing photographic stills in his work

Camera Lucida, Roland Barthes borrows the Latin word 'punctum' in order to designate signification that goes beyond the surface narrative of the image:

> It is this element which rises from the scene, shoots out of it like an arrow, and pierces me. A Latin word exists to designate this wound, this prick, this mark made by a pointed instrument; the word suits me all the better in that it also refers to the notion of punctuation. [...] This second element [...] I shall therefore call *punctum*.[28]

The French theorist picks up stills from Eisenstein's films to illustrate his point. A reference to ancient tragic literature is more befitting to illuminate Barker's dramatic tactics of figuration. My choice is the descriptive passages of the blinding scene of Oedipus as they are handled by Sophocles and Seneca respectively. Sophocles gives no more than five lines to the atrocious act of blinding and quickly moves to the philosophical contemplation of blindness, which forms the bedrock of the dramatic situation of the play. Seneca, on the contrary, takes vast pleasure – and time – in prolonging the action of inflicting pain to the self, giving priority to sado-masochistic sensation almost exclusively. The difference in the figurative capacities of the two images is telling. The former is very much in the mode of Auerbach's 'figura' or Barthes's 'punctum'. In the latter the drama is played on the surface: in modern terms this is a graphic sample of 'in-yer-face' art.

Nietzsche also gives a wonderful example of artistic figuration. It concerns the transformation of physical pain into figurative language and therefore it is very apt to our discussion here:

> I have given a name to my pain and call it 'dog'. It is just as faithful, just as obtrusive and shameless, just as entertaining, just as clever as any other dog – and I can scold it and vent my bad mood on it, as others do with their dogs [...] [29]

This excerpt from *The Gay Science* is striking both for the vivacity and the variety it gives to the concept of pain through the figurative use of the word 'dog' and the poor animal it stands for. In our contemporary culture we are familiar with a long list of dog compounds: 'Dogville', 'Straw Dogs', 'Reservoir Dogs', 'Yellow Dog', 'Top Dog/Underdog'.[30] The history of this word's figurative deployment goes back to the Bible and classical antiquity. Howard Barker has entitled one of his earlier plays *The Power of the Dog* (1982) after a quote from the Bible.[31] In many of his other works he makes ample use of metaphorical and ambiguous dog imagery; most tragically striking is the image of the bandaged and eventually slain dogs in *Found in the Ground* (2001).[32] In *Gertrude* the dog imagery retains the full power of conflicting ambiguity that we have noted in the quote from Nietzsche's *The Gay Science*. In Barker's play the expansion of canine imagery is effected through its double application to the murdered king and his murderer, Claudius. The latter's contradictory diction reflects this duality:

> LET THE DYING DOG'S EYES SWIM IN YOUR
> *Pause.*
> He's not a dog
> *He shrugs.*
> I called him a dog
> […]
> If anyone's a dog
> […]
> It's me [33]

In another situation Claudius identifies himself as Gertrude's dog, her hound, thus expanding further the ambiguity of figuration. The figurative spectrum of 'dog' is completed through a reference to mad dogs and also through a possible reversal of the word 'god', reminiscent of similar Beckettian word puns. In another play, *Und*, the protagonist reflects studiously and exhaustively on the different nuances of the word dog and its visual associations:

> A WORD CAN BE DISHEVELLED
> Oh yes not only hair a word take DOG
> *She scrawls.*
> It won't be dog dog would imply resentment dog would cause him to conclude he has offended me an aristocrat is never offended no not dog I chose dog out of the blue I chose dog at random [34]

Later on she continues to ruminate on further possible nuances of meaning, again reflecting a Nietzschean wit and perspicacity:

> The word dog
> On its own
> Solitary
> And even underlined

Would not

NOT NECESSARILY

Constitute

Pause.

Offence

Pause.

Oh no

Oh no

I like dogs

So do many

Dogs are also faithful

Dogs are also loyal

Teeth yes

And some are curs but

IT ISN'T SIMPLE IS IT

Pause.

How I hate simplicity [35]

'Dog' is just one example of how Barker's poetic language gains figurative value, attains a 'punctum'. Usually a linguistic metaphor is combined with an image for associative thinking that sends the imagination to all possible directions. Thus 'dog' in Und's delirious speech leads to 'mat' and 'mat' leads to 'grass,' as the mind reels off, generating image upon image, emotion against emotion. In *Gertrude*, too, words and gestures of utter cynicism are later inverted to a softer meaning. The Queen's early, lustful invitation to Claudius, 'fuck me', on the very spot of her husband's murder, seems to have hampered many critics' receptive ability for the rest of the performance.[36] Ironically, however, if one peruses the whole play closely, one will notice a surprising change of mood, a shift in the signification of the same four-letter word 'fuck', due to a change of context. When, towards the end of the play, Gertrude has that extraordinary vision of archaic life, she closes her speech of mourning for her grey state of existence with a fierce, capitalised and doubly repeated 'HE'LL RUSH TO FUCK'. This stark statement is so much imbued with regret and disappointment that it stands in complete opposition to the passionate cry of the opening 'fuck me', which was burning with ecstatic, shameless desire. In this way, through linguistic displacements of a figurative nature, Gertrude is invested with a complex sensibility of her tragic state, revealing a genuine pain that bites into the soul and creates a 'punctum' to the spectator.[37]

Barker is a real connoisseur of all the secrets of injurious language.[38] If *Und* is, among other things, a thorough study of delicate linguistic battles with an imaginary (or just scenically invisible) adversary, *Gertrude* attests, additionally, to a more phenomenological aspect of language, which aligns itself with actual physical force. Says one of the characters:

> How it gratified me when I came here
> The sheer saying
> What liberty
> The sheer saying
> The thought straight to the mouth
> And no queuing
> No queuing up behind the teeth
> OUT THOUGHT
> OUT INJURY [39]

Thus, the performativity of language, the force and the intentionality that speech act theory has spotted in the modality of utterances,[40] is highlighted by Barker through direct reference to the very physicality of speech and the bodily organs that assist in its articulation. It is the same vibrant imagery of corporeal articulation that has come down to us through the linguistic vivacity of the Homeric epics and that of the Greek tragic writers.[41]

However, in Barker it is not only language that escapes literal meaning. There are other means of figuration as well. Very often it is the juxtaposition of antithetical images that displaces the initial situation and creates the true tragic emotion of the play. One such instance can be quoted from *Judith*. It is the poetic speech that the heroine delivers at the end of the play, when she has recovered from her real or hypothetical – certainly miraculous – encounter with Holofernes that Barker has elaborated out of the familiar Apocryphal story:

> Dawn! Yes! This is the hour sin slips out of the sheets to creep down pissy alleys! Morning, cats! Did you slither, also? Morning, sparrows! Rough night? Hot beds cooling. The running of water. WELL, IT HAS TO END AT SOME TIME, LOVE! But its smell, in the after hours… MAGNIFICENCE!

She laughs, with a shudder. A cracked bell is beaten monotonously.

[…]

The cracked bell stops. Sounds of naturalistic conversation, the clatter of pots, the rising of a camp. [42]

It is this movement from the extraordinary to the ordinary, from the 'divine' of the Judith-Holofernes encounter to the mundane of the outer world, that is so painful, so insufferable for the heroine. This is what constitutes the real moment of tragedy in the play. The representation that Barker has given us of the unspeakable stays – on the fictional level – locked in the consciousness of the heroine. The frustration she communicates to the spectator is how to translate the unspeakable to the surrounding indifferent world. It is the inexpressibility of the event, as experienced by the heroine, after the completion of the personal contact and the murder, that seals the tragic in this contemporary version of the Apocryphal story. The total dismay at the expressive limitations of speech is also beautifully captured in *Gertrude*:

> In a strange and sinister equation the more we tell the more the untold becomes agony
> and even that which was once said becomes unsayable
> *Pause.*
> Strange
> And
> Probably
> Only
> An
> Aspect
> Of
> Our
> Impenetrable
> Solitude [43]

Also in *Und* there is a powerful image of a darkening sensibility, similar to the one quoted from *Judith*. This is the grim variation of an earlier and happier vision of the protagonist's invisible lover in a café. This new version is the counter-narrative of death, set against the earlier narrative of romantic perception:

A little grave I saw him yawning in a café the newspaper slipping from his hand and
morning this was morning sun streamed through the curtain and his mouth was oh a
cave his hair unwashed his face unshaven no collar marks of dinner on his sleeve dark
brows dark hair he's dead this is his grave [44]

What creates a tragic anti-climax here is the passage from the anticipated familiar and
the cosy to the unfamiliar and the threatening; from the assumption of a happy, protected
existence to the dreadful finality of death. Tragedy comes, as also in *Judith* and *Gertrude*,
when the reverie turns into nightmare, the sweet dream into harsh reality. Barker has a
very special way of playing on the tight rope between reality and illusion, cynicism and
romance; admitting the absurdity of the latter but also its irresistible fascination – a very
human psychic necessity. In *Und*, in particular, the protagonist is transformed into a model
of an *ars moriendi* and the play becomes a reflection upon the *aesthetic* of a personal and
collective death, of a disintegrating, dying culture as a whole – much in the vein of T S
Eliot and, more recently, of Heiner Müller:

> […] and what was the horizon for want of a better word the horizon rose and fell in
> constant motion fountains geysers boiling plunging liquid volatile and seen through
> tidal heat and rolling clouds of toxins livid bile and copper green *and this acquired a*
> *certain beauty so he said* into this he walked walked walked he did not run and where he
> encountered obstacles lifted his leg placing the sole of his boot firmly in the ground
> neither stooping nor attempting to present the narrow profile of his body to the front
> his shirt unbuttoned and wearing a soft cap not a helmet in one hand a cane and in
> the other nothing nothing nothing in the other hand but let hang loosely fingers idly
> vertical *as if* [my emphasis] [45]

With Und's 'as if' we come full circle to the 'as if' and the 'what if' of the 'figura' and
the 'punctum' that formed the basis of my approach to Howard Barker's *oeuvre* – a work
invested with the 'seriousness' and the 'magnitude' that Aristotle's definition attributed
to the tragic genre. It is also invested with the ironising attitude, the spirit of parody, that
Nietzsche and, recently, Calasso attach to any modern revision of the tragic. In *Gertrude*
the dark shadows of unidentified gods and the mysterious call of distant, chthonic cries
suggest the writer's even closer approach to the blurred borderline between the tragic and
the barbaric, while parody recedes to the background. [46]

   I started this essay with a reference to contemporary art exhibitions and I will close
it with yet another. One of the outstanding items in the 'Outlook' exhibition in Athens in

autumn 2003 was a larger-than-life statue of a crippled girl holding a box for donations, entitled 'Charity', by the controversial British artist Damien Hirst. In Athens, which in the distant past had been the site of such proud, oversize representations of the human body as the famous archaic Korae and Kouroi,[47] this subversive, present-day alternative gains a more telling significance. In anticipation of the Olympic games hosted in Athens in the summer 2004, Hirst's 'Charity' seemed to open an ironic forum of debate between our crippled contemporary culture and the (hypothetically) healthier cultures of antiquity, by challenging the classical robust athletic body with that of the diseased and the disabled. Yet the mere *size* of Hirst's statue [48] or the pity it might arouse are not enough to provide tragic magnitude to his provocation. Almost thirty years ago Barker maimed his Helen of Troy and challenged us by naming her female descendants *Gay* and *Charity*, launching a loftier and more profound provocation and interrogation.[49] His 'stories' are larger than life; they are extreme. Like Heiner Müller's, his theatre knows no bounds; it flies beyond. Its action exceeds human dimensions; it challenges the divine.[50] It negotiates between the mythologies of a proud, glorious past and a sensuously self-pitying present. It lives in the interstices between the symbolism of the arrogant, impervious Kouros and the trauma of the crippled girl, engaging us in dialogue with both.

NOTES

1.   This essay has been based on a talk I gave at the Barker Symposium held in Paris-Nanterre from 29 to 31 January 2004. An extended, French-language version of the essay appears in E Angel-Perez (ed) *Howard Barker et le Théâtre de la Catastrophe* (Paris, Editions Théâtrales, 2006).

2.   Of the four finalists for the Prize Anya Gallaccio displayed her installations of real gerberas ('preserve "beauty"', 1991) and real apples strung on the branches of a metal tree ('because nothing has changed', 2000), both exposed to natural decay; Jake and Dinos Chapman played ambiguously with the ideas of sex and death by crossing meaning and representation in their provocative installations 'Sex 2003' (a new return to Goya and a reappropriation of their earlier 'Great Deeds Against the Dead', 1994) and its companion piece 'Death' (comprising two inflatable sex dolls engaged in fellatio); and Grayson Perry's extraordinary vases challenged vehemently thematic decency and aesthetic value by mixing sex, crime and child abuse with romance on the one hand and kitsch art with traditional pottery art on the other.

3.   Thierry De Cordier, 'Asperges Me', figuring a male organ shooting sperm at a toppling cross.

4.   Thanasis Totsikas, 'Untitled', depicting a naked man engaged in sexual intercourse with a watermelon.

5.   Since Aleks Sierz adopted the term as a provocative, selling title for his book (*In-Yer-Face Theatre: British Drama Today*, London, Faber, 2001), he legitimised its scholarly use as a label – as catchy and comfortable as Esslin's 'the theatre of the absurd' for a previous generation of writers – for the new generation of British playwrights of the 1990s such as Sarah Kane, Mark Ravenhill and others.

6.   H Barker, *Gertrude – The Cry* in *Gertrude – The Cry* and *Knowledge and a Girl* (London, Calder, 2002). There are three relevant references in the play: 'archaic' (p 46), 'archaism' (p 50) and 'antiquity' (p 52)

which all work on two levels of meaning: as a negative statement for the fossilised ethics of the Danish Court (in the context of the story of Hamlet) and as a vague nostalgia for a higher form of civilisation long lost in myth. Barker attempted a similar deconstruction of heroic stories of the past (this time drawn from the world of Homer, which actually preceded the archaic period) in his earlier play *The Bite of the Night*.

7. T Eagleton, *Sweet Violence: The Idea of the Tragic* (Oxford, Blackwell, 2003), p ix

8. R Calasso, *Literature and the Gods* (London, Vintage, 2001), pp 3, 74

9. *Ibid.*, p 193

10. In his brief but thorough introduction to a recently published English anthology of Heiner Müller's work, *A Heiner Müller Reader: Plays, Poetry, Prose* (C Weber, Baltimore and London, Johns Hopkins University Press, 2001), the American playwright Tony Kushner attributes to the German dramatist characteristics amazingly similar to many attitudes and forms that characterise Barker's drama: a fearless and unforgiving intelligence, the refusal of catharsis, the invocation of love to cover appalling crimes, a focus on the intricate relationship between the murderer and the murdered, a dark dialogue with the dead and a preoccupation with the rubble of European history. A more fundamental likeness, however, seems to be the striking similarity in their concept of the tragic, given in a mixed style of seduction and despair.

11. Barker, *Gertrude – The Cry*, p 15

12. *Ibid.*, pp 15–16

13. *Ibid.*, p 89

14. Similarly in *The Bite of the Night* Helen accuses Homer of withholding the truth concerning female representation; for omitting horror out of pity; H Barker, *The Bite of the Night* in *Collected Plays vol 4* (London, Calder, 1998), p 25

15. In the Wrestling School production of the play Gertrude first appeared on stage in a stunning, bright yellow long dress and a matching hat.

16. Similar high-fashion costumes were used again in *13 Objects* (2003) but they were more savagely treated as they reappear wrinkled, torn and misshapen after their first immaculate appearance, in line with Barker's heightened dark satirical mood.

17. Barker, *Gertrude – The Cry*, pp 91–2

18. *Ibid.*, p 92

19. *Ibid.*, p 93

20. L Gardner, *Guardian*, 25 October 2002 in *Theatre Record*, 22 October – 4 November 2002, pp 1419–20

21. It must be this dark, solemn, brooding pessimism in Howard Barker's art that alienates him from the wider British audiences, who refuse to accept the idea of a profound tragic vision of the world threatening their own existence. Lyn Gardner's view in her review of *13 Objects* is a key to this mistrustful attitude: 'The happy people among us will not entirely buy this doleful thesis'; L Gardner, *Guardian*, 20 October 2003 in *Theatre Record*, 22 October – 4 November 2003, pp 1463–4

22. This comparison to the classical writers of antiquity is not intended to minimise or doubt Barker's affinity to the English dramatic tradition, especially that of Elizabethan and Jacobean tragedy, but to enrich it.

23. H Barker, *Arguments for a Theatre* 3rd edn (Manchester, Manchester University Press, 1997), p 19

24. Auerbach had treated this term exhaustively in an earlier long essay under the same name, *Figura*; E Auerbach, *Figura* in *Scenes from the Drama of European Literature* (Manchester, Manchester University Press, 1984)

25. E Auerbach, *Mimesis: The Representation of Reality in Western Literature* 50th anniversary edn (Princeton and Oxford, Princeton University Press, 2003), p 49

26. In a marvellous moment of (self-) parody Barker has Hamlet observe sardonically: 'I think these people are not shocked […] It is so hard to shock them' (Barker, *Gertrude – The Cry*, p 14). He then focuses more on the skills and techniques of provocation: 'Or is shocking a career? / A vocation? / A profession worthy of the finest minds?' (p 15)

27. H Barker, *Und* in *Collected Plays vol 5* (London, Calder, 2001), pp 224, 225

28. R Barthes, *Camera Lucida* (London, Jonathan Cape, 1982), pp 26–7

29. F Nietzsche, *The Gay Science* (New York, Random / Vintage, 1974), pp 249–50

30. Here I am mainly drawing from recent titles of films and literature.

31. Psalm 22: 20

32. Examples include the end of Barker's poem, 'Mates of Wrath' (in *The Ascent of Monte Grappa*, London, Calder, 1991), 'But still I call my art / As a man whistles his lingering mongrel'; Gabriele's dogs in *12 Encounters with a Prodigy* (in *Collected Plays vol 5*, London, Calder, 2001), and Kisster's posing as one to be beaten; Leopold's pose in *The Europeans* (in *Collected Plays vol 3*, London, Calder, 1996); *Christ's Dog* (written 2004) and *A Living Dog* (written 2006). H Barker, *Found in the Ground* in *Collected Plays vol 5* (London, Calder, 2001)

33. Barker, *Gertrude – The Cry*, p 10

34. Barker, *Und*, p 224

35. *Ibid.*, pp 227–8

36. It is characteristic of this critical attitude that Lyn Gardner's review in the *Guardian* (25 October 2002) begins with this crass impression: '"Fuck me," cries Gertrude, offering up a knickerless crotch as Claudius pours poison into her sleeping husband's ear.'

37. Here, I think, Barker's own poetic title of his earlier tragic play *A Bite of the Night* constitutes the ideal description of the specific quality of his version of tragedy.

38. Judith Butler gives useful insights on this language dynamic in her book *Excitable Speech: A Politics of the Performative* (London and New York, Routledge, 1997).

39. Barker, *Gertrude – The Cry*, p 85

40. J L Austin's groundbreaking book *How to Do Things with Words* (Oxford, Oxford University Press, 1962) gave rise to a strong research interest in the performative aspect of language, developing recently into an actual theory of performativity with ample application in the study of literature and drama.

41. For an extensive discussion of a performative language of pain in Sophocles and in Artaud and some references to Barker see E Sakellaridou: 'Millennial Artaud: Rethinking Cruelty and Representation' in Z Detsi-Diamanti *et al.* (eds) *The Flesh Made Text Made Flesh: Bodies, Theories, Cultures in the Post-Millennial Era* (New York, Peter Lang, 2006 (forthcoming)).

42. H Barker, *Judith* in *Collected Plays vol 3* (London, Calder, 1996), p 265

43. Barker, *Gertrude – The Cry*, p 42

44. Barker, *Und*, p 236

45. *Ibid.*, pp 236–7

46. Interestingly it revived again, in an openly satirical form, in his subsequent play *13 Objects* (in *Plays Two*, London, Oberon, 2006), a collage of shorts, in which Barker reveals his artistic interest in objects by offering, in the mode of performance, a theatrical critique, a parody, of contemporary art industry and our culture's fascination with installation art. The role of the artist in society and a biting contempt for art mediators have been frequent themes in Barker's work.

47. One such gigantic Kouros statue (580BC), held in the archaeological museum of Samos, is of an estimated original height of 4.8m.

48. Approximate height 6.7m.

49. I am referring to his seminal play *A Bite of the Night*.

50. Claudius dramatically declares in *Gertrude*, 'Gertrude, it is god I'm fighting when I fight in you' (*Gertrude – The Cry*, p 44). Also the servant in *Judith* addresses the eponymous heroine as 'my divine' and 'goddess' (Barker, *Judith*, pp 257, 258).

'DEMOLITION NEEDS A DRAWING, TOO...'

Case Histories of The Lurking Truth Theatre Company's
Engagements with Barker

ROGER OWEN

I first encountered the work of Howard Barker in Aberystwyth in 1985, as part of what was intended to be a student production of *Victory: Choices in Reaction*, his play based in the aftermath of the English Civil War. This production eventually spawned the Lurking Truth Theatre Company, which has claimed two stage premieres of Barker's work, and whose efforts became the subject of a Barker poem, 'To the Aberystwyth Students' (published in the 1987 volume *Gary the Thief / Gary Upright*). Whilst this in itself might be cause for temperate (one might even suggest, private) rejoicing, this chapter reflects on the ways in which this production, and subsequent ones, influenced my thinking about Barker, and how the company – and I myself – attempted to make sense of the demands implicit in Barker's notion of a 'Theatre of Catastrophe', which was emerging during the early stages of the Lurking Truth's life as a company.

The Lurking Truth's first encounter with Barker's Theatre of Catastrophe came in 1986 with his play *Victory*, a production which might serve as an exemplar of Barker's assertions about the vexation caused by his theatrical style. It was originally intended that the play should be presented by a group of my fellow Welsh-speaking students at Aberystwyth, as a first attempt to create a settled ensemble group which would stage challenging work in Welsh and English. At the first read-through and discussion of the potential production of the play, however, a deep but lyrical silence overtook a number of the assembled company: this was a piece which, at the very best, was going to polarise the audience's response; at worst, it would incite outright hostility; or so they seemed to fear. Little wonder, then, that more than half of them did not present themselves at the next meeting, and, as far as *Victory*, Barker and challenging work in English and Welsh were concerned, were never seen again.

Before it even began rehearsal, then, the play had already forced a number of 'choices in reaction'. Here was proof of a dividing line – which I had never previously acknowledged – between those who were prepared to engage with a play's offence but still commit to it (and even study it),[1] and those who were not; those who felt Barker's theatre to be potentially inclusive, notwithstanding the inherent turmoil of its action, and those who (to use the current parlance) 'felt excluded by it'. Speaking later, a number of the 'deserters' affirmed their sense of the power or legitimacy of the events and language in *Victory*, but could not bring themselves to act as conduits for those experiences before a paying public.

Their failure of nerve was, to a certain extent, understandable: *Victory* was undoubtedly a difficult project for a young – and desperately green – company in the middle 1980s. It ran counter to some of the main imperatives of the theatre of that period (particularly the 'radical' or 'political' varieties), namely the tacit reaffirmation of the interrelatedness and continuity of social life and a rejection of the competitive ethics of Thatcherism. It rebuffed that theatre's wan utopianism and its increasing tendency to operate merely as a glib declaration of allegiances, and affirmed instead that theatre could be a completely different means of engaging with the world. Barker himself had given up on the utopian affirmative (or, as he described it, the 'Royal Court' style) and, by the time of *Victory*, was beginning to assert Catastrophe as the foundational moment of his theatre's experience and expression, in which all conventional signposts towards an 'approved' position relative to the work were removed. Thus, the play did not present itself as an amenable ally or tool in the imaginative struggle against Conservative ideology. Although it made many of the noises and gestures of heroic non-compliance, it certainly didn't favour my desire to possess or be associated with a narrative of resistance.

There was almost nothing in my sense of theatre which had prepared me for this. I, along with most of the others in that initial company, had been brought up in a Welsh-speaking culture which, outwardly, prized not only a collectivity of expression and aspiration, but also a certain docile social respectability. Being Welsh had almost always been a matter of 'doing things together'. The world of Barker's play, conversely, was individualistic, unapologetically combative and wholly unpredictable. By their actions, and their penchant for contradiction (or just contrariness), his characters refused commoditisation. They made themselves exceedingly difficult to 'buy into'. They could not be worn as badges of honour.

Back at square one, with the original brief torn up, the instigator of the project thus far, Richard Lynch, met David Ian Rabey, and the rest was, if not history, then anything but silence. The Lurking Truth Theatre Company / Cwmni'r Gwir sy'n Llechu was born. Events quickly acquired a momentum of their own: suddenly, the production was back on, meetings and auditions were being held. No one, it seemed, was being turned away.

No one was bottling out either. From having been intended as a close-knit community of Welsh actors, we were now an international company – Welsh, English, American, Luxemburgish (the Luxemburger, Eric Schneider, ended up playing the poet Milton – how, God only knows; but it was inspired casting. His astonishing otherness brought a necessary iconicism to the role, and I've never since been able to think of the author of *Paradise Lost* as anything other than an urbane yet Nietzschean middle European. Scrope's line, 'This is John Milton, you bitch,' has probably never since been required to perform quite the same explicatory function, either).

In the event, the production – at Aberystwyth's unheated and imminently defunct Barn Theatre, in February 1986, with the dramatist himself in attendance – was as much a test of the audience's resistance to hypothermia as it was of their appetite for an 'unapologetic intimacy with the forbidden',[2] as Barker later described his Theatre of Catastrophe. Whatever they gained by that production of *Victory*, it was for me the beginning of a full-scale theatrical (re)education, particularly in terms of attempting to comprehend the implications of Barker's Catastrophism. Whilst I understood – how could one fail to do so? – that he opposed the conventional morality and politics of the age, as well as many of the dominant traditions of dissent within contemporary English drama, it was some time before I – and, I believe, the Lurking Truth too – fully realised how transgressive of some of the normatively collective habits of contemporary theatre practice Barker himself was determined to be.

'The Lurkers', galvanised around Barker's work and celebrating their fearlessness in tackling such a beast of the stage, became a clique unto themselves. We were renegades, the fabulous Barker boys. I have no doubt that other companies at the time, and since, have similarly indulged themselves as result of their engagement with Barker's work. Beneath the froth of camaraderie and bravado, however, it was altogether a tough call to conflate the play's difficult knowledge with the sense of group solidarity produced by venturing to present it on stage. Though many of the Lurking Truth's members (myself included) desperately wanted to declare themselves Barker 'fans', or at least to be identified as such, Barker's work resisted adulation. What, after all, was one avowing? What exactly was one favouring? Having one's preconceptions shattered? Living in a condition of catastrophic refusal to conform, to submit? Barker's characters habitually operated beyond conventional narrative morality, and Barker dissociated himself from instruction:

> This is a theatre which abolishes debate, in which the play is a substitute for debate, and without obligation to notions of entertainment or enlightenment, neither 'delightful' nor

instructive, it resolves nothing – on the contrary, resolution is anathema: it is tragedy without catharsis, tragedy in which the audience is implicated in the acts of cruelty it witnesses, and from which there is no relief or refuge in the reiteration of the utilitarian concept of the public good.[3]

In 1986, to anyone looking for an affirmation of class solidarity, or an avowal of some form of social cohesion not already claimed by the Right, Barker's Catastrophism was a chilling abnegation. Its most memorable manifestation in *Victory*, for me, was the exchange between Bradshaw and Scrope, when, starving and dishevelled, they encounter some old republicans burying a gun in a field. Bradshaw takes advantage of them first of all by declaring who she is in order to excite their charity, and secondly by relieving one of them of his purse; Scrope, appalled by her betrayal of their former allies (but grateful nonetheless for the dinner thus acquired), turns on her:

> SCROPE: You must not injure people in their faith.
>
> BRADSHAW: Why not? What's so precious about faith? Why can't it take a kicking like anything else? I do them a favour. They get an education, and I get a wallet. Cheap at the price…
>
> SCROPE: A man may be beaten, and his wife violated, and his house burned, and his children murdered by his enemies, and yet stay whole. But to be so treated by his friends…you encourage madness.
>
> BRADSHAW: I DO KNOW THAT. Do you think I found it easy? It wasn't easy. But that's my triumph. Any man can rob his enemies. Where's the victory in that? [4]

The implications of Bradshaw's actions were not necessarily easy to interpret or to accept. Clearly, I sensed, they seemed to be an attack on the vacuousness of solidarity, a comment on the failure of the Left in contemporary British politics; but even the callow nineteen year old in me knew that successful dramatists did not tend to write convoluted and dense dramatic action if they wanted to say something so essentially simplistic.[5] Was Bradshaw's act, then, an image of the necessity of sacrifice in times of crisis? No doubt, but this would again be to reduce the action to a mere existentialist parable, a non-specific example of an extreme action at an extreme time, too imprecise a way of dealing with the specific nature of Bradshaw's theft. Was it an affirmation that conventional morality could not hold our impulses in check, and that this amoral truth was good no matter what the contentions of our peers? Well, it could be; but, distressingly, this would fail to distinguish – depending upon the impulse – between a radically conscientious challenge to the self and downright

Thatcherite economic opportunism. As Sartre might have put it, to make the world according to your own will is all very well and good, but there is always the question of bad faith. In Bradshaw's case, it seemed as if the question of bad faith either had no time to arise or was simply flung aside. This action did not exemplify any system of thought with which one could easily identify. For me, this scene left a scar on the play (and that in a drama where violation in one form or another was a constant motif). It seemed to be an act of outright hostility against its audience, utterly indifferent to the conventional need in contemporary theatre for a consensual act of moral contemplation. It refused to reassure me that my appreciation of its inherent poetic would eventually allow me that sense of moral ease so beloved of the young man in search of palatable certainties. It left me with nothing but a constant return to scour the action itself.

This was, of course, the point. But the effect was curious. Since there could be no safe or 'approved' point of view on the action of Barker's Theatre of Catastrophe, I felt there to be a great difficulty in describing it at all (without first blundering through wholly inappropriate tropes of conventional theatre practice) and in presenting a defence of it which did not either simply antagonise one's interlocutor (not always an undesirable prospect, of course) or else ape Barker's own critical tone, usually with a certain ineptitude of exposition in comparison to the real thing. During *Victory*, I soon realised, I was by dint of my education and temperament wedded to the kinds of expectations which Barker himself was later to criticise variously as preoccupations of the 'Humanist Theatre', 'Critical Theatre' or 'Theatre of Clarity'. To engage with Barker's work in a more meaningful way would require a quite different performative resolve.

In September 1986, the Lurking Truth rode again, this time with Barker's most recent full-length stage play, *The Castle* (and with Rabey's performance of *Don't Exaggerate* by way of overture). The circumstances of this production were different: this time, the University's Department of Drama offered us their (mercifully heated and fully rooved) Theatr y Castell; and we were *known*. We were the company that 'did Barker', and our general demeanour as an ensemble suggested that we wanted to be acknowledged as such. Unsurprisingly, a certain level of hostility thus arose between ourselves and other groupings within the Department – trivial enough in the grand scheme of things, but sufficient to make me aware that the virtue of our efforts would have to be energetically asserted, rigorously defended, and ultimately speak for themselves as well.

This was never going to be easy. *The Castle*, like *Victory*, was a profoundly uncompromising piece. And again, if anyone within the Lurking Truth sought refuge from their peers' disdain for the game of theatre-as-existential-combat, there was precious little shelter offered by the material of the play. *The Castle* was a more expansive piece than *Victory* (anticipating the reach of experience in later plays such as *The Bite of the Night*), a fact which intensified the audience's exposure to the calculated excess of the action. In simple terms of utilising the conventional range of emotion, rhetoric, sensation and shock, the first Act of *The Castle* could, in itself, be regarded as enough of a play to startle most audiences. Whilst the second Act obviously operated as a means of completing the narrative arc of the play as a whole, its more important theatrical function was to deepen, and then to explode, the potent anxiety implicit in the erection of Stucley's castle. It showed Barker's rapidly developing aptitude with the Catastrophic, particularly his insistence on digression as a necessary narrative technique, and the refutation of dramatic resolution.

I had been given the role of Batter, Stucley's servant; a character charged with enacting Stucley's wish to restore his demesne after seven years of woman rule. This gave me a perspective on the action which precluded much of the eroticism in the play, and thence one of its chief components of Catastrophe, namely the love-complex between Stucley, Ann, Krak and Skinner. As in *Victory*, one of the main devices in *The Castle* is an intense sexual attraction across a social and political boundary, in this case between Stucley's wife and his Arab prisoner (in *Victory*, it is between Bradshaw and the cavalier Ball); however, unlike the earlier play, there is no sense in *The Castle* in which that sexual attraction occupies a comic structure. In *Victory*, in spite of his copious brutality, Ball is presented as 'sonnet mad for Bradshaw',[6] a victim of his own involuntary priapism (and it is no coincidence that, once satisfied, he does not communicate with her until the very final scene, by which time his body has been broken and mutilated, and his tongue cut out). In *The Castle*, conversely, Ann's desire for Krak contains no inherent comedy, not even as a means of stimulating the dramatic shock value that it does in *Victory*. Rather, the whole affair creates intense pain: for Stucley, it is symptomatic of the loss of his power as a knight (in this respect, there is some parallel with Ball); for Skinner, it is a betrayal and – because of Krak's preoccupation with drawing cunt – an objectification of her love for Ann, which she asserts as synonymous with her own life; and for Krak, it exacerbates the rage and displacement of his condition as prisoner and enslaved genius. The audience sees the erotic pain of this complex as a phenomenon with almost boundless emotional, psychological and political consequences.

In the midst of this complex, and suffering a certain displacement of my own, I found Batter to be an extraordinary, forceful and personally liberating voice, and – shamefully, possibly – relished the licence which the role gave in terms of its physical violence and reactionary zeal for reconstruction. Playing Batter (especially after having previously played a series of quasi-Chekhovian defeatists with low personal status) was an exposure to an astonishing level of eloquence. This may be a rather ironic statement about Batter – he, after all, complains about his inability to comprehend Krak ('you bilingual fucker, you have more words in a foreign tongue than I have in English'[7]) – but here was my first experience of having to submit to the inherent dynamism of a text, and to let it sweep me to places which I had had no intention to visit, and frequently beyond. This was text beyond the will; and it changed my notion of acting completely. Psychologically, this liberation of a repressed verbosity in me was no doubt also precipitated by the simple fact that I remained anonymous throughout, playing the entire piece swathed in black leather and with a hood over my head. The socially adjusted part of my psyche was thus effectively inked out, and something more licentious and predatory revealed instead. In fact, I became a living embodiment of Barker's notion of theatre without conscience: 'Inside the black box [or, in my case, 'bag'] the imagination is wild and tragic and its criminality unfettered. The unspeakable is spoken.'[8]

The fusion of the sexual and the architectural in *The Castle* created a powerful sense of disturbance in the play, and, again, as in *Victory*, severely undermined any capacity to see the play as a programmatic political statement. Whereas the action presented obvious parallels to the arms race, and with what was known at that time as 'the terror gap' (between the sizes of the USSR's and USA's nuclear arsenals), it did not expand upon this issue, far less offer any 'useful' resolution to it. Indeed, the end of the play deepened the inherent antagonism between the remaining characters. Skinner is offered a demesne in ruins, overlooked by the Fortress, its previous ruler having been assassinated and its women consumed by mass suicide. Whether or not she accepts Batter's offer, the prospects for Stucley's former realm are not good – a grand terror, or a continuing paranoia. Krak's insistence that she take up the keys that she has previously discarded provides neither authority nor hope, for it is Krak's aptitude for architectonics which has helped to create the castle in the first place; and Skinner's contempt for his fixation with abstract design as a means of implementing his sense of beauty and the erotic is absolute:

> KRAK: Got to.
>
> SKINNER: Who says?
>
> KRAK: Got to!
>
> *Pause. She looks around.*
>
> SKINNER: Out the shadows, who thinks the only perfect circle is the cunt in birth…
>
> *KRAK emerges from a cleft in the wall.*
>
> KRAK: Demolition needs a drawing, too…[9]

Across this dispute, however, the sound of jets streaking low overhead punctures the action, providing a final digression rather than resolution. Here, as in *Victory*, was an extraordinary explosion of the conventions of historical playwriting, and a highly unnerving encounter between the actors and the audience. The turmoil of these plays' erotic imagination, the viscerality of their language and politics, and many characters' appallingly lucid engagement with the world, even at the risk of their own obliteration, was a step into the beyond for all of us and, I guessed, at the very furthest reach of our powers as performers. In both of these plays, there was little scope here to feel that one had discovered a secure home for one's ideas. Rather, the plays insisted upon alienating themselves from even their most ardent admirers. They cared nothing for the shape of the world as we knew it, and in the end could visit the criminality of their imagination on us too.

In October 1990, the Lurking Truth produced the stage premiere of Barker's radio play *The Early Hours of a Reviled Man*, once again at Theatr y Castell, Aberystwyth. As director of this production, I was attracted to the play by the dangerous ambiguity of the main character, Sleen. Based on the French writer and physician Louis-Ferdinand Céline, Sleen was an inveterate Catastrophist, a recalcitrant, pugnacious, anti-Semitic misanthrope who utterly refused to be silent and remorseful in the face of the overwhelming judgement of history upon him. However, Sleen's inherent Catastrophism notwithstanding, there were important distinctions between this piece and our earlier productions of Barker. This was a radio play, and had been written primarily as a soundscape; it was also less extreme in its violent and erotic content than previous Barker plays, and consequently it suggested a partial retreat from Catastrophism. It was another digression in a series of digressions within Barker's career.

Between *The Castle* and *Early Hours*, Barker had been seriously productive, not only as a dramatist and poet, but also as a theorist of the theatre. The first edition of his seminal *Arguments for a Theatre* had been published in 1989, and had done much to establish a critical discourse for his work. Tellingly, it also revealed some points of comparison between Barker himself and Sleen. For example, both were defiant in the face of the rejection of their work by the cultural authorities and scornful of its disregard by the approved narrators of literary history; and both were determined to remain 'difficult' writers from a moral and political standpoint. In *Arguments for a Theatre*, Barker had noted that his work had been consistently refused by the National Theatre, and had been viewed and treated with increasing unease by the Royal Court and the RSC: thus, he had been forced to pursue his career without any reliable endorsement by two of the most powerfully legitimated theatres in the country.[10] Of course, this rejection had hardly dealt a fatal blow to his career as a writer, but it was a clear snub to his work, and an assertion that it lay outside an 'approved' contemporary canon. Comparable to that of Sleen (and Céline), Barker's excision by some arbiters of public taste was not the end of the story, but the slight to his work was evident and deeply felt.

His response was characteristically theatrical and uncompromising – the monstrous Sleen, scratching his reviled work into life at dead of night; brutal in his most intimate relationships as well as in his conviction that the world was insufficient to the task of appreciating his genius; sentimental, self-aggrandising and self-pitying in his struggles against his detractors and the angel of history; and dishonourably, uncleanly loquacious in the face of his persecutors' righteous fury. Here was a kind of ironic Christ figure, pictured at several stations on his inadvertent journey (again, an ironic debasement of the sanctified will) towards his '...last experience of / Silence'.[11] To elevate his rejection to such a hyperbolic condition may or may not have been typical of Barker, but it would certainly be typical of Sleen, whose recourse to a self-fortifying mythology is revealed during the play, including his construction of a heroic structure for his own biography.

I sensed *Early Hours*, therefore, as a confrontation between the dramatist's bruised, necessarily arrogant and highly articulate ego and the ghosts of his interlocutors. Sleen was thus an avatar or projection of the ultimate authorial controller of the action, and hence – the spectacle being impossible without the cynosure – his pursuers had little hope of fulfilment in their conflict with him. Significantly, at the end of the play, Barker maps the destruction of Sleen onto the termination of the action itself: there is no image of Sleen's demise, but rather the cessation of his articulacy. Whoever within the dramatic action (if anyone) may be supposed to dispatch Sleen at the end of the play, it is still an authorial, narrative device, rather than a climactic act of retribution, which ultimately silences him.

This terminal silence is notable for its conflation of the author's intercession with the audience's final experience of the cityscape. Sleen is confronted by a presence which is announced (and in that respect, embodied) only by an inrush of sound from the outside, and thus it is the city itself which finally assaults him. On radio, the disembodiment of the action at this point strongly reinforces not only the dramatist's intervention to snuff out his protagonist but also the sense of the urban soundscape as an intrusion into and extension of the emotional conflicts of the play and the physical substance of the characters. Throughout the play, there has been an antipathy between the city as a civic space and Sleen as an ostracised trespasser, by which he acquires an iconic quality of separation from his environment. Thus – as noted earlier – one of the most appropriate scenographic styles for the play in stage production would seem to be the Stations of the

Cross, with Sleen as an ironicised, inadvertent and distinctly unbiddable Christ. As in the visual representations of Christ's progress to Crucifixion, the cityscape is suffused with a sense of the enactment of a higher will, a fact which restrains the journey from becoming a directionless picaresque, and provokes a sense of it as a continued passage towards destiny. Here, of course, that higher will is not that of God but of History; but the suggestion of a sentient city, impelling the action towards the restoration of moral order through the excision of the Chosen One, makes the urban landscape of *Early Hours* a very different proposition from Barker's more overtly Catastrophist cities, such as Troy in *The Bite of the Night* or Vienna in *The Europeans*.

Nonetheless, *The Early Hours of a Reviled Man* does maintain some important aspects of Barker's Catastrophist theatre style of the late 1980s and early 1990s. It could be argued, for example, that the city in *Early Hours* does have parallels with Troy in *The Bite of the Night*, in that it provides a continuous series of digressions, and that, far from being closely structured in the conventional sense, *Early Hours* is a play whose narrative is thrown off its axis, to career hither and thither to a highly ambiguous conclusion (which is presented as a digression from Sleen's concluding monologue). Sleen himself has certain affinities with more Catastrophic characters, such as Fladder in *The Bite of the Night*, who embodies a Catastrophic personal narrative in that play in one of its earliest scenes by appointing the volatile Savage as a judge and declaring himself guilty of a capital crime. Thus, the play plunges itself and its audience into the crisis of witnessing a leader who insists on his own self-abasement (even to the point of death), and a theatrical spectacle which refutes the traditional notion of a developing action by choosing to be excessive from the outset. Similarly, in *Early Hours*, Sleen accedes to his objectification as 'the reviled man' early in the play, rejoicing (albeit bitterly) in his status as a manifestation of excess and a refutation of history's urge to order. In that sense, although it deviates in terms of manner from the Theatre of Catastrophe, *Early Hours* is still, in essence, a spectacle built upon a profound theatrical disturbance, and cannot be viewed – or presented – from a point of moral certainty.

In 2001/02, the Lurking Truth returned to Barker with a co-production (with Íomhá Ildánach) of *The Twelfth Battle of Isonzo*. This production marked a coming of age for the Lurking Truth, in that it was directed by Barker himself, and in that it toured to several venues, mainly in Ireland. Barker's staging for the play set up the action as a quasi-Dadaist cabaret, complete with grotesque exordium as a prelude to the main action, in which the male protagonist traversed the back of the stage, reaching for two white sticks which floated in the air just out of his grasp, to accompaniments of distinctly unnatural effects of lighting and sound. The ensuing sparseness of visual effect on this stage and the extremity of the play's content – concerning the attempted consummation of a marriage between a blind seventeen year-old girl, Tenna, and an allegedly blind and 'very old' man, Isonzo – created a theatrical environment which was considerably more compact than such Catastrophist works as *The Castle*, *The Bite of the Night* and *The Europeans*. Where they used violence, intense eroticism and a general sense of historical tumult (of living in ruinously 'interesting times') as a means of explosively projecting the dramatic action out of its narrative containment, *Isonzo* never created a sense of a completed, insulated dramatic world. The stage was set for a ritual act, not for the dramatic proposition and depiction of action in some other place.

In that sense, the play has parallels with a number of other liminal combats, such as that in Sam Shepard's *The Tooth of Crime*. However, the most informative counterpoint to the play and production seemed to me to be provided by the work of Samuel Beckett. There are obvious visual similarities, for instance, between Isonzo and Hamm in *Endgame* – both are presented as blind and restricted in terms of their mobility (Isonzo by his apparent old age and Hamm by the fact that he is paralysed). But the treatment of the degenerated physical is quite different in both cases. In Beckett, it is congruent with his emphasis on the traditional Cartesian notion of dualism, whereby the characters' minds remain (sometimes almost distressingly) active in spite of the body's confinement or inertia. Indeed, on occasion, his characters appear to have no knowledge or heed of their constraint – as in *Play*, where they appear as heads confined within urns, or as with Nagg and Nell in *Endgame*, who are incarcerated in dustbins. Conversely, in Barker's play, Isonzo's physical degeneration is acknowledged and attracts comment from the outset: Tenna's first speech opens with a declaration of her impending marriage to a 'very old' man, and a defence of the allure of the old against the 'nauseating strategies / Evasions / Refuges' of the young.[12] Isonzo's first entrance confirms the image of decrepitude which Tenna has created, but this physical manifestation of the inappropriate object of desire is accompanied by Isonzo's bold assertion of his beauty as 'Infinite', which draws Tenna's admiring affirmation.

The refutation of aesthetic convention, implicit in the discord between the image of physical decomposition and the affirmation of its beauty and desirability, has been foreshadowed by the youthful Tenna's previous description of herself as 'a winter of anticipation',[13] which suggests a Beckettian complementarity between the two characters. But the proposal of the two as symbiotic opposites does not persist; rather, it becomes strained by the persistently active tension of sexuality at play, and this provides a significant counterpoint between *Isonzo* and the work of Beckett. In Beckett, where there is no such sexual tension, the plays tend to dissolve notions of dramatic space and time, with a uniformity or complementary coupling of characters and a generally static dramatic scenario which gradually strips them of a distinctive individuality. They become enclosed within the cyclical dynamics of their situation. Conversely, Isonzo and Tenna's mating dance resists its enclosure, existing instead as a constantly arrested yet energetic performance which accomplishes the creation of temporary and ever-uncertain bridges between the characters' respective desires and their expression through language. The play's abiding dramatic tension occurs as they constantly tear down these bridges, through subterfuge, deceit, denial and delay. *Isonzo* forces a confrontation with the risks implicit in the demand that language encompass and properly articulate the nature of the physical.

Isonzo was also markedly different from Barker's earlier Catastrophist plays in terms of its scenography. In those plays, the characters' scenic presence is highly volatile, in that their actions often explode the parameters of the drama, through outrage, pain or the overt articulation of desire. As an audience we are forced to imagine that it may be *possible* to think and feel like this, and, moreover, to recognise that we *do* feel and think with all the unlicensed criminality of Barker's characters, without generally acknowledging the fact. In *Isonzo*, however, there is no such extrapolation from the action on stage to an implicit 'real world'. In Barker's production, the setting created a visual sense in which the characters were (to some extent because of their relative stasis) part of the scenography, growing into the stage rather than being projected out to the audience. Consequently, the action was not tied to any social milieu, and existed on the theatre stage rather than in an analogous dramatic location. The sense of space thus created was very fluid, and its reference to places within the dialogue (such as the department store, where Tenna purchases her underwear) operated as an overtly poetic effect rather than as a 'locating' device.

In addition to this resistance to dramatic location, there was a significant emphasis within the production on a discontinuity of action. The use of sound and lighting effects often disproportionately stressed the impact of certain moments, such as Tenna's gasps of anticipation, and Isonzo's discarding of his sticks. The sounds here were amplified and stood out from the continuity of the action and of the narrative. They were moments apart, and the production carried within it a sense that any subsequent moment could be equally removed from a general continuity. This was also true of the actors' mainly slow, steady declamation of the text (again a prevalent Beckettian device), which created a rhythmic anticipation of the completion of the meaning of the next phrase or sentence – a constant dynamic of attempted consummation within the theatrical action which also made manifest the principal dramatic tension. Here the theatrical dynamic of delay and deflection became the medium for the relationship between Tenna and Isonzo.

In many ways, the pervasiveness of *Isonzo*'s soundscape was redolent of that of *Early Hours*, and emphasised a number of links with that play which suggests its prescience as an indicator of later developments in Barker's theatrical style. As noted earlier, in *Early Hours* Sleen was in conflict not only with his pursuers but with the city itself, an environment in which space and sound were conflated. The same kind of conflation was in evidence in *Isonzo*, where the sound effects displaced the action and suggested (in the case of Tenna's initial gasps, for example) a cavernous, impossible interior space on a different plane of hearing. Isonzo himself could also be seen as a shadow of Sleen – an aged, duplicitous figure at the heart of a play which described an indefinitely delayed consummation: in Isonzo's case, sexual intercourse; in Sleen's case, death.

The putative link between these two characters, separated by over ten years and by different dramatic media (radio and stage), points the difficulty of tracing a critical line through Barker's output in any kind of chronological sense. There are conversations, other than those which might be identified as sequentially progressive, between the dramatist, his medium and his audience, and his plays do not always suggest the development of an artistic vision – often, indeed, there is a sense of Catastrophist digression, rearticulation and refutation about his work as a whole. In that sense, and as noted earlier, the problem posed by Barker's Catastrophist theatre, and the development of/from it in plays such as *Early Hours* and *Isonzo*, is not, I believe, with accepting the content of the work; the notion that they ought to be presented to the public as shocking or 'difficult' in terms of content is a gross distortion of the plays themselves and of the public's appetite for representations of transgression. Rather it is that the plays pose deeper problems in terms of their challenges to contextualisation; and the attempt to describe and distil them for the purposes of critical comparison, or to describe them as phenomena in the public domain, so often wrecks any sense of the experience that they present to an audience. One is left – as I was in the face of Bradshaw's astonishing theft in *Victory* – with nothing but a constant return to scour the action; and thus it is, perhaps, only in production that one can genuinely encounter these plays' inherent dynamic of digression, refutation and moral demolition.

NOTES

1. See H Barker, 'Radical Elitism in the Theatre' in *Arguments for a Theatre* 3rd edn (Manchester: Manchester University Press, 1997), p 35: 'A public has emerged for my theatre which does not appear to suffer offence in the way its guardians do, or more precisely, it is prepared to study its offence.'

2. *Ibid.*, p 123

3. *Ibid.*, p 120

4. H Barker, *Victory* in *Collected Plays vol 1* (London, Calder, 1990), p 161

5. See also H Barker, 'Theatre Without a Conscience' in *Arguments for a Theatre*, p 75. There, he criticises a production which 'humiliated the text by using it as a means to an end, a starting point for the endless curse of debating things, wrecked the invention of [its] actors, turning them into mere didactic instruments, and liquidated any possibility in the audience that their structure of feeling and thought could be inflamed by what they had witnessed – [it] reduced the non-cerebral event of a play into a pack of arguments'.

6. Barker, *Victory*, p 176

7. H Barker, *The Castle* in *Collected Plays vol 1* (London, Calder, 1990), p 216

8. H Barker, 'Theatre Without a Conscience' in *Arguments for a Theatre*, p 78

9. Barker, *The Castle*, pp 248–9

10. See the essay 'Radical Elitism in the Theatre' in *Arguments for a Theatre*, p 34

11. H Barker, *The Early Hours of a Reviled Man* (stage production 1990, unpublished)

12. H Barker, *The Twelfth Battle of Isonzo* in *Collected Plays vol 5* (London, Calder, 2001), p 241

13. *Ibid.*, p 242

THE BODY TURNED INSIDE OUT

Sight, Insight and the Senses in *He Stumbled*

CHRISTINE KIEHL

SUBVERSION ECLIPSED BY DISCOMFORT

After hacking Helen's body in *The Bite of the Night*, chopping Holofernes's head in *Judith*, beheading a dozen virgins in *Ursula*, eating up Lvov's body in *The Last Supper*, the Theatre of Catastrophe bursts open the carnal frame of the body in *He Stumbled*. The play invades the spectator's intimacy by transgressing the primitive taboos of sex and death: the performance of anatomy is seasoned with acts of copulation next to the dead body.

And yet the dramatic treatment of abjection and intimacy in *He Stumbled* deceives the audience's voyeuristic instincts: it seems the spectators are made to stumble over their atavistic visual perspective sustained by centuries of Cartesian enlightened 'in-sight'. The obscure intrigue and complex argument elude obvious meaning as if the play resisted the current tyranny of transparency. If the themes of sex and death propose the body as a tragic hero in the play, the performance challenges blunt voyeurism. The display of the body in *He Stumbled* shifts from abject imposture to a tragic posture guaranteeing a new audience-stage relation, from visual representation to visual imagination. The appeal to physical perceptions other than the visual induces an imaginary and sensuous vertigo verging on a poetical Sublime.

Howard Barker claims, '*He Stumbled* is a most subversive play because it goes against science and stands up against science.'[1] To understand this claim for a play of harrowing uneasiness, it is useful to redefine the concept of subversion in our society numbed by media sensationalism. Subversion questions the values and principles of a given system by turning them upside down. Does it still make sense in drama today? Since the 1990s, so-called 'In-Yer-Face' dramatists have relied on predominantly naturalistic images of extreme violence, voyeuristic in their claim to make the private scene public. This 'New Brutalism', which defines itself as subversive, has paradoxically wiped out subversion by entering the mainstream theatre market. The visual shock effects of sex and violence rival those dispensed by the television and film industry. Subversion no longer meets its target: instead of urging the audience to think, 'In-Yer-Face' theatre may nourish voyeuristic compulsion and consumption. Against this dubious complicity with an economic market crushing man's free will, Barker offers an alternative form of drama that redefines subversion: a theatrical event which causes unpredictable and unspeakable unease, compelling reflection after the performance. The Theatre of Catastrophe provocatively aligns itself with a radical elitism in its uncompromising rejection of opportunistic naturalism – 'Tragedy resists the trivialization of experience' – and shunning of delusional clarity and meaning:

> People will endure anything for a grain of truth.
> But not all People. Therefore a tragic theatre will be elitist.[2]

'New Neo-Jacobean drama' [3] frequently involves images of the taboo, and lurid scenes of violence and sexuality may have become conventional hallmarks rather than something deeply shocking. What, then, is the nature of the persistent discomfort prompted by *He Stumbled*? Jerzy Klesyk, a noted director of Barker plays, has found as yet no support from French theatres to stage the play. Producers dither not so much over explicit imagery as over the play's evasion of 'signification' amidst rhetorical lushness.[4] The meaning refused by Barker for his drama is that of morally secure answers: his plays are not meant to be an ethical scrutinising of cruelty or transgression. Barker's tragedies subvert the form of Classical and Elizabethan tragedies ('Traditional tragedy was a restatement of public morality over the corpse of the transgressing protagonist'): exit the father-figure of morality allowing safe purgation from crime and guilt. The Theatre of Catastrophe has no ethical project but 'the suspension of moral predictability': 'My plays do not operate as models of behaviour, recommendations or exhortations'.[5]

He Stumbled resists both conventional catharsis and 'In-Yer-Face' sensationalism. It proposes intimacy as the ultimate sphere of political resistance, against the consensual consumerism of violence and flesh. A live performance with flesh-and-blood actors cannot compete with the filmed horror produced – co-produced – by TV news broadcast and snuff movies. The Theatre of Catastrophe rejects the inflationary tactic, as it is pointless to heap violence on violence: reduplicating subversion makes it impotent. Barker's project is to wake the audience up from the merchandising of passivity sustained by the media and film industry. Conversely he avoids resorting to shock effects such as Edward Bond's 'aggro-effect',[6] which urge the audience to look for answers *inside* the play. Barker urges the audience to construct their own meaning for the play after the performance, as no answers are provided inside the play itself. Barker's drama makes the audience less reactive than creative.

The focus on anatomy in *He Stumbled* is not a pretext to stake a scientific claim to ontological truth. The opening of the body is a metaphor for the exploration of intimacy – an intimacy threatened by today's tyranny of transparency.

ANATOMY AS A 'BREAKTHROUGH' IN THE VISION OF THE BODY

The dissection of the body in *He Stumbled* is performed as a dramatic parody of the scientific and religious crisis that marked Early Modern Europe: the rise of anatomy introduced by Andreas Vesalius (1514–64) in the 16th Century [7] and the religious alarm caused by the exploration of a corpse's insides. The main action is set in a castle hall turned into an 'operating theatre', where 'The organs are sealed in their caskets […] rapidly acquiring those aspects of religiosity with which all relics are endowed'.[8] *He Stumbled* provides a carnival version of the historical breakthrough of anatomy as recorded:

> [Historian] Piero Camporesi evokes quite humorously the meticulous carving up of Nun Chiara de Monfalco who died in the odour of sanctity in 1308 at the Augustinian Convent. The various viscera were carefully placed in an earthenware jar and the heart was set apart.[9]

Although the play deftly juggles with anachronisms, it implicitly anchors the main action in a Renaissance atmosphere tainted with Middle-Age obscurantism. It parodies the ritualistic removal of a king's organs to be sent as relics to the holy sites of Christianity:

> BALDWIN: The lungs are going to Jerusalem…!
> […]
> No, the lungs are staying, it's the brain that must be going to Arabia…
> […]
> And label everything…! Because how silly if how idiotic and infuriating if the organ
> […] should on arrival be discovered to have accidentally been exchanged the lungs in
> Lapland and the brain in Ireland for example.[…] (pp 259–60)

Doja's parody of ceremonious dissection recalls Rembrandt's paintings of anatomy's début; his well-known 1656 portrait shows a beautiful young man lying on the anatomy table, gazing under his own chest at the large cavity where the viscera have been removed.[10] This famous reference suggests that the play owes not so much to historical truth as to the artistic recreation of history. The staging of anatomy in *He Stumbled*, positioning Doja and his assistants Pin and Suede in relation to spectators Baldwin and Turner, burlesques graphic dissection scenes such as those depicted in *Chirurgica Magna* (1363) by Guy de Chauliac, a most eminent surgeon in Early Modern Europe:

> The magister stands beside the table where the corpse rests, reading aloud from the consecrated text [Galien's work] held in his left hand whilst pointing at the organs with his right hand. Two kinds of barbers are to be seen: the cutting up of the body devolves onto the illiterate and the extracting of the organs is the privilege of the more literate. Several church dignitaries are present: a nun and a priest are praying as anatomical surgery is performed under the aegis of the Church.[11]

Doja's ostentatious aping of ritual gestures (he *'lifts out the heart and suspends it in the manner of a priest raising the host. It leaks blood'*, p 259), together with his profane Latin designating the various organs, humorously subverts the historical scene.

The question of anatomy, and the association with holy relics, brings us back to the ontological crisis which altered the perception man had of his body in Early Modern Europe. With his mechanistic vision of the body, Vesalius introduced the concept of 'the body' as isolated and distinguished from man:

> Breaking the body to pieces is a way of destroying human integrity: […] the body, studied as itself and for itself, is dissociated from man. […] From Vesalius to Descartes, from *De Humani Corporis Fabrica* to *The Discourse of the Method*, the body has been purified from any reference to nature and to the previous man he embodied.[12]

The modern man appeared between the sixteenth and seventeenth century, a man cut off from his own self, from the others, from cosmos. The dialogue between Doja and the king's son Baldwin opposes the anatomist's dualistic vision of body and soul to the Prince's sense of the body as undistinguished from the self:

> BALDWIN: What's that…?
> *The ASSISTANTS look at one another.*
> On the table what is it…

DOJA: It is the degenerate and spoiling prison of a dead man's soul… […] But I must
cut him all the same… […] And you must watch without exclaiming…

BALDWIN: I will I said so didn't I…

DOJA: The flesh is not the man… […]

BALDWIN: Stop…! […] The flesh is not the man…?

He looks at DOJA.

The flesh is not the man…? What is the flesh then? Is the flesh not this man's and no
other's? If the flesh is not the man, why are you here? (pp 256–7)

The Church contemplated the relics removed from Saints as a metonymy of the mystical
body. When the first anatomists searched the insides of the human body, they considered
it as separate from the subject that lived in it. Both Christian and Cartesian ethics stem in
their own ways from Plato's dualistic vision opposing the body to the soul and/or the mind.
French philosopher Merleau-Ponty challenges this view by arguing for the inseparability
of subjectivity, the body and the world.[13] *He Stumbled* provides a similar perspective.

CARTESIAN INSIGHT REVISITED

He Stumbled rejects the view of the body as a symbol for God. In Barker's *The Last Supper*,
the Eucharist is comically subverted into the literal absorption of a guru's body. Conversely,
He Stumbled does not celebrate the body as a material object; the play contemplates the
body as the substance of the self. Touching the flesh means touching the self, its senses and
sensibility. If the play does not make a case against anatomy, neither does it celebrate it:
anatomy *is not* the central issue in *He Stumbled*. The question of anatomy is subverted into
a dramatic speculation on the *modern* perspective of man introduced in the Renaissance,
which 'opposes the body to the subject himself'. Ever since Vesalius and Descartes the
body has been considered as 'an alter ego, a kit, a sum of parts potentially detachable and
at the free disposal of the individual':

> In contemporary scientific discourse the body is considered as indifferent matter, a mere
> prop for the person. Ontologically distinguished from the subject, the body has become an
> object to be handled and improved, a raw material in which personal identity is dissolved.
> Estranged from the man it embodies as an object, the body is emptied not only of symbolical
> character but also of any value.[14]

The play questions the mechanistic perspective still in force today in a world ruled over by the dictate of sciences threatening man's *integrity*, particularly through the presumption that 'In today's world, the body no longer incarnates the subject…the body is a construction, a transient object to be manipulated'.[15] With the advent of 'post-humanity',[16] the manipulation of man's body – from aesthetic surgery to genetic treatment and the commerce of organs – is a scientific ethos which reinforces the cult of transparency. Society promotes the belief that truth is unveiled when the body is publicly exposed. This ruling principle is ethically worrying as it endorses the political claim to the transparency of man's mind. Therefore, beyond exhibition, intimacy takes on a political dimension in Barker's plays. *He Stumbled* tackles the scientific disruption of man's integrity – his unity as both a body and a subject. The ethical distrust of science is in keeping with Merleau-Ponty's reflection on the body: 'Science has encouraged us to contemplate the body as an assembly of parts and experience its disintegration in death.' [17]

He Stumbled is like an odyssey of the modern man searching his lost 'integrity' out of the wreckage of his physical and hence mental disintegration; 'integrity' is to be taken literally as wholeness and completion in a body alive to its perceptions. Doja's autopsy of the king is the initial catastrophe that sets in chaos the perceptions that relate him to himself, to others and to the outside world, by rupturing the bond between man and his body. *He Stumbled* probes intimacy as the obscure site of man's complexity, the mystery of his emotions which resist rationalisation. Dissection is a catastrophic act causing disruptive chaos among the characters compelled to reinvent themselves on the corpse of dead values. Catastrophe urges them to make unexpected decisions. Barker:

> […] Decision being the key to tragedy […], for the word 'decision' means literally 'to cut', and cutting ends one life and compels the individual to reach for another'.[18]

Dissection in *He Stumbled* is a metaphor explored literally to 'speculate' on the landscape of the body, of man's humours, his desires and passions. 'Speculation' in Barker's theatre means probing the aftermath of catastrophe. Here, anatomy is not the central issue but its 'introduction'. The play depicts the entering of the flesh to scrutinise the emotional havoc of the protagonists as onlookers of the dissection. In other words the audience's interest is deftly diverted from the autopsy scene to that of the characters' intimacy.

BEYOND TRANSPARENCY: INTIMACY LAID BARE

In *He Stumbled*, a celebrated anatomist is performing his last autopsy before the bewildered gaze of the dead king's son. The prince goes mad at the sight of his father's opened corpse and takes revenge on both the anatomist and his treacherous mother by urging them to make love next to the corpse before ordering Doja's death.

Baldwin responds to Doja's manipulation of his father's insides by manipulating him in return. He urges Doja to put his hands onto his mother's body before his very eyes ('BALDWIN: I witnessed one, why not the other…? […] TRESPASS AND BE DAMNED…', p 274). The dissection of the body is the initial scene, which launches a second scene: that of squirming sex. The plot against Doja and Turner turns into a three-act initiation rite for Baldwin. The prince first responds to the autopsy of the king as a trespassing on his own self. By laying his father's insides bare ('You put your hands into my father, Mr Doja', p 274), Doja not only infringes the limits of the self ('This man has turned my father inside out', p 259), he violates the vital organs that engendered Baldwin's life. The transgressing dissection is a catastrophic rupture, which operates as a symbolic rebirth for Baldwin via the abject spectacle of combined death and sex.

The Prince is drawn to a harrowing site of abjection where the repellent sight of bodily fluids commands morbid sexual attraction. Doja is the central focus of an Oedipal triangle reminiscent of *Hamlet* as he embodies a father-figure in two respects: first as the Master of anatomy performing for Baldwin the symbolical murder of his father, and second as the usurper of the father's part in the sexual act with the mother. The prince's passion for Doja is an intricate mixture of hatred and love:

> BALDWIN: Oh Mr Doja everything conspires to make me intimate with you
> […]
> It's me you love
> […]
> BALDWIN *flings himself on* DOJA *and drags the sheet with him.*
> Kiss, I said […] (pp 274, 290)

The second act in Baldwin's initiation is the spectacle of his mother's sexual union with his father's 'butcher'. The confusion between sex and death is complete: by watching both his father's organic insides (in death) and his mother's intimacy (in sex), Baldwin satisfies a morbid desire to return to the womb. Julia Kristeva analysed the paradoxical character of abjection as a combination of organic decay and sexual drive stimulating contrary attraction and repulsion:

> The interior of the body makes up for the breaking-down of the boundary between the inside and the outside – as if the skin was a frail container no longer guaranteeing the integrity of what is 'proper'. Once flayed or transparent, invisible or taut, the skin yields to the evacuation of the contents. Urine, blood, sperm, excrement comfort the lack of what is 'proper'. The abject fluids spilling out from inside the body suddenly become the sole 'object' of sexual desire – an absolute 'abject' – where man, out of fear, penetrates the mother's dreadful womb [...]. But this immersion also gives man an almighty power, that of owning – if not being – the wrong object which inhabits the maternal body. Abjection is then seen to play the part of the other, arousing sexual pleasure [...] [19]

The sight of his mother's ecstasy is unbearable for Baldwin, literally seen to stumble when watching her physical union with Doja:

> *TURNER kisses [DOJA]... BALDWIN is a miracle of balance for the second time, a picture of curiosity and repulsion, in which by degrees, the repulsion triumphs until he throws himself from the stool, and, close to suffocation, runs offstage* (p 275)

Baldwin's turmoil illustrates Kristeva's description of the painful rupture of the self when confronted with abjection:

> Abjection causes a violent and obscure upsurge of the whole being against some threat originating from an overwhelming outside or inside [...]. Fright urges him to turn his back, disgust makes him reject. [...]A being haunted by abjection is literally thrown off balance by a pole of attraction and repulsion.[20]

The sight of his father's death is conjugated to the fantasised re-enactment of Baldwin's conception: that death (including the small death of orgasm) should breed life is a climactic epiphany for the prince, hence his fear of change: 'I dread maturity / The nakedness of things will scald my soul' (p 273).

The third stage in the prince's initiation to maturity tests the character's visual powers; Baldwin claims 'When I come near people they undergo some change, some mineral disintegration, colour, structure, odour, a puddle underneath my gaze' (p 280). In this premature claim of kingly charisma, Baldwin competes with Doja's rational insight as the skilled Master keeping the 'most clinical and frozen distances between [him] self and the material remains of the –' (p 292). Baldwin's tragic flaw consists in believing he can watch the forbidden sexual scene with similar scientific detachment, overlooking the emotional turmoil caused by the taboo spectacle. The distance of intellectual insight is at variance with the painful immediacy of intimacy made public:

> BALDWIN: Oh, melancholy
>> Intuitive to an inordinate degree
>> My skin
>> So thin
>> […]
>> And vision
>> Vision, oh
>> My sight is such agony to me I could court blindness for a day's relief from this
>> PITIFUL TRANSPARENCY OF OTHERS (p 273)

Baldwin has his eyes opened to the supremacy of the senses over intellectual insight. Baldwin has inflicted on himself the 'obscene' spectacle of abjection ('obscene' in the etymological sense of 'ob-scene, 'offstage', beyond the visible). Baldwin's ritual of initiation sees the emergence of his subjectivity – the truth of the self – as rooted in his physical perceptions unleashed by a visual experience:

> Consciousness, manifest as an act of self-conception – idea (from *idein*, 'to see') – begins in the act of visual perception. Eye becomes 'I', the self perched at the edge of the body.[21]

Both Doja and Turner go through similar rites of passage involving a new definition of sight. Doja is diverted from the scientific observation of the corpse to the revelation of his emotional senses in sexual encounter: 'Violation might be…the doorway to a different liberty…' (p 274). His erotic union with Turner turns him away from the rational control of the intellect and the illusory supremacy of intellectual insight. Doja – who has performed the dissection in cold blood – loses his head in a passionate embrace which ushers him to a sensorial experience so far inhibited by analytical distance. The 'penetrating gaze' of intellectual insight dissolves in the desire to penetrate Turner's flesh. An upsurge of humours and perceptions draws Doja to the queen's odour reminiscent of organic death:

DOJA: Her skin…

[…]

I can only describe it as possessing the identical extreme of fecundity and death
associated with…[…]

Compost…

Manure…

Ordure…

[…]

Intoxicating…

Nauseating (pp 289–90)

Turner's naked body ('a football field of fornication / […] A sodden quarry of copulation')
thrusts Doja into the site of conjoint abjection and ecstasy. 'Can't look at her – but looking
is love' (p 308) is the Faustian knowledge granted Doja. Doja's falling in love with the
Queen parallels Baldwin's death and rebirth as a new self.

Beyond the moral humanism of Shakespearean tragedy and against the reductive
psychological rooting of the Freudian heritage, *He Stumbled* revives the organic and
visceral man of the Renaissance. The play is a flesh and blood opera inventing its own
'theory of humours' in the line of Robert Burton's *Anatomy of Melancholy*. Turner is the
central figure of subversion 'returning' Doja to his senses – that is, to his live body. She
subverts his blindness to flesh into a compelling commitment to ecstasy, which alters her
own perceptions in return: 'EVERYTHING THAT OCCURRED WAS NOVEL TO ME / […] I WAS
A STRANGER TO MYSELF' (p 284). Intimacy stands as the last recess of man's freedom to
invent himself.

BEYOND EXHIBITIONISM: THE REFLEXIVE DISTANCE

If the protection of man's secrecy against audio-visual exhibitionism is a vital cause, intimacy
remains the ultimate sphere of resistance. The dramatic representation of intimacy is a
political project in Barker's drama: it reveals without necessarily showing it all. How can
the performance transgress the limits of the body whilst resisting voyeurism?

In a voyeuristic situation the spectator co-operates in a manipulation game whose
rules are foreseeable, leaving him safe in spite of a conspicuous absence of distance. In
He Stumbled, 'reflexive' distance is guaranteed within the dramatic situation itself: the
audience watch characters watching a forbidden scene. 'Reflection' both designates the

mirror-image sent back to the audience and the activity of the mind – the latter continuing beyond the end of the play. Indeed, the lush complexity of the text, the relentless rhythm of almost surreal action and the agonising pain of the protagonists allow no time or space for intellectual reflection. The audience is given a rough handling, diverted as it is from safe mimesis to the unguarded exploration of human passion. Voyeurism is subverted into discomfort. The exordium which the text specifies to open the play combines excruciating abjection with pantomimed copulation. The spectator's libidinous desire to SEE is excited but voyeurism is repeatedly diverted: the scenes of abjection and ecstasy lashed at the protagonists' gaze remain partially concealed from the audience, converting voyeuristic consumption into creative imagination. In the Wrestling School production of *He Stumbled* (2000), the corpse was not materially visible on the anatomy table, the edges of which helped to conceal the imaginary body from our sight so that it existed entirely in the audience's mind. The organs taken out of the body came already sealed in plastic bags: hyper-realistic imitation was averted and visual expectation is ironically deceived. In the same vein, the erotic scenes remain suggestive:

> *He unhitches her dress... her breasts are exposed...* […] TURNER *kisses him* […] *The light fades on the scene'* (p 275)

> DOJA *sinks to the floor with* TURNER *in his embrace. He takes her from behind in a faltering light* […] (p 305)

Sight is sublimated into imagination. Instead of satisfying the spectator's visual craving to penetrate the forbidden obscene, the performance conjures up his desire to fantasise it: The protagonists' powerfully organic speech is highly suggestive, drawing the audience from the visual to the perceptive. The characters' sensorial ordeal is an intimate, irrational experience whose only true expression is the chaotic rhetoric of emotions. The lush spilling out of carnal language invades the spectator's intimacy. The play humorously hinges on a strong 'sense of humour' evincing both an uneasy whiff of abjection and the playful distance of acting all this. The language of the senses makes more sense than 'sensible' language, a perspective close to Merleau-Ponty's reversal of the Cartesian and Platonic intellectual traditions 'in which the intellect is dissociated from the senses and where the intellect reigns supreme over the senses which are hence devalued'.[22]

He Stumbled explores the consequences of man's alienation from himself, from his body as the substance of his senses, his 'sense', his essence. The essential and meaningful relation of man to himself and the outside world is achieved through the body, as Merleau-

Ponty has suggested, but our modern world has reduced the body to a tool, a disposable prop severed from man as a subject. *He Stumbled* is a dramatic reflection on the tragic chaos which results from the divorce between the body and the self, the flesh and the mind, the flesh and the soul. The structure of the play deftly handles the visual perspective so as to hold the audience breathless. For instance when suggestion is preferred to blatant exhibition, the audience is not given the time to fantasise at leisure: the roused desire is interrupted by a brutal juxtaposition of fragmentary scenes which rush the audience into the next dramatic act. No comfort is allowed in the overall dislocated structure which thwarts expectation. However, the deception of voyeuristic desire is not dramatised systematically – in which case the audience would understand it as a predictable governing principle and remain emotionally unconcerned. The scene of Doja's coercing Turner into drinking the bodily fluids of her late husband is as unexpected as harrowing:

> DOJA: (*He forces her head steeply back.*)
> [...] Drink your husband [...]
> *He continues to grip* TURNER *with one hand, and with the other lifts a beaker of fluid from the anatomy table to* TURNER's *lips... A long pause...*
> DRINK
> DRINK
> *She gulps the fluid...*
> DRINK
> *The sound of her swallowing. She drains the beaker. It falls to the floor.* DOJA *sinks to the floor with* TURNER *in his embrace. He takes her from behind in a faltering light as the dead priests whisper...* (pp 304–5)

The precise choreography leads to climactic obscenity in the combination of brutality, abjection, and love. This highly visual scene exhibits the primitive taboos previously tackled: sex, death, and food – food being a substantial paradigm in the play. At this point, a powerfully visual spectacle makes sense.

He Stumbled does not reject voyeurism but opposes its economic merchandising sustaining benumbed passivity. And logically enough, the play remains open-ended on the issue. Tortmann's spectral appearance – a subverted figure of the slain commander in Mozart's *Don Juan* (Doja?) – makes a final ambiguous pronouncement, supporting voyeurism as both ecstasy and reflexive distance:

TORTMANN: An obsession… What's an obsession, Mr Doja…but a privilege…? […]

because I was a king my ecstasy has been…extraordinary… […]

I kept my distance…oh, distance Mr Doja, distance is everything…to know…to

see…what's that but sordid witnessing… (p 314)

NOTES

(*I have translated the quotations from French myself.*)

1. Interview with Howard Barker, Brighton, November 2004

2. H Barker, *Arguments for a Theatre* 3rd edn (Manchester, Manchester University Press, 1997), p 18

3. The labels 'New Neo-Jacobean drama' and 'New Brutalism' were dropped in favour of 'In-Yer-Face Drama' (see A Sierz, *In-Yer-Face Theatre: British Drama Today* (London, Faber, 2001)

4. Interview with Jerzy Klesyk, stage director, Paris, 11 July 2005

5. Barker, *Arguments for a Theatre*, pp 58, 203

6. 'Aggro-effect': expression coined by Edward Bond in 1979 for shock tactics: 'Shock is justified by the desperation of the situation or as a way of forcing the audience to search for reasons in the rest of the play.' In A Sierz, *In-Yer-Face Theatre*, p 19

7. A Vesalius, *De Humani Corporis Fabrica* (On the Fabric of the Human Body), 1543

8. H Barker, *He Stumbled* in *Collected Plays vol 4* (London, Calder, 1998), pp 260–308. Subsequent page numbers indicate quotations from this edition until otherwise indicated.

9. D Le Breton, *Anthropologie du corps et modernité* (Paris, PUF, 1990), p 37

10. H van R Rembrandt, 'The Anatomy Lecture of Dr Nicolaes Tulp', oil on canvas, 1632. 169.5 x 216.5 cm, Mauritshuis, The Hague; 'The Anatomy Lecture of Dr Deyman', oil on canvas, 1656. 100 x 134 cm, Rijksmuseum Amsterdam.

11. Le Breton, *Anthropologie du corps et modernité*, p 52

12. *Ibid.*, pp 55–8

13. See M Merleau-Ponty, *La Phénoménologie de la perception* (Paris, NRF Gallimard, 1945), especially p 467

14. D Le Breton, *L'Adieu au Corps* (Paris, Métailié, 1999), p 9

15. Le Breton, *Anthropologie du corps et modernité*, p 23

16. For the concept of 'Post-Humanity', see D-R DuFour, *L'Art de réduire les têtes. Sur la nouvelle servitude de l'homme libéré à l'ère du capitalisme total* (Paris, Denoël, 2003).

17. Merleau-Ponty, *La Phénoménologie de la perception*, p 493

18. Barker, *Arguments for a Theatre*, p 156

19. J Kristeva, *Pouvoirs de l'horreur, essai sur l'abjection* (Paris, Seuil, 1980), p 65

20. *Ibid.*, p 9

21. S Lobanov-Rostovsky, 'Taming the Basilisk', quoted in D Hillman and C Mazzio *The Body in Parts, Fantasies of Corporeality in Early Modern Europe* (New York, Routledge, 1997), p 200

22. I Matos Dias, *Merleau-Ponty une poïétique du sensible* (Toulouse, Presses universitaires du Mirail, 2001) p 17

IMAGES OF DEATH

in Howard Barker's Theatre

HEINER ZIMMERMANN

Howard Barker's theatre is 'crucially an art of death', as he recently emphasised once more in *Death, The One and the Art of Theatre*.[1] Death lies at the heart of his idea of tragedy, which he conceives of as a 'labour of death'. This makes it an *ars vivendi* rather than an *ars moriendi*, in which death confers meaning on the life preceding it. He bases his plays on the premise that only a life lived in the face of death is a life lived consciously and fully. Aristotle, who focuses on suffering as a characteristic of tragedy, makes little mention of death. Yet Barker's concept of tragedy is basically anti-Aristotelian. His theatre is explicitly amoral, refusing to serve any utilitarian purpose. In his concept of tragedy, catharsis, the purging of passions, is inverted; rather, Barker's Art of Theatre provokes the unlocking of the drives, instincts and desires of the unconscious; *anagnorisis*, which reasserts rationality and morality, is refused, as his Theatre of Catastrophe promotes the discovery of forbidden knowledge and the assertion of human irrationality: the protagonists' self-confident indulgence of their instincts and passions disregards rationality and moral norms. Any discussion of the images of death in Barker's tragic theatre must bear this in mind. His plays liberate *thanatos*, the irresistible, unconscious death-drive frequently interlocked with *eros*. The territory of death is, however, unknown and unknowable; it cannot be represented from within. As the great Unknown it defies the imagination. If at all, it can only be imagined in terms of the known.[2] The signs of death, the symptoms of dying, the semblance of a corpse can indeed be shown on stage, where death is given a body and silence a voice; but they are signifiers without a referent. Simulating death, they, however, permit a confrontation with the incomprehensible and unforeseeable. Barker's theatre accordingly neither serves enlightenment nor is it representational,[3] since the realm of death lies beyond knowledge.

In the following I shall explore some of the images referring to death in Barker's plays, regarding them from different perspectives and in different connections, such as *thanatos* and *eros*, death and agony, ecstasy, mourning, sacrifice, martyrdom and revolution, murder or the idea of the absence of death.[4] Death not only figures as the climax of plays such as *Claw*, *Hated Nightfall*, *The Last Supper* or *Und*; it also stands at the beginning of other plays or precedes the action, as in *Victory*, which starts with the disinterment of a corpse or in *Scenes from an Execution* and *The Europeans*, where war and rampant death determine the course of the play. In *Ego in Arcadia* the realm of the pastoral with its absence of death is surrounded by the clamour of war and destruction, just as Lvov's doctrine of love in *The Last Supper* is set in a context of killing and war.

A TRAVESTY OF SACRIFICIAL DEATH

The early political satire, *Claw*,[5] already exemplifies the crucial significance of the death motif in Barker's work. The drama highlights a young working-class rebel's campaign against the hated bourgeoisie, a campaign that culminates in his death. Claw, the unloved, illegitimate son of a Stalinist communist, battles for wealth and power by fighting the corrupt, capitalist society with its own weapons. In this world, where dog relentlessly eats dog, he pursues his aims as viciously and mercilessly as all the others. He exploits his fellows, whose uncontrolled desires, rapacity and lust render them vulnerable. As a pimp catering for the rich and mighty he makes prostitution a weapon in his class war.[6] But he queers his own pitch when he himself loses control over his passions. When he is disturbed while copulating with the Home Secretary's wife on a by-pass, the partners' sexual ecstasy is transformed into orgiastic rage and they revel in fantasies of killing and castrating the interfering policeman. In his craving for revenge Claw almost beats him to death. But he overestimates his power when he attempts to blackmail the Home Secretary into saving him from prosecution. The Home Secretary simply eliminates him by having him locked away as a dangerous pervert and subsequently murdered. The suicidal drive underlying Claw's struggle is revealed in a daydream, when he imagines himself as a revered pop star destroying himself in order to disrupt the public spectacle: 'And then, in front of everybody…I would disembowel myself…and chuck my innards in Mick Jagger's gob' (p 31).

Barker's early political satire anticipates his Theatre of Catastrophe by exploring a society composed exclusively of amoral characters. Claw the reckless rebel is a travesty of the selfless socialist revolutionary and his death parodies the self-sacrifice of the political martyr. His ritual drowning by two criminals working for the Secret Service in the guise of male nurses provides the climactic image for the perversion of human relationships satirised by the play. Ignoring his appeals to humanity and pity – qualities he never displayed himself – the two henchmen impassively set about their job. The scene in which Claw has a vision of his dying father predicting his son's death is a reference to the drowning of Clarence in a butt of malmsey wine by two murderers in the pay of his brother Gloucester and to his premonitory dream in Shakespeare's *Richard III* (I: iv). This makes Claw's death a stage death inviting comparison with its historical model. The juxtaposition underlines the alienation of human relations in Barker's fundamentally amoral world, where, as Claw's father points out in his testament to his son, God does not exist. Not so in Shakespeare, where one of the assassins is troubled by pangs of conscience when Clarence appeals to his compassion. In Barker's play, the inhuman cruelty of the scene is heightened by the complete absence of communication between the killers and their victim. Claw's desperate rhetoric goes unheeded. Human relationships have been totally alienated and functionalised. The victim has become a mere object to be eliminated. This trivialises the murder, which in the Home Secretary's memorandum becomes the accidental death of a psychopath, and annihilates the pathos of Claw's willing acceptance of his death by undressing himself and stepping into the bath tub, where he is drowned. Claw's murder hardly arouses any sympathy in the audience since he is just as ruthless as his killers. His elimination by the Home Secretary is a logical outcome in the given context of amoral power play. The death of this rebel provokes not hope but despair in the face of human relationships devoid of all the constraints imposed by morality. It is, however, in Barker's later Theatre of Catastrophe that we find the full range of his speculations and reflections on death. The following explorations focus on a number of plays in which death, as in *Claw*, forms the culmination of the action and is frequently linked with sacrifice and renewal.

THANATOS AND EROS

In most of Barker's plays that culminate in the protagonist's death, this motif is tightly interleaved with that of desire and love. His theatre probes the relationship between the two opposing instincts which, according to Freud, dominate the human being.[7] Parallels between Georges Bataille's philosophy of death and the idea of death in Barker's drama suggest that this philosophy may have played a part in the development of Barker's ideas. Accordingly, a brief outline of the French philosopher's thoughts on this point may enhance the clarity of the points I wish to make.[8] The assumption of an inter-textual relationship between Bataille's writings and Barker's tragedy of catastrophe is supported by the affinity between the ethics of his characters and the ethics proposed by Bataille, determined by instinctive spontaneity, the refusal of all prohibitions and limits and the desire for transgression by way of excess.

According to Bataille, a disciple of Nietzsche, the dictates of reason, which enforce the principles of self-preservation and the survival of the individual, should be abandoned. As all existence derives from the inevitability of non-existence, the human being is rooted in the not-being of death. Living to the full only becomes possible by virtue of the experience of death, which enables the finite individual to immerse him/herself in the infinite continuity of not-being. This leads to a reunion with nature in a mystical experience of ecstasy akin to an excess of being in a moment outside the dimension of time. For Bataille death always belongs to life and true life is lived on the level of death, since the acceptance of the impossibility of unlimited continuity liberates us from the fear of death. Bataille's enthusiasm for death is thus an enthusiasm for a species of life that neither fears death nor seeks to plunge into it and considers ecstatic encounters with death to be nothing other than paroxysms of life. The ability to live presupposes the ability to die. Bataille pits his ideas on the ecstasy of encountering death, on excess and the enthusiastic squandering of the self both against the principle of economy pervading life in a capitalist system and against its decree of survival.

In his view, religious sacrifice and eroticism are the two most powerful ways of affirming death. As eroticism is the voluntary expropriation of the self through devotion to another, it brings death in the midst of life. By contrast, the all-pervading 'sexualisation' of contemporary life is mere decadence, as it stands in the service of survival. Eroticism is a kind of sacrifice of the self implying the dissolution of the individual's uniqueness in fusion with the other, or, as Bataille expresses it, *'L'érotisme, il est possible de dire qu'il est l'approbation de la vie jusque dans la mort'*.[9] Considering orgasm as *la petite mort*, just as in Renaissance English to die also meant to have sexual intercourse, he sees the union of lovers as inclusive of death, of the desire to kill or to commit suicide. In this context the unclothing of the lovers (*mise à nu*) is compared with killing (*mise à mort*), and the enthusiastic waste of the self in the lovers' union implies the desire for death. The ecstasy of orgasm as an instant of being nothing results from the conjunction of eroticism and death. Baudrillard adopted this crucial idea in *L'échange symbolique et la mort*,[10] making the union of eroticism and death the fundamental form of symbolic exchange. Bataille's idea of infinite continuity implies the universal participation of all in all, in the moment of ecstasy. The encounter with death in love shapes his idea of community. It is for him a community of love that includes death, in particular sacrificial death, and thus also becomes a community of death. It brings a return of the sacred and a rebirth of tragedy, which in its basic conflict opposes community and society and culminates in the tragic festivity of death.

For Freud, as for Bataille, non-being precedes life and the organism therefore strives towards death as its initial state and its origin. Freud also recognises parallels between the sexual act and dying. In his view, eroticism derives its supreme satisfaction from the extinction of excitement and tension (whereas the eroticism in Barker's plays and productions compounds, and is compounded by, anxiety and tension). Freud's speculations on *eros* and *thanatos* are, however, grounded in biology and anthropology and have little in common with Bataille's mystical metaphysics asserting that the 'little death' of orgasm implies a union with boundless continuity, nature and all life.

These ideas are echoed in Barker's theatre as the following thoughts on the plays are designed to show. They not only shed light on his revival of tragedy and on the ethics of his tragic characters, they also suggest a philosophical grounding for his decision in the 1980s and 1990s to rework myths such as Christ's sacrificial death and the Eucharist in *The Last Supper*, the Apocryphal narrative of Judith or the mediaeval legend of the martyrdom of St Ursula in the eponymous plays.

Judith[11] and *Ursula*, two plays which are strikingly similar in design, scrutinise different fusions of love and death. According to the author's programme notes, both were inspired by paintings portraying killing scenes. Artemisia Gentileschi's 'Judith Beheading Holofernes' (1620)[12] looms behind Barker's remodelling of the Apocryphal myth, just as Lucas Cranach the Elder's 'The Martyrdom of St Catherine'[13] influenced his reworking of the legend of St Ursula. Both plays subvert the traditional stereotypic images of sex and death and their marginalisation of women. In both dramas gender clichés are inverted as a female protagonist disinherits the male hero as the warrior and executioner cruelly dealing death with the sword. The female protagonists recover and redefine their femininity 'over the dead body' of the male hero (in *Judith*) and of the virgin martyrs (in *Ursula*).[14]

In Artemisia Gentileschi's painting, Judith's brutal butchery with the blood spurting from the victim's veins stands in stark contrast to her womanly beauty. Her appearance as a rich, bejewelled bourgeois lady in a refined gold damask dress recalls her role as seductress but shows no trace of her sacrificial prostitution. Barker seems fascinated above all by the way the picture blends the expressions of the life and the death drive. Like its model, his play focuses on the juxtaposition of intimacy and distance in the gory bedroom scene where the couch of love becomes a death bed, where tenderness and desire are intermingled with cruelty and aggression, and seduction and desire turn into blood-shed and death. In the author's staging of *Judith* (1995), the middle of the stage (a structure of black strings suggested a tent) was occupied by a camp bed as the focal point of the action. In Barker's version, Gentileschi's maid-servant holding Holofernes down whilst Judith cuts off his head – a deviation from the Apocryphal narrative – possibly suggested her tricking of Judith into performing the execution. Here she personifies Judith's single-minded, patriotic alter ego. The Wrestling School's staging of the killing scene also echoed Gentileschi. As in the painting, Holofernes lay supine on his camp bed with his face turned upside down towards the viewer. Barker's Holofernes, however, does not display the desperate horror familiar from pictorial representations of the scene by Gentileschi and other painters. His last words to his slayer are, 'My dear. My loved one.' (p 60). Elizabeth Sakellaridou drew attention to the pictorial quality of the scene in which Judith hesitates with the sword over her head before she brings it down, leaving the act of severing the head to the servant.[15] The arrest of the movement, as if it were a still in a film, interrupts life and anticipates death. In Barker's production the act of beheading was symbolically suggested by pantomime, while the head of one of the two busts flanking the general's tent fell into the servant's basket – another reminder to the audience that they were not witnessing a mimesis of reality. This death was to be perceived as an artefact.[16] The sacrificial bloodshed, the festivity of death, in Bataille's sense of the term, was aesthetically distanced.

Barker's Judith, who is conscious of being a citation herself, feels relieved that Holofernes is 'simply an element in a fiction' (p 58), an artificial construct, because of the liberties this opens up for her.[17] Both rebel against the blueprint of the myth. Barker transforms the morally justified execution of the tyrant aggressor into an encounter between love and death echoing Bataille's idea of eroticism. The lovers' hesitant ritual unclothing evokes the act of self-exposure as the reduction to a state of defencelessness anticipating the *mise à mort* which Bataille imagined it to be. Both court death by opening themselves to each other. Admitting their deceitfulness they tear apart a tissue of lies and counterfeit if only to find an insecure ground of sincerity for their mutual desire. They approach each other so closely that the anonymous confrontation between the aggressor and Judith as the defender of her people is dissolved. The murder of the tyrant, justified by tradition, no longer appears 'natural'. Judith's confession that she has come to kill Holofernes, only to deny it immediately afterwards, implies a declaration of love: 'I intend to kill you, how is that for a lie? And that must mean I love you!' (p 58) As a widow, she has found independence from social norms through the experience of death, loss and mourning. She feels free to follow the urgings of her desire. It is not her mission that makes her kill Holofernes. Her servant exhorts her in vain. Only when she makes her believe for an instant that Holofernes' discourse of love is merely a power strategy does she accomplish the deed.

Barker's Holofernes is a philosopher general who confronts death with a meditation on the countless dead and dying bodies surrounding him on the battlefield and inspiring him both with wonder and fascination. The tragic irony of his references to the death of others is manifest. Killing and the danger of death fascinate him and transport him to ecstasy like a true disciple of Bataille. He is fully aware of the fact that his death-drive prevails over his sexual desire, that he is cruel but cannot love. He is, moreover, convinced that he cannot be loved and yet he yearns for another's fear for his own death that is for love. Aware of the certainty of his death, he anticipates it and thus liberates himself for it, so that in the end he can deliberately choose it by refusing to leave it to chance.

Holofernes deplores the arbitrariness of death, which empties life of sense, makes killing as meaningful as praying, and the reproduction of the species the only reason for existence. Drained of all tension, he abandons himself to Judith in his erotic ecstasy, pretending to sleep. At the moment of his execution Holofernes thus wilfully exposes himself to death in order to conquer love by voluntarily accepting the destiny predetermined by the myth.[18] His slaying is the logical end of a life in pursuit of death, a life centred on dealing death to others. His submission to it is, however, an act of love.

At the crucial moment of the play both protagonists refuse the political role which the myth proposes and follow their instincts with complete disregard for the consequences. Judith does not need to triumph over the male hero nor does she care about her people's injunctions. Her killing of Holofernes is a mistake resulting from a momentary deception about his real feelings. Her destruction of the object of her desire drives her into a catatonic state, an ecstatic encounter with death outside of time, making her lose all consciousness of time; love, like death, desires eternity. Her servant seizes Holofernes's severed head as a trophy, the token of his death. It has become the emblem of victory over the enemy, exorcising fear and guaranteeing Israel's salvation.[19] Judith, however, turns to his body. Since what made him her enemy has now been severed, she can abandon herself to her feelings. Her desperate attempts to copulate with his dead body mingle eroticism and death in accordance with Bataille's ideas. They are, however, a parody of what she desires, i.e. a life-creating union. Steeped in the timelessness of sexual desire and the encounter with death she loses for a long moment all sense of time – for as Nietzsche says, 'Alle Lust will aller Dinge Ewigkeit'.[20] Judith's trauma and the frustration of her sexual desire boost her ego- and death-drive.[21] She displays an aggressive, authoritarian form of discourse asserting her will to power. With the appropriation of Holofernes' sword she assumes his role, claiming 'I could cut off a million heads and go home amiable' (p 66). The sacrifice of her desire transforms Judith into a national hero. She no longer owns her body, which like Holofernes's head, is converted into a symbol. Her new body is Israel.

DEATH AND VIRGINITY

Barker's version of the medieval legend of St Ursula in his eponymous play pits mystical love against sexuality and martyrdom against lust. Once more he questions modern hedonism's dearest values, sex and pleasure, by confronting them with eroticism and sacrifice, which – if one follows Bataille – affirm death and integrate it into an exalted experience of life. By their vow of virginity and the love of Christ, the saint and her followers abnegate the corporeal self in order to devote themselves entirely to a metaphysical ideal. Thus they include death in the centre of their lives. Their idea of eroticism is the opposite of self-preservation. Willingly accepting the death of the body as a precondition for their mystical union with Christ, they squander themselves and their lives in a moment of mystical ecstasy as finite consciousness dissolves into unconscious continuity.

In a programme note for the Wrestling School's production in 1998, the dramatist defines virginity as 'the fear of…the hell of a vertiginous desire for another'.[22] Sexual desire is vilified by his female protagonists for its false promise of the 'annihilation of the self'[23] in the 'little death' (*la petite mort*) of orgasm. This criticism is obviously grounded in the opposition between sexuality and Bataille's concept of eroticism as the extinction of the self and the dissolution of existing forms. In the play, the theme is metaphorically highlighted by the subtitle, 'Fear of the Estuary' and the leitmotif of the river losing itself in the sea. After her conversion to womanhood, Placida, the mother superior of Ursula's convent, speaks of her lover's pouring '[h]is river in my sea' (p 80). Ursula's self-dedication to virginity is borne out by her wish 'to be parted from herself', that is from her nature as woman. It is thus akin to self-hatred. Only the spiritual love of God can deliver Ursula from herself: the saint's wish to be parted from her self is absolute, wanting its extinction to be definitive. Whether this means a loss of reality of life is a question of perspective. The virgins disdain Placida's experience of sexual ecstasy as a failure, since afterwards '[t]he self comes back again' (p 66). Replacing 'the pleasure of sex with the agony of desire', virginity leads to a higher form of ecstasy 'which is the outcome of pain' (programme note) and overcomes the determinism of the subject through her body by raising love to a spiritual level – an endeavour that mysticism shares with Platonism. Ursula's intrepid acceptance of the spiritual love of God in contrast to her anxiety concerning sexual desire implies her acceptance of death. The annihilation of the body in martyrdom is the gate she has to pass through in order to achieve her mystical union with God. *Thanatos* is a driving force of virginity, which takes a vision for reality and spurns the earthly life, hoping for bliss hereafter. This self-aggressive loss of reality is perverted to political aggression by suicidal terrorism. The non-violent virgins, however, become the victims of the reality principle they disparage.

In Barker's drama, the Prince of the Estuary's frustrated sexuality does not turn into aggression as it does in the legend. Like a true protagonist of the Theatre of Catastrophe he refuses to subscribe to the convention of the male cult of honour and searches for a new discourse, a new code of behaviour seeking to gain strength from humiliation and the purification of the soul from shame. This transformation of the pre-text was inspired by Lucas Cranach the Elder's painting 'The Massacre of the Virgin Martyrs'[24] in Dresden, which shows the Prince 'leaning on his unused sword and observing the massacre with the moral detachment of the SS Officer'.[25] Ursula's negation of the Prince's masculinity by preferring virginity to marriage with him unmans him. He can no longer wield the oversized, symbolic 'sword of execution' that looms large in the last part of the stylishly formalised drama, anticipating the tragic end. Neither he nor his soldiers kill Ursula and the virgins, who are wheeled onto the stage on steel mortuary trolleys – an anachronistic image recalling both the position of the sacrificial victim on the altar in antiquity and a current image of death in modern times.[25] The hospital is of course also a place of 'butchery' in the service of survival. Placida, the mother superior, assumes the part which in the legend is performed by men. She adopts the roles of bride and mother that Ursula has refused. As she has seduced the prince and opposes virginity by ecstatically living out her sexuality, his sword is offered to her. Thanks to her newly acquired carnal knowledge she perceives her former companions' devotion to virginity in the light of her awareness as lover and (potential literal) mother. It is thus her assignment to destroy those who have evaded the symbolic control of society. She 'helps' them to fulfil their desire to part from themselves and to consummate their marriage with Christ. By ritually cutting their necks she produces a sacrificial bloodbath which is mopped up by a stagehand. Barker's modification of the legend renders the final stage image radically ambivalent. It testifies to the triumph of nature and the body as much as to the triumph of virginity, that is to the triumph of the spirit over the body in seeking the ultimate annihilation of the self. If, as Elisabeth Bronfen observes, 'the dead feminine body' is 'a trope of castration *par excellence*',[27] it here refers both to male castration through female virginity and to female self-castration by virginity. Martyrdom has eliminated the virgins from society and transformed their bodies into symbols of the love of Christ. In a symbolic exchange they are thus restored to society as saints.[28]

DEATH AND RESURRECTION AS MYTH

The Last Supper [29] provides an alternative version of the central Christian mystery of Christ's death and the Eucharist, by returning to archaic practices of sacrificial death and ritual cannibalism underlying the sublimated, symbolic consumption of flesh and blood in the form of bread and wine. As we have seen, sacrifice and the consumption of the sacrificed body is in Bataille's view the most powerful affirmation of death besides eroticism, and for Baudrillard it is the ultimate instance of symbolic exchange characterising the attitude of 'primitive' societies towards death.[30] Barker transforms the biblical sacrifice of Christ by God the father into the self-sacrifice of his protagonist, Lvov. As a leader, Lvov realises that he has exhausted his resources for impressing his followers and that he is about to be demystified by them. They are disappointed by his ordinariness and start to parody him. He knows that he owes his authority to their projections. In order to survive as a myth, he asks his disciples to kill him and to consume his body as proof of their love. It is not death he fears, but oblivion. Eating Lvov will preserve his body from decomposition and render him sacred. By leaving no corporeal trace behind he will become pure myth, which will be disseminated by his followers because he will live on in their memory. The personal connection will thus be transmuted into a symbolic relationship. Barker's play thus goes back to an insight which originally underlay the rite of the *pharmakos* and suggested 'that non-being is the only path to true identity and that to embrace this dissolution can be life-giving rather that annihilating'.[31] He thus not only parodies the myth of Christ's sacrifice, in which He takes on the sins of the world as a scapegoat to expiate them,[32] but also the conviction that the disappearance of Christ's body after his death and its substitution by the word of the gospels constitutes the proof of his resurrection.

Lvov, whose message is love, has to be killed by those who love him so that his words can survive. His death suggests that the killing of the human body resides at the core of his doctrine of love. His strategy strips love of human weakness and makes it purely metaphysical. Lvov commissions Judith to adopt the role of Judas and organise his killing. The *mise-en-scène* of the disciples' stabbing of their leader in accordance with his desires and partly against their wishes is reminiscent of the murder of Julius Caesar in Shakespeare's tragedy (III: i). They are, however, just as uncertain as Shakespeare's Brutus about whether their deed really is an act of liberation. The ritual stabbing is as much an ordeal for them as for their victim. They are all the same animated by a sense of equality and feel that too much power and authority are concentrated in the person of Lvov and have thus been prevented from circulating in the group. They are also curious about what the world will be like without him. As is only to be expected Lvov cannot keep his promise to communicate his experience of death to Judith. The ritual act of eating his body, an ecstatic immersion in infinite continuity, is not presented on stage. The secret must not even be talked about, as they impress on one another in their last words: 'DON'T DARE DESCRIBE IT!' (p 56). A tableau vivant parodying Leonardo's 'Il Cenacolo' highlights the disciples' exhaustion, their dejected, bewildered and guilt-ridden condition after these acts of sacrifice and cannibalism, their dissension, and the absence of the centre formed by the figure of Christ in the Italian model.[33] The scene looks like a staging of the Madman's complaint in Nietzsche's *The Gay Science*:

> God is dead. God remains dead. And we have killed him! How can we console ourselves, the murderers of all murderers? The holiest and mightiest thing the world has ever possessed has bled to death under our knives: who will wipe this blood off us? With what water could we clean ourselves? [34]

However, their guilt and the secret they share finally bind them together – like the soldiers who tie them together at the end of the play – and will be the source of their power.[35] Their community of love is renewed by the integration of death. The sacrifice of Lvov confers on his myth a continuity no longer subjected to the temporal limitations of the body.

JEWISH DESIRE FOR DEATH

After this discussion of *Judith* and *Ursula* it does not come as a surprise that, in his meditation on the *Shoah* in *Und* [36] (1999), Barker imagines the relationship between a Jewish victim and a fascist executioner as a tragic love affair. The play superimposes and intertwines two situations: that of a woman waiting in vain for her lover and that of a Jew assaulted in her house by fascists during a pogrom. As Elizabeth Sakellaridou [37] has pointed out, the play offers a variation on Roland Barthes's comparison of the deserted lover's state of panic and violent despair, which he calls 'catastrophe amoureuse',[38] to the desperate state of a prisoner doomed to death in a concentration camp. Barker adopts the metaphor proposed by Barthes to speculate on the psychology of the rapport between Jews and Nazis. Barthes himself had doubts as to the meaningfulness of conceiving the Holocaust in terms of individual, psychological experience. The question remains whether the deserted lover's feeling of total annihilation of the self can be equated with the corporeal pain and the despair caused by physical torture – not to mention the difference between the liquidation of the body and the feelings involved in the annihilation of the self.

Barker's drama inverts the structure of *Judith* and once more mingles desire and hatred, tenderness and cruelty, courteous consideration and brutal violence, *eros* and *thanatos*. The protagonist's soliloquy presents the victim's perspective, which is complemented, commented on and contradicted by mostly nonverbal interventions supposedly coming from her invisible lover and a servant off stage. The expected meeting with her fascist lover never materialises. Instead, it turns into a lethal encounter with death. As she is dressed to seduce her lover Und meets death like a bride. The fact that loving a fascist means loving her own death is something she represses almost until the end of the play. The dissolution of her identity, the destruction of her self as a rejected lover is complemented by the torture of her emotions and final liquidation of her body in the form of a sacrifice.

In the ecstatic wanderings of her mind, Und oscillates between the repression of reality and moments of lucidity. She idealises her absent lover, and whitewashes the brutal attacks on her room and on her body. Though they both frighten and pain her, she desperately clings to the fiction of a mutual love relationship. Her self-deceit drives her to a dissolution of the dualism of perpetrator and victim by imagining her fascist lover with a *kipa*. Intermittently, however, she also perceives the terror to which she is exposed and relates it to her lover. Her contradictions are complemented by contradictory signs sent to her anonymously from off stage including tea and flowers as well as a heap of earth. The assaults on her escalate from the insistent ringing of her doorbell to the breaking of her windows and hammerings on the door. They culminate in her being drenched with sordid fluids and stifled with smoke. But even when she weeps and suffers from the cold and the heat inflicted on her in the course of these attacks, this in itself also implies a parody of the ecstasies of the Petrarchan lover. She suggests this idea herself when she interprets the assault on her person as 'desire expressed as rage' (p 218). Her assertion 'we are destined for each other' (p 222) is as ambiguous as her last words 'let him in' (p 238), with which she admits her executioner into her room in terms that could also suggest penetration by her lover.

Whilst, like Judith, she cannot keep her distance from the beloved enemy, he depersonalises their relationship by refusing all communication, stigmatising her in a note as a 'Jew', which provides the pretext for her torture and liquidation. Although she is aware of his persecution of Jews, she is fascinated by his intrepidity in the face of death and his contempt for life. Far from relating the fascist death drive to herself, she admires the sublime beauty of apocalyptic spectacles of destruction and the lacerated, dismembered corpses produced by Nazism. As an aristocrat and a member of God's chosen people she feels akin to the fascist superman. When the attacks are finally directed at her own body, her rhetorical glosses on the situation become more and more eccentric. She understands, however, that 'this man intends to murder [her]' (p 234), and plans to show her aristocratic contempt for life by committing suicide, which would also be a means of stopping the torture that transposes her into a continuous state of dying. But even then she is still eager to believe that her fascist cavalier actually loves her. In the fantasies incited by being sent a heap of earth from off stage, she wards off the intimation of her own death, superseding the image of her fascist lover by that of a Jewish intellectual whom she remembers as having died as a victim of anti-Semitism. With her Jewishness she accepts her role as victim, sacrificed on the altar of the Fascists' racist mania which demonises the Jews as the terrible other. A Jacob van Ruysdael painting (of 1655–60) is let down from the flies beside the reflection of her tortured image in a mirror. Gazing at it, she enters a Jewish cemetery with sarcophagi, ruins and dead trees, thus contrasting the aristocratic finesse of Jewish art, its peaceful image of death, to the fascist barbarity that destroys her. She finally accepts the sight of her enemy/lover knowing that cognition will be her death.

THE ABSENCE OF DEATH

The title of Barker's *Ego in Arcadia* (1992)[39] is a citation from Nicolas Poussin's famous painting 'The Arcadian Shepherds', a variation on the enigmatic inscription 'Et in Arcadia Ego' on the sarcophagus in the centre of the picture.[40] The personal pronoun *ego*'s reference to a subject is ambiguous in both cases. According to E Panofsky and L Marin *ego* could stand for a dead shepherd buried in the monument, or for Death – as corroborated by the death's head in the Chatsworth version of the painting – or for the artist who imagines Arcadia and is both present and absent in his work.[41] In Barker's drama, *ego* evokes Death and the dramatist/narrator, but also refers to the dramatis personae. Poussin's elegiac picture shows three shepherds and a shepherdess mourning in front of a monument. This affirmation of the presence of death in Arcadia provoked Barker to a speculation on what Arcadia would be without death. However, personified Death, bearing the pseudonym Tocsin, is one of the play's characters.[42]

Barker's Arcadia is a landscape of dereliction, a refuse dump full of the trash produced by a technological civilisation in which nature has been destroyed long ago. It is a ghetto to which a group of refugees have escaped from the eternal war outside and which they can no longer leave. These refugees are artists and politicians, artificial constructs somewhere between citation and allegory. Arcadia, tradition insists, is the locus of love and therefore 'a place of infinite suffering' (p 271); for love, which is in general unrequited, is conceived of as a loss of self, causing pain, despair, aggression and self-hatred. The painter Poussin, one of the protagonists, paraphrases Roland Barthes when he describes 'the absolute of love' as a state in which 'you would turn yourself inside out…and maim your very perfect parts…and hack your soul…for another who remains…implacable' (p 300).[43] Sexual desire is the only impulse which drives these characters. It makes the henchman of the revolution covet the queen he is ordered to execute, the dancer love the old novelist who reviles her, and the model adore the painter who ignores her. It absurdly persists in the decrepit body, as is demonstrated by Poussin's mother, who solicits sexual relations with most of the male characters. The suffering and pain of rejected love provoke hatred and aggression. The urge to annihilate the beloved or the rival is as omnipresent as unrequited love. As the characters in the Theatre of Catastrophe obey no moral norm but only the spontaneous impulse of the moment, the attempts to kill are numerous. When Verdun, the model, stabs Poussin, whom she adores, and slashes his painting, because he only loves his art, this is an attempt to appropriate the elusive object of her love. By mourning him she hopes to make him her own. Sansom, the revolutionary, suffocates Dover, the ex-queen, to appease his unrequited longing, and Mosca, her lover, stabs him out of revenge at the end of the play after having knifed him out of jealousy at the beginning. Even Tocsin, the personification of death, is hanged by Poussin, who, like his historical model, invited him to Arcadia. But in Barker's Arcadia no one is killed permanently (except Tocsin). This is both the rule of the game, and the horror of the place. The act of killing has no consequence. It does not change the victim's state of being. Like an actor on a stage, which is of course the case, he/she gets up and continues as before. Thus emptied of meaning, the gesture of destroying the other becomes a sign without a referent. On the meta-dramatic level this implies an ironic comment on the impossibility of representing the acts of killing and dying. In the context of the play it means that the act of annihilating the other does not produce the desired release from suffering. Frustrated desire and pain will continue for ever, as in J P Sartre's *Huis Clos*. This makes the inmates of Arcadia wonder, whether they have not already died. They realize that life without the possibility of death is no real life. Unlike Poussin's pastoral elegy, where death is evoked indirectly through the shepherds' mourning and the sarcophagus, violent acts continue in Barker's Arcadia like a reflex, although they remain without consequence; the idea of death continues as a nostalgic memory of reality. Unable to live out their aggressions, the protagonists turn their hatred against themselves and dream of redemption through suicide. Some of them succeed in killing their desire, but the absence of passion and pain only means that they have 'ceased to live' (p 316) and merely exist. They court Tocsin, the dispenser of relief, who could grant them oblivion. The wooing of Death culminates in a song contest reminiscent of Spenser's *Shepherds' Calendar* to identify which of them is the most deserving of the grace of Death. Poussin, who only loves his art, does not want to die. Death therefore singles him out, but after wrestling with him in a lethal dance Poussin triumphs over Death as he does through his art. It is the artist, not Death, that rules in Arcadia. The play closes with Poussin drawing the dead bodies of two unhappy lovers. Death and pain are indispensable for the fullness of life, love and art, in Arcadia as anywhere else.

THE WORK OF MOURNING AS EMANCIPATION FROM THE PAST[44]

I should like to conclude the observations above with some remarks on the rapport between the living and the dead: that is, on the work of mourning in Howard Barker's theatre. In *Victory: Choices in Reaction* [45] the disinterred corpse of the regicide Bradshaw constitutes the play's crucial symbolic image.[46] It visualises the challenge to the living posed by the dead. The widow's quest to recover the scattered remnants of her husband's corpse is the outward equivalent of her work of mourning. It opposes King Charles's desecration of Bradshaw's remains as a way of parading his victory over the puritan revolution. Moreover, the contrary ways of dealing with the body of the Commonwealth's chief ideologist illustrate different ways of facing up to the memory of the revolution, as is indicated by the play's subtitle. The vengeful exhumation of the regicide by the royalists at the play's opening is contrasted by the republicans' ritual burial of their arms in Act One, Scene 5, representing their hope for a future resurrection. Whilst in ancient cultures, as for instance in Greece, death was conceived as a passage, a journey to the realm of the dead, here the widow sets out on a journey to restore her husband's corpse to the peace of the grave. In pursuing this aim, Bradshaw projects the psychic effort involved in the work of mourning onto the external plane. Just as Antigone honours the holiness of the ties of blood and ignores the reasons of State and public order, Bradshaw honours her physical love for her husband's body and ignores puritan pieties.[47] She has done with shame, conscience, duty, guilt and power (p 18) altogether, but she suffers intensely when she is confronted with the sight of her husband's rotting brain, his impaled head, and dismembered body publicly exhibited by order of the king. In order to retrieve his corpse she exposes herself to humiliation, pain and torture. By making this quest the object of her life, she renounces her self and shows 'responsibility' in Derrida's sense of the word.[48] In the course of this labour she accepts the fact of his death and gradually withdraws her libido from him, which is nourished by her memories. This psychic liberation enables her to gain emotional distance from the dead body, which she gradually accepts to be an object. Bradshaw invents her ritual of mourning as a rite of passage. The loss of her husband also sends her on a journey of rediscovery dedicated to her own lost self, which was annihilated by her marriage. Thus the process of recovering and reassembling the remains of her husband's dead body dispersed by the royalists also represents the process of recovering the submerged parts of her own ego. By maintaining a constant relation with her dead husband, Bradshaw reinvents herself. The experience of death makes her life real. She openly repudiates her husband's life-denying, rationalist work ethic, its hostility to sexuality and pleasure and his purely theoretical advocacy of equality between the sexes. Her labour of mourning is a struggle for emancipation from the internalised decrees of puritan doctrine. The slap she gives the poet Milton is a final act of liberation projecting her aggressive feelings for her husband onto the figurehead of republican philosophy. She obeys no moral commands and pragmatically adapts to her situation in a Machiavellian manner. Her metamorphosis brings her near to the position of the Cavaliers, which, however, does nothing to weaken her unflinching resolve to save her husband's corpse from royalist abuse. The new principles underlying her behaviour entirely preclude a conflict of loyalties to opposing moral laws, like the dilemma that destroyed Sophocles's Antigone.

King Charles's repudiation of the memory of the revolution knows no taboos. His vengeful irreverence and derision make a mockery of his posthumous punishment of the judge who condemned his father to death. He orders his corpse to be hanged and decapitated, his head to be impaled, and the parts of his dismembered body to be exhibited in different public places as a deterrent. He vindictively demonstrates his disdain of the dead enemy by playing skittles with his skull and making Nell Gwynn kiss the chaste lips of the dead puritan – an image reminiscent of a baroque *memento mori*. Since these sacrileges are performed on the defenceless body of one who is already dead and in the hands of God, they discredit the king. Only when he makes the skull 'lick' the blood of his murdered friend – suggesting that the murder of the capitalist was fully in line with the revolutionary's intentions – does Charles realise the *memento mori* implicit in his gesture and become melancholic. When at the end of the drama Bradshaw has at last recovered her husband's remains, she has exorcised his spirit and annihilated his power over her. Not so her daughter, who learnt Latin in order to read and translate his treatise *Harmonia Britannia* and to spread his message.

It is of course impossible even to sketch a morphology of the death motif in Barker's theatre. His work is too extensive and death is almost ubiquitous in his drama. My choice of plays, which have death at their core, is therefore arbitrary and reflects my own encounters with his work. Other dramas would have merited the same attention. In *Hated Nightfall*, for instance, the protagonist's commission to kill the Romanov family leads to a dance of death which locks the executioner and his victims in an ever closer embrace as both sides attempt to seduce each other in order to conquer the other's love. More recently *Dead Hands* (2004) has explored the power of the dead over the living and the way this power fashions their lives.

It is equally impossible even to outline the meaning of death in Barker's theatre in a short essay like this one. The author himself dedicated a whole volume to this question (*Death, The One and the Art of Theatre*). This essay has highlighted only some aspects of this vast issue, such as the meshing of death and love, the necessity of a consciousness of death for a full experience of life, the role of death as a doorway to survival as myth, the life-giving and life-taking ecstasy of martyrdom, the erotic relationship between the executioner and the victim (even in the case of the Holocaust) or the work of mourning as emancipation from the power of the dead. Death in the Theatre of Catastrophe is always a histrionic event. As in Nietzsche, it is a sacrifice by life to life and a symbol of the inexhaustible fertility of life. The cycle of birth and death, in which the desire to destroy corresponds to the ecstasy of creation, is eternal. It is no coincidence that most of my interpretations have started out from a crucial image of death or killing. Barker's theatre galvanises its audience's imagination as much by its fascinating pictorial quality as by the power of the word.

NOTES

1. H Barker, *Death, The One and the Art of Theatre* (London, Routledge, 2005)

2. *Ibid.*, p 30

3. *Ibid.*, p 53

4. For an excellent study of the role of death in contemporary British drama, to which my following observations are much indebted, see A Pankratz, *'Death is... not.' Repräsentationen von Tod und Sterben im zeitgenössischen britischen Drama* (Trier, Wissenschaftlicher Verlag Trier, 2005)

5. H Barker, *Claw* in *Collected Plays vol 1* (London, Calder, 1990), first production 1975. Page numbers in the text refer to this edition until otherwise indicated.

6. C Lamb, *Howard Barker's Theatre of Seduction* (Amsterdam, Harwood Academic, 1997), p 3

7. Freud expounds his theory of the life-preserving and life-renewing sexual drive and its opposite number the ego- or death-drive in 'Jenseits des Lustprinzips' (1920) and 'Das Ich und das Es' (1923). He also

observes that both drives are always blended, so that we only encounter mixtures containing different proportions of each. See S Freud, *Psychologie des Unbewußten*, Studienausgabe vol III, (Frankfurt, Main, S Fischer Verlag, 1975), pp 308, 348

8. Bataille developed his philosophy of death in *L'Erotisme* (Paris, Editions de Minuit, 1957), *Les Larmes d'Eros* (Paris, Editions J J Pauvert, 1961), *L'Expérience Intérieure* (Paris, Gallimard, 1943), *La Part Maudite* (Paris, Editions de Minuit, 1947), and *Théorie de la Réligion* (Paris, Gallimard, 1948). My following outline is also indebted to G Bergfleth, 'Baudrillard und die Todesrevolte', J Baudrillard, *Der symbolische Tausch und der Tod* (Munich, Matthes & Seitz Verlag, 1982), pp 365–430.

9. G Bataille, *L'Erotisme*, *Oeuvres complètes vol X* (Paris, Gallimard, 1987), p 17

10. J Baudrillard, *L'Echange symbolique et la mort* (Paris, Gallimard, 1976)

11. H Barker, *Judith* (London, Calder, 1990). Page numbers in the text refer to this edition until otherwise indicated.

12. Florence, Galleria degli Uffizi. Criticism interpreted the image as the artist's revenge on her rapist teacher, Tassi. This is more plausible concerning the version of 1612/13 in the Museo di Capodimonte at Naples, which she painted only a few years after her lawsuit against her rapist. According to the author, Artemisia Gentileschi served him as model for his Anna Galactia in *Scenes from an Execution*.

13. The right wing of the altar of St Catherine (1506) at Dresden shows St Ursula in the company of St Barbara and St Margaret. In his programme note to the Wrestling School's production of the play, Barker refers to a representation of the 'massacre of the virgin martyrs' with the prince in the centre leaning on his sword, which is in fact the picture of 'The Martyrdom of St Catherine' in the centre of the triptych.

14. E Bronfen, *Over Her Dead Body* (Manchester, Manchester University Press, 1992)

15. E Sakellaridou, 'La qualité picturale des pièces récentes de Howard Barker' in *Alternatives théâtrales* 57 (1998), 69–72, p 72

16. Judith's complementary gesture of pouring red wine from a bottle into a bath tub, however, had the effect of melodramatic 'overkill'. Barker repeated this in his production of *Hated Nightfall* having Romanov's son, Christophe, pour red liquid from a watering can on similar occasions.

17. She admits that what she says is not original (p 50) and claims that this is also true of Holofernes's discourse (p 56). See C Lemke, 'Widerstandsfähigkeit des Zitierens in Judith Butler's *Bodies that Matter* und Howard Barker's *Judith*' in A Gutenberg and R Poole (eds) *Zitier-Fähigkeit. Findungen und Erfindungen des Anderen* (Berlin, Erich Schmidt Verlag, 2001), pp 123–35.

18. His ecstatic self-abandonment recalls the helplessness on the warrior's face in Gentileschi's painting.

19. For Elizabeth Sakellaridou in 'La qualité picturale des pièces récentes de Howard Barker' (p 72) this calls up visual reminiscences of numerous representations of severed heads in the fine arts such as those of St John the Baptist, Goliath or the Medusa – all *iconae verae* of death.

20. 'All lust desires eternity for every thing' (my translation) from F Nietzsche, 'Das trunkne Lied', stanza 11, *Also sprach Zarathustra*, *Werke in drei Bänden vol 2* (Cologne, Könemann Verlag, 1994), p 415

21. See also Lamb, *Howard Barker's Theatre of Seduction*, p 75

22. H Barker, programme note, *Ursula* (The Wrestling School production, 1998)

23. H Barker, *Ursula* in *Collected Plays vol 5* (London, Calder, 2001), pp 29–30. Page numbers in the text refer to this edition until otherwise indicated.

24. See note 13 above.

25. Barker, programme note, *Ursula*

26. According to the author's programme note, the motif of the unfeeling onlooker at a scene of slaughter is one of the 'continuities that shock and dignify European culture'. Goya plays this role in *Terrible Mouth*. In *Ursula* Lucas watches the massacre from backstage. Only after its accomplishment does he advance to the front 'mesmerised'. On a meta-dramatic level the play invites the audience to reflect on their role as 'voyeurs' and to compare their viewing of the aestheticised 'sweet violence' (Terry Eagleton, see note 30) of the stage ritual with the watching of images showing thousand-fold death on the television screen.

27. Bronfen, *Over Her Dead Body*, p 138

28. J Baudrillard, *Der symbolische Tausch und der Tod* (Munich, Matthes & Seitz Verlag, 1982), p 218

29. H Barker, *The Last Supper* (London, Calder, 1988). Page numbers in the text refer to this edition until otherwise indicated.

30. Baudrillard, *Der symbolische Tausch und der Tod*, pp 206–9, 217–20

31. T Eagleton, *Sweet Violence* (London, Blackwell, 2003), p 280.

32. *Ibid.*, p 283: 'In the Christian eucharist as in ancient sacrifice, symbolic identification with the *pharmakos*…takes the literal form of actually eating the body of the scapegoat.'

33. cf. Barker, *The Last Supper* p 55, stage direction; Howard Barker's front cover drawing; and H Zimmermann, 'Les tableaux dans le théâtre de Howard Barker' in E Angel-Perez (ed) *Howard Barker et le Théâtre de la catastrophe* (Paris, Éditions théâtrales, 2006), pp 65–91, 215–24

34. F Nietzsche, *The Gay Science* book 3, 125, ed. B Williams, tr. J Nauckhoff (Cambridge, Cambridge UP, 2001), p 120.

35. Lamb, *Howard Barker's Theatre of Seduction*, p 51.

36. H Barker, *Und* in *Collected Plays vol 5* (London, Calder, 2001). Page numbers in the text refer to this edition until otherwise indicated.

37. E Sakellaridou, 'A Lover's Discourse – But Whose?: Inversions of the Fascist Aesthetic in Howard Barker's *Und* and Other Recent English Plays' in *European Journal of English Studies* 7 (2003), pp 87–109

38. R Barthes, *Fragments d'un discours amoureux* (Paris, Éditions du Seuil, 1977), p 60

39. H Barker, *Ego in Arcadia* in *Collected Plays vol 3* (London, Calder, 1996). Page numbers refer to this edition until otherwise indicated.

40. There exist two versions of 'The Arcadian Shepherds', one in the Chatsworth Collection in Devonshire of 1630 (?) and a later one in the Louvre. Barker mainly refers to the second.

41. E Panofsky, 'Et in Arcadia Ego: Poussin and the Elegiac Tradition' in *Meaning in the Visual Arts* (New York, Doubleday & Co, 1955), pp 295–320; L Marin, 'Toward a Theory of Reading in the Visual Arts: Poussin's "The Arcadian Shepherds"' in S Suleiman and I Crosman (eds) *The Reader in the Text: Essays on Audience and Interpretation* (Princeton, Princeton University Press, 1980), pp 293–324

42. Pancratz (*'Death is…not.'*, p 115) points out that Starhemberg in *The Europeans* is identified as personified death by the other characters. Meeting him is deadly.

43. 'I have projected myself with such a force into the other that I cannot recover or recuperate myself when I am without him: I am lost forever' (my translation) in R Barthes, *Fragments d'un discours amoureux*, p 60: 'je me suis projeté dans l'autre avec une telle force que, lorsqu'il me manque, je ne puis me rattraper, me récupérer: je suis perdu, à jamais.'

44. I understand work of mourning in the sense defined by Freud in 'Trauer und Melancholie' (1917) in S Freud, *Psychologie des Unbewußten* (Frankfurt, S Fischer Verlag, 1975), pp 194–213.

45. H Barker, *Victory: Choices in Reaction* (London, Calder, 1983). Page numbers in the text refer to this edition until otherwise indicated.

46. In *The Castle* Skinner, the militant feminist witch, who murdered a builder of the fortress, is sentenced to carry the rotting corpse of the victim in front of her. From now on she lives facing death. At the end of the play the corpse has decayed to a skeleton. Her self-knowledge gained in the process of expiation finally helps her to reject the offer of governing the new community as she is aware of her cruelty and desire for revenge.

47. The fable also recalls the Egyptian fecundity myth of Osiris.

48. J Derrida, in *Donner la mort* (Paris, Galilée, 1999, p 76), speaks of 'the rapport with the other, a response to the other: the experience of personal kindness and an intentional gesture [...] a gesture of making a gift which is a renunciation of the self' (my translation): 'le rapport à l'autre, une réponse à l'autre: experience de la bonté personnelle et mouvement intentionnel [...] un mouvement de don qui renonce à soi'.

A CHRONOLOGY

of Howard Barker's Work

Dates indicate first stagings, broadcasts or publications (not subsequent productions in the same medium).

Place of publication is London, unless otherwise noted.

[JC]   John Calder

[OB]   Oberon Books

First staging occurred in Britain, unless otherwise noted.

[HB]   production directed by Barker

•   indicates that this unpublished text is summarised and considered in Rabey (1989)

†   indicates a non-professional university production

1970   *One Afternoon on the 63rd level of the North Face of the Pyramid of Cheops The Great*: broadcast BBC Radio; unpublished•

Cheek staged; published in *New Short Plays: 3* (Eyre Methuen Playscripts 1972, volume credited to Barker, Grillo, Haworth and Simmons)

No One Was Saved staged; unpublished•

1971   *Henry V in Two Parts* broadcast BBC Radio; unpublished•

1972   *Herman, with Millie and Mick* broadcast BBC Radio; unpublished•

Edward – The Final Days staged; unpublished•

Alpha Alpha staged; unpublished•

Faceache staged; unpublished

1973   *Skipper* staged; unpublished•

My Sister and I staged; unpublished•

Rule Britannia staged; unpublished

Bang staged; unpublished

1975   *Claw* staged; published with *Stripwell* 1977 [JC]

Stripwell staged; published with *Claw* 1977 [JC]

1976   *Wax* staged; unpublished•

Heroes of Labour unproduced television play; published in *Gambit 29* [JC]

1977   *Fair Slaughter* staged and published [JC]

That Good Between Us staged; published 1980 with *Credentials of a Sympathiser*, unproduced television play [JC]

1978 *The Love of a Good Man* staged; published 1980 with *All Bleeding*, unproduced
television play [JC]

The Hang of the Gaol staged; published 1982 with *Heaven*, unproduced television
play [JC]

1980 *The Loud Boy's Life* staged; published 1982 in *Two Plays for the Right* [JC]

Birth on a Hard Shoulder staged (Stockholm, Sweden); published 1982 in *Two Plays for
the Right* [JC]

1981 *No End of Blame* staged and published [JC]

The Poor Man's Friend staged •

1983 *Victory* staged and published [JC]

A Passion in Six Days staged; published 1985 with *Downchild* [JC]

Crimes in Hot Countries staged†; published 1984 [JC]

1984 *Pity in History* staged†; published in *Gambit 41* [JC]; broadcast BBC TV 1985

The Power of the Dog staged and published [JC]

Don't Exaggerate (performance poem) staged, published with other poems 1985 [JC]

1985 *The Castle* staged and published with *Scenes from an Execution* [JC]

Scenes from an Execution broadcast by BBC Radio; published with *The Castle* [JC]

Downchild (written 1977) staged

The Blow unproduced filmscript •

1986 *Women Beware Women* staged and published [JC]

The Breath of the Crowd (performance poem) staged and published with other poems
[JC]

1987 *Gary the Thief / Gary Upright* (performance poems) published with other poems
[JC]

1988 *The Possibilities* staged and published [JC]

The Last Supper staged and published [JC]

The Early Hours of a Reviled Man broadcast by BBC Radio

The Bite of the Night (written 1985) staged and published [JC]

Lullabies for the Impatient poems, published [JC]

The Smile published in *New Plays: 2*, ed Peter Terson, Oxford University Press

1989 *Seven Lears* staged and published with *Golgo* [JC]

Golgo staged and published with *Seven Lears* [JC]

The Europeans (written 1987) staged (Toronto, Canada) and published with *Judith*
[JC]

Arguments for a Theatre (essays) 1st edn [JC]

1990 *Scenes from an Execution* stage production

The Early Hours of a Reviled Man stage production†

Collected Plays vol 1 (*Claw, No End of Blame, Victory, The Castle, Scenes from an
Execution*) published [JC]

1991   *The Europeans* (written 1987) staged[†]
         The Ascent of Monte Grappa (poems) published **[JC]**

1992   *A Hard Heart* staged, broadcast by BBC Radio, and published with *The Early
            Hours of a Reviled Man* **[JC]**
         Ego in Arcadia staged (Sienna, Italy) **[HB]**
         Terrible Mouth (opera libretto) staged and published (Universal Edition)

1993   *Collected Plays vol 2* (*The Love of a Good Man, The Possibilities, Brutopia, Rome,
            (Uncle) Vanya, Ten Dilemmas*) published **[JC]**
         Arguments for a Theatre (essays) 2nd edn, Manchester University Press
         All He Fears (marionette play) staged and published **[JC]**

1994   *Hated Nightfall* staged **[HB]** and published with *Wounds to the Face* **[JC]**
         Minna staged (Vienna, Austria) and published, Alumnus, Leeds

1995   *Judith* staged **[HB]**
         (Uncle) Vanya (written 1992) staged[†]

1996   *(Uncle) Vanya* staged **[HB]**
         Collected Plays vol 3 (*The Power of the Dog, The Europeans, Women Beware Women,
            Minna, Judith, Ego in Arcadia*) published **[JC]**
         The Tortmann Diaries (poems) published **[JC]**
         Defilo (Failed Greeks) written

1997   *Arguments for a Theatre* (essays) 3rd edn, Manchester University Press
         Wounds to the Face staged
         An Eloquence (film) written
         The Blood of a Wife (film) written

1998   *Ursula* staged **[HB]**
         Collected Plays vol 4 (*The Bite of the Night, Seven Lears, The Gaoler's Ache, He Stumbled,
            A House of Correction*) published **[JC]**
         Ten Dilemmas staged[†]

1999   *Und* staged **[HB]**
         Scenes from an Exexcution staged **[HB]**
         A House of Correction broadcast, BBC Radio
         Albertina broadcast, BBC Radio
         The Swing at Night (marionette play) written

2000   *The Ecstatic Bible* staged (Adelaide, Australia) **[HB]**
         He Stumbled staged **[HB]**
         Animals in Paradise staged (Malmo, Sweden)
         The Twelfth Battle of Isonzo staged (Saint-Brieuc, France, in French)
         The Swing at Night (marionette play) staged and published **[JC]**
         Stalingrad (opera libretto) written
         All This Joseph written

2001   *The Twelfth Battle of Isonzo* staged (Dublin, Ireland, in English) **[HB]**

A House of Correction staged **[HB]**

Collected Plays vol 5 (*Ursula, The Brilliance of the Servant, 12 Encounters with a Prodigy, Und, The Twelfth Battle of Isonzo, Found in the Ground*) published **[JC]**

2002   *Gertrude – The Cry* staged **[HB]**; published with *Knowledge and a Girl* **[JC]**

Knowledge and a Girl broadcast **[HB]**, BBC Radio; published with *Gertrude – The Cry* **[JC]**

Stalingrad (opera libretto) staged (Denmark)

Brutopia staged (Besançon, France, in French)

Five Names written

2003   *13 Objects* staged **[HB]**

2004   *The Ecstatic Bible* published **[OB]**

Dead Hands staged **[HB]** and published **[OB]**

N/A (Sad Kissing) (written 2002) staged (Vienna, Austria)

The Moving and the Still (written 2003) broadcast, BBC Radio

The Dying of Today written

Acts Chapter 1 written

2005   *Death, The One and The Art of Theatre* (essays) published, Routledge

Animals in Paradise staged (Rouen, France, in French) **[HB]**

The Fence in its Thousandth Year staged **[HB]** and published **[OB]**

Christ's Dog (written 2004) staged (Vienna, Austria)

Two Skulls (written 2001) broadcast (Danish Radio)

Dead, Dead and Very Dead (libretto) written

Heroica (film) written

Adorations Chapter 1 (film) written

Let Me written

Eduardo Houth: *Howard Barker: A Style and its Origins* written

2006   *The Seduction of Almighty God* (written 1997) staged and published **[OB]**

The Road, The House, The Road broadcast, BBC Radio

A Living Dog staged (Odense, Denmark)

Plays One (*Victory, Scenes from an Execution, The Possibilities, The Europeans*) published **[OB]**

Plays Two (*The Castle, Gertrude – The Cry, 13 Objects, Animals in Paradise*) published **[OB]**

The Forty (Few Words) written

A SELECTION OF FURTHER CRITICAL READING

on Howard Barker

IN ENGLISH

Full-length Studies

C Lamb, *Howard Barker's Theatre of Seduction* (London, Harwood Academic Press / Routledge, 1997)

C Lamb, *The Theatre of Howard Barker* (London, Routledge, 2005).

D I Rabey, *Howard Barker: Politics and Desire: An Expository Study of his Drama and Poetry, 1969–87* (London, Macmillan, 1989)

D I Rabey, *Howard Barker: Ecstasy and Death: An Expository Study of his Plays and Production Work, 1988–2007* (London, Palgrave Press, forthcoming, 2009)

Articles and Essays

D Barnett, 'Howard Barker: Polemic Theatre and Dramatic Practice, Nietzsche, Metatheatre and the play *The Europeans*', in *Modern Drama* 44.4 (Winter 2001), pp 458–75

G Bas, 'The Cunts, the Knobs and the Corpse: Obscenity and Horror in Howard Barker's *Victory*', in *Contemporary Theatre Review* 5 (1996), pp 33–50

R Boon and A Price, 'Maps of the World: "Neo-Jacobeanism" and Contemporary British Theatre', in *Modern Drama* 41 (1998), pp 635–54

A Cornforth and D I Rabey, 'Kissing Holes for the Bullets: Consciousness in Directing and Playing Barker's *(Uncle) Vanya*', in *Performance and Consciousness* 1.4 (1999), pp 25–45

R Cotterill, 'Military empires and military republics: Howard Barker's *The Bite of the Night*', in Tony Howard and John Stokes (eds) *Acts of War: The Representation of Military Conflict on the British Stage and Television since 1945* (Aldershot, Scolar Books, 1996), pp 164–78

D Gallant, 'Brechtian Sexual Politics in the Plays of Howard Barker', in *Modern Drama*, 40 (1997), pp 403–13

K Gritzner, 'Catastrophic Sexualities in Howard Barker's Theatre of Transgression' in M Sönser Breen, and F Peters (eds) *Genealogies of Identity: Interdisciplinary Readings on Sex and Sexuality* (Amsterdam and New York, Rodopi, 2005), pp 95–106

G Klotz, 'Howard Barker: Paradigm of Postmodernism', in *New Theatre Quarterly* 7. 25 (Feb 1991), pp 20–6

C Megson, 'Howard Barker' in M Luckhurst (ed) *A Companion to Modern British and Irish Drama* (Oxford, Blackwell, 2006)

M Morel, '*Women Beware Women* by Howard Barker (with Thomas Middleton): the "Terrible Consistency"', in N Boireau (ed) *Drama on Drama: Dimensions of Theatricality on the Contemporary British Stage* (New York, St Martin's Press, 1997), pp 59–71

I Neubert, 'The Doorman of the Century is a Transient Phenomenon: the Symbolism of Dancer in Howard Barker's *Hated Nightfall*', in B Reitz (ed) *Drama and Reality. Contemporary Drama in English 3*, (Trier, Wissenschaftlicher Verlag Trier, 1996), pp 145–53

D I Rabey, 'For the Absent Truth Erect: Impotence and Potency in Howard Barker's Recent Drama', in *Essays in Theatre / Études théâtrales* 10 (1991), pp 31–7

D I Rabey, '"What Do You See?": Howard Barker's *The Europeans*', in *Studies in Theatre Production* 6 (December 1992), pp 23–34

D I Rabey, 'Howard Barker', in W W Demastes (ed) *British Playwrights, 1956–95: A Research and Production Sourcebook* (London, Greenwood Press, 1996), pp 28–38

D I Rabey, 'Barker: Appalling Enhancements', in D I Rabey, *English Drama Since 1940* (London, Longman Literature in English series, Pearson Education, 2003) pp 182–90

D I Rabey, 'Two Against Nature: Rehearsing and Performing Howard Barker's Production of his play *The Twelfth Battle of Isonzo*', in *Theatre Research International* 30.2 (July 2005), pp 175–89

E Sakellaridou, 'A Lover's Discourse – But Whose? Inversions of the Fascist Aesthetic in Howard Barker's *Und* and Other Recent English Plays', in *European Journal of English Studies*, 7.1 (April 2003), pp 87–108

G Saunders, 'Missing Mothers and Absent Fathers: Howard Barker's *Seven Lears* and Elaine Feinstein's *Lear's Daughters*', in *Modern Drama* 42 (1999), pp 401–10

R Shaughnessy, 'Howard Barker, The Wrestling School, and the Cult of the Author', in *New Theatre Quarterly* 5.19 (August 1989), pp 264–71

A Thomas, 'Howard Barker: Modern Allegorist', in *Modern Drama* 35 (1992), pp 433–43

L Tomlin, 'The Politics of Catastrophe' in *Modern Drama* 43, 1 (2000) pp 66–77

L Tomlin, 'Howard Barker', in J Bull (ed) *Dictionary of Literary Biography vol 233: British and Irish Dramatists Since World War II*, 2nd series (New York, Buccoli Clark , 2001), pp 9–21

R Wilcher, 'Honoring the Audience: the Theatre of Howard Barker', in J Acheson (ed) *British and Irish Drama Since 1960* (Basingstoke, Macmillan, 1993), pp 176–89

H Zimmermann, 'Howard Barker's Appropriation of Classical Tragedy', in S Patsalidis and E Sakellaridou (eds) *(Dis)Placing Classical Tragedy* (Thessaloniki: University Studio Press, 1999), pp 359–73

H Zimmermann, 'Howard Barker's Brecht or Brecht as Whipping Boy', in B Reitz and H Heiko Stahl (eds) *What Revels Are in Hand: Assessments of Contemporary Drama in English in Honour of Wolfgang Lippke* (CDE-Studies 8. Trier, Wissenschaftlicher Verlag Trier, 2001, pp 221–6

H Zimmermann, 'Howard Barker in the Nineties' in 'British Drama of the 1990s': *Anglistik & Englischunterricht* 64 (2002), pp 181–201

IN FRENCH

Alternatives Théâtrales 57 (mai 1998). Numéro spécial Howard Barker, coordonné par Mike Sens. Avec des articles de Mike Sens, Jérôme Hankins, Bernhard Reitz, Heiner Zimmermann, Charles Lamb, David Ian Rabey, Corinne Rigaud, Safaa Fathy, Elizabeth Sakellaridou, Ofra Henig, ainsi que des entretiens avec Howard Barker, ses metteurs en scènes (Ian McDiarmid et Jerzy Klesyk notamment) et ses traducteurs (Sarah Hirschmuller).

E Angel-Perez (ed) *Howard Barker et le Théâtre de la catastrophe*, éd (Paris, Editions Théâtrales, 2006)

E Angel-Perez, «L'espace de la catastrophe», G Chevallier (éd) *Cycnos* 12 (1–1995)

E Angel-Perez, «Pour un théâtre de la barbarie: Peter Barnes et Howard Barker», É Angel-Perez et N Boireau (éd) *Études anglaises* 52, 2 (avril–juin 1999), 198–210. Rééd. en *Le Théâtre anglais contemporain (1985–2005)* (Paris, Klincksieck, 2006 (à paraître))

E Angel-Perez, Préfaces aux volumes 1–5 des *Howard Barker: Œuvres choisies* (Paris, éditions Théâtrales)

E Angel-Perez, Notice sur Howard Barker de l'*Encyclopédie Universalis* (Paris, Encyclopædia Universalis, 2003)

E Angel-Perez, «Howard Barker: de la catastrophe à l'épiphanie» en E Angel-Perez, *Voyages au bout du possible. Les théâtres du traumatisme* (Paris, Klincksieck, 2006)

N Boireau, «Le paysage dramatique en Angleterre: consensus et transgression» en *Alternatives Théâtrales* 61 (1999), pp8–10

N Boireau, «Dystopies» en N Boireau, *Théâtre et société en Angleterre des années 1950 à nos jours* (Paris, PUPS, 2000)

S Hirschmuller, «Howard Barker ou la déconsécration du sens. À propos de Maudit crépuscule.» J-M Lanteri (éd) *Écritures contemporaines* 5 (2002) pp 25–42

M Morel, «La 'catastrophe' selon Barker» G Chevallier (éd) *Cycnos* 18, 1 (2001), pp 65–76

The editors would like to express their gratitude to Elisabeth Angel-Perez for assistance in compiling this bibliography.

INDEX

of Names and Main Subjects